What Colleagues Say About *Assessing English Language Learners: Bridges To Educational Equity: Connecting Academic Language Proficiency to Student Achievement*

"This practical book provides excellent background information and practical guidance for educators interested in improving the assessment of English learners (ELs) and connecting academic language proficiency to academic achievement. Its format of using reflections throughout each chapter offers opportunities for readers to think more deeply about topics and helps guarantee that they will be engaged and apply what they are learning to their own settings. Sharing the reflections with colleagues will help readers gain multiple perspectives related to the assessment of language proficiency in ELs. The practical resources at the end of each chapter will help educators apply what they learned."

—Diane August
Managing Researcher
American Institutes for Research
Washington, DC

"While we know that first-hand teaching experiences cannot readily be substituted by reading about the work and practice of others, with evocative scenarios of teachers, students and schools used throughout Assessing English Language Learners: Bridges to Educational Equity, *Margo Gottlieb comes close to making this happen. This is critical in two ways: first, the book is lively and interesting—serving as a welcome, well-designed text for teacher preparation courses, and second, the scenarios with their companion reflection questions can serve as an excellent stand-alone reference and thought-provoking resource for the increasing number of classroom teachers who find themselves responsible for the instruction and assessment of students acquiring English alongside their content area learning."*

—Alison L. Bailey, EdD
Professor of Human Development and Psychology
Department of Education, UCLA and
Faculty Research Partner, CRESST
Los Angeles, CA

"Margo Gottlieb's new book brings together research and policy on assessment and ELLs with practical tools for implementation. Her framework "Assessment as, for, and of learning" helps educators understand how assessment shapes teaching and learning and identifies concrete steps that educators can take to ensure that assessment practices are equitable for this group of students. The consistent application of the lens of the culturally and linguistically responsive classroom makes this book a must-have for teachers, school and district administrators, and teacher educators alike."

—Ester de Jong, EdD
Professor & Director, School of Teaching and Learning
University of Florida
Gainesville, FL

"Assessing English Language *Learners is an important contribution to the field for the many educators who believe that assessment for second language learners is important, but only if it is valid. This book lays out a clear and compelling argument that assessment and equity are not mutually exclusive concepts in educational programs for the nation's burgeoning population of multilingual learners. Its breadth is impressive and includes important discussions about language proficiency assessment, but also adds ideas for content area assessment practices. Important reading for practitioners and educational leaders."*

—Kathy Escamilla, PhD
Professor, Division of Educational Equity and Cultural Diversity
University of Colorado, Boulder
Boulder, CO

"Assessing Language Learners: Bridges to Educational Equity *is a great resource for teacher education programs and professional learning opportunities for schools. The book presents a new vision about assessment in the 21st century, which is influenced by new standards, accountability and technological advances in education. The new concept of Assessment as, for, and of learning that Gottlieb presents will transform education and provide a different perspective of assessment to all stakeholders. This is definitely a book that all educators should read."*

—Miguel Fernandez, Ph.D.
Associate Professor
Chicago State University
Chicago, IL

"This book lays out a much needed practical process for instructional professionals to design equitable access to educational opportunity for English learners! The author both responds to and promotes growing awareness of the critical importance for teachers and instructional leaders to ensure English learners' meaningful engagement with content through academic English. This authentic evolution of appropriate assessment as, for and of learning answers the "how" part of the clarion call for English learners to participate in rigorous curricula and instruction."

—Jonathan Gibson
Title III English Learner Program Director
Nevada Department of Education
Las Vegas, NV

"Framed by a lens of equity, Gottlieb makes the complex landscape of assessment accessible for classroom practitioners of English language learners. Readers will walk away with a crystal clear understanding of the instructional conditions they can create for English language learners, promoting linguistically responsive assessment practices."

—Trish Morita-Mullaney, Ph.D.
ELL Assistant Professor
Purdue University
West Lafayette, IN

Assessing English Language Learners: Bridges to Educational Equity

Second Edition

DEDICATION

To language learners and their families, whose linguistic and cultural wealth enhances our classrooms and communities every day.

To teachers who embed the linguistic and cultural richness of their language learners and families into teaching and learning so that school is an exceptional and exciting experience for students every day.

To school leaders and administrators who rejoice in the languages and cultures of their schools and districts every day.

To all the language learners, teachers, school leaders, and educators who have enriched my life with their languages and cultures every day.

Assessing English Language Learners: Bridges to Educational Equity

Connecting Academic Language Proficiency to Student Achievement

Second Edition

Margo Gottlieb

Foreword by
Margaret Heritage

CORWIN

A SAGE Publishing Company

FOR INFORMATION:

Corwin

A SAGE Company

2455 Teller Road

Thousand Oaks, California 91320

(800) 233-9936

www.corwin.com

SAGE Publications Ltd.

1 Oliver's Yard

55 City Road

London EC1Y 1SP

United Kingdom

SAGE Publications India Pvt. Ltd.

B 1/I 1 Mohan Cooperative Industrial Area

Mathura Road, New Delhi 110 044

India

SAGE Publications Asia-Pacific Pte. Ltd.

3 Church Street

#10-04 Samsung Hub

Singapore 049483

Program Director: Dan Alpert

Senior Associate Editor: Kimberly Greenberg

Editorial Assistant: Katie Crilley

Production Editor: Laura Barrett

Copy Editor: Shannon Kelly

Typesetter: C&M Digitals (P) Ltd.

Proofreader: Eleni Georgiou

Indexer: Teddy Diggs

Cover Designer: Candice Harman

Marketing Manager: Charline Maher

Copyright © 2016 by Corwin

Printed in the United States of America

Library of Congress Cataloging-in-Publication Data

Names: Gottlieb, Margo, author.

Title: Assessing English language learners: bridges to educational equity: connecting academic language proficiency to student achievement / Margo Gottlieb.

Description: Second Edition. | Thousand Oaks, California: Corwin, A SAGE Company, [2016] | Includes bibliographical references and index.

Identifiers: LCCN 2015045167 | ISBN 9781483381060 (pbk. : alk. paper)

Subjects: LCSH: English language—Study and teaching—Foreign speakers. | English language—Ability testing.

Classification: LCC PE1128.A2 G657 2016 | DDC 428.0071—dc23 LC record available at http://lccn.loc.gov/2015045167

This book is printed on acid-free paper.

20 10 9 8 7 6 5

Contents

Foreword

While college and career ready standards (CCRS) represent challenges for all students and their teachers, the challenge for English Language Learners (ELLs) is particularly significant. Already, ELL students have to learn subject matter content while simultaneously acquiring a new language. Moreover, the CCRS place a strong emphasis on extensive academic language use to engage in deep and transferable content learning and analytical practices. For example, mathematics CCRS ask students to explain, conjecture, construct viable arguments, and critique the reasoning of others, while the English language arts CCRS require students to engage with complex texts and write to inform, argue, and analyze.

With the rising population of ELL students in the United States and their stubbornly persistent low educational outcomes, like it or not, educational equity will depend in large part on *all* teachers taking responsibility for their ELL students' continuing language development in the context of learning demanding content-area material. This means that teachers will need to have a deep understanding of the content standards they teach, as well as complementary English language development (ELD) standards, and the skills to integrate them effectively, lesson-by-lesson, to provide optimal learning opportunities for their ELL students.

And to be able to successfully engage their ELL students in content-area and language learning, teachers must also have the knowledge and skills to use assessment information, a critical part of teaching, for making sound decisions to keep their students' learning moving forward. Furthermore, it cannot just be teachers who engage in assessment. Learning is the property of the learner, and while teachers and peers can help students learn, in the end, it is only they who can actually do the learning. Effective assessment practices can enable students to become agents in their own learning. By understanding what they are learning, why they are learning it, and how they will know if they've learned it, students can engage in self-assessment in ways that lead them to regulate their own learning, a core skill for college and career readiness.

All of this is easy to say but much harder to do. Fortunately for teachers of ELLs and those who support them, Margo Gottlieb, well known for her passionate advocacy for language-minority students, has used the theme of "bridges" in this book to clearly move us to a conception of equity for linguistically and culturally diverse students. Importantly, these students are not treated as a homogeneous group. Rather, there is recognition that each student comes to school with his or her own ethnic heritage, experiences, interests, language, exposure to English, and variations in the time spent in U.S. classrooms. It follows then that a one-size-fits-all approach to supporting ELLs' learning will not meet the needs of all students, underscoring the necessity for effective assessment practices that help teachers be responsive to their students.

Assessing English Language Learners: Bridges to Educational Equity—Connecting Academic Language Proficiency to Student Achievement uses the conception of assessment *as, for,* and *of* learning as a useful heuristic to capture the range of functions that assessment serves within a comprehensive system. There is a clear and helpful differentiation of assessments, and who uses them for what purposes, along with a recognition of the interdependence of the assessments to support decision making by administrators, teachers and students.

Each chapter tackles an important topic, ranging from the changing demographics of the U.S.'s school population, to detailed considerations of assessment for ELLs, to placement decisions for ELLs, to how ELD and content standards can work together to produce successful outcomes. To add to this, the book is full of practical advice that stems from research and contemporary theory, and there are many helpful resources throughout that provide support for thinking about the chapter topics and for taking action. The result is a 360-degree view of not only what needs to be in place but how to put it in place, to achieve educational equity for ELLs.

While this book reminds us how complex and challenging teaching and assessment for linguistically and culturally diverse students is, Margo Gottlieb has marshaled her commitment to social justice and combined it with her deep expertise to lead the way, across bridges, to an educational environment where success can be achieved. We should all heed her wise counsel.

Margaret Heritage
Senior Scientist
WestEd

Preface

It's strange. The opening to this preface is as relevant today as it was a decade ago when this book was first conceptualized. So I repeat: In his seminal book, *The Structure of Scientific Revolutions* (1962), Thomas Kuhn envisions a paradigm shift as the point in time when an overwhelming mass of accumulated knowledge reaches a critical point that forces us to adjust our way of thinking. The United States continues to undergo a paradigm shift in the field of educational assessment, albeit of a slightly different nature than in the early years of the new millennium. This transformation can be attributed to changes in demography, policy, theory, and practice.

Assessing English Language Learners: Bridges to Educational Equity—Connecting Academic Language Proficiency to Student Achievement (Assessing English Language Learners) is organized around a series of bridges that leads educators toward a vision of educational parity for all students. Each chapter highlights an equity issue that educators face and illustrates how we can promote positive change through assessment in reasonable and practical ways. By examining assessment through a social justice lens, the overall intent is to generate, interpret, and share data that more fairly reflect what language learners, and particularly English Language Learners (ELLs), can do.

ORGANIZATION OF THE BOOK

This edition of *Assessing English Language Learners* presents information about assessment and provides numerous examples of assessment strategies in eight chapters. The major updates reflect (a) the growing recognition of academic language as central to both language development and conceptual development, and therefore to assessment as well; (b) the increased role of technology in our lives and assessment; (c) the broadening of literacy to include multiliteracies and its measurement in authentic ways; (d) the influence of academic content standards, including college and career readiness standards and their facsimile on curriculum, instruction, and assessment; and (e) the emphasis on the important roles of students, teachers, and school leaders in the design and implementation of classroom or instructional assessment. Unless we provide all students opportunities and equitable access to standards-referenced, technology-driven curriculum, instruction, and assessment, these lofty twenty-first-century goals will not become a reality.

Part I sets the backdrop and rationale for a new vision of assessment. Chapter 1, *Assessment of English Language Learners: The Bridge to Educational Equity*, paints the current assessment landscape by identifying its key players—the students and their teachers. Working from the premise that all students are language learners who are in the process of acquiring grade-level academic language, this chapter outlines the purposes of assessment for a variety of stakeholders, describes a comprehensive assessment model, and suggests that without linguistically and culturally responsive schools, assessment data cannot be relevant for the new majority—our minority students. Chapter 2, *Assessment of Academic Language Through Standards: The Bridge to Systemic Equity*, discusses the influence of content and language standards in shaping curriculum, instruction, and assessment. It explains how multiple sets of standards, representing expectations for learning, work together to promote academic success for students.

The midsection of the book addresses how language learners and their teachers are to be involved in all forms of assessment within and across classrooms. Chapter 3, *Assessment of the Language of the Content Areas: The Bridge to Academic Equity*, offers assessment ideas related to key uses of academic language in the core curricular areas of language arts, mathematics, science, and social studies. Chapter 4, *Assessment of Oral Language and Literacy Development: The Bridge to Linguistic Equity*, speaks to the expansion of performance activities, tasks, and projects within and across listening, speaking, reading, and writing, including multiliteracies and translinguistic transfer, or translanguaging, as part of meaning making and communication for language learners.

Part II introduces a relatively new paradigm in assessment in the United States that speaks to students, teachers, and administrators—assessment *as, for,* and *of* learning. The comprehensive, standards-referenced model points to the relationship among three approaches and six forms of assessment. Chapter 5, *Assessment as Learning: The Bridge to Student Equity*, focuses on the voice of learners and how, through self-assessment and reflection, our students contribute to and help shape the assessment process. Student agency and advocacy demonstrated in assessment *as* learning frames this and the remaining chapters. Chapter 6, *Assessment for Learning: The Bridge to Teacher Equity*, illustrates how classroom teachers, by carefully planning and enacting an assessment process, can contribute sound evidence for standards-referenced decision making. Chapter 7, *Assessment of Learning: The Bridge to Administrator Equity*, points to the shifts in testing since the onset of college and career readiness standards and their impact on the new generation of assessment. The last chapter, *Assessment Results: Feedback, Standards-referenced Grading, and Reporting: The Bridge to Sustained Educational Equity*, summarizes how documentation of assessment *as, for,* and *of* learning within a standards-referenced system can yield rich results for educators, students, and family members, especially when supported through student-led conferences and assessment portfolios.

Reflections are interspersed throughout the chapters (consider *Reflections* as embedded self- and peer assessment or assessment *as* learning for yourself and your colleagues). They offer opportunities for you, either individually or as a member of a grade, department, or professional learning team, to grapple with some of the issues surrounding the instruction and assessment of language learners and evaluate the potential use of these ideas in your setting. *Resources* extend chapters by providing forms, surveys, and rubrics as well as support materials for instruction and assessment. Many of these exemplars have been adapted from the *Academic Language in Diverse Classrooms* series (Gottlieb & Ernst-Slavit, 2013, 2014a, and 2014b) and are meant to inspire thoughts on how best to approach classroom-embedded or instructional assessment. In addition to the expanded *References* section, there is an extensive *Glossary* of words and expressions.

AUDIENCES

A broad range of audiences will hopefully find this book useful. First and foremost are teachers—each and every teacher who works with language learners, particularly ELLs, now or in the future. Potential teachers who will soon enter linguistically and culturally rich classrooms will also hopefully see the benefits of examining assessment through an equity lens. School leaders, such as counselors, program directors, and curriculum coordinators, can find some ideas for supporting valid assessment for students, especially ELLs and ELLs with learning disabilities. Preservice and in-service teacher educators, whether working for a school district or university or independently, can use this updated edition in a hybrid course, with a professional learning community, or in a traditional face-to-face venue.

As schools move to more collaborative models for instructional planning and delivery, we would encourage individual educators to pair with other professionals to delve deeper into issues related to assessing language learners. There are a number of ways that professional learning can be a springboard for teachers to work with other teachers as critical friends, thought partners, coaches, or mentors. Hopefully this book will spur collaboration among grade-level team members or content and language teachers within and across departments.

Bridges are the pathways that lead to equity and, subsequently, educational success for all students, in particular ELLs. The accomplishments of current and future generations of students rest on teachers forging new ground today. *Assessing English Language Learners* provides teachers and teacher educators with the motivation, ideas, and tools to cross those bridges.

Acknowledgments

What started off as a simple update of my inaugural Corwin book somehow morphed into quite an overwhelming project. This edition would not have come to fruition if it were not for the vigilance and guidance of Dan Alpert, who has always been there for me for the better part of the past decade. As program director of equity and professional learning, Dan's advocacy for educational and social justice is far-reaching and, as is evident in this book, has personally influenced my thinking. For that, I cannot thank him enough.

There are other folks along the way that make the transformation of a manuscript into a book a reality. Kim Greenberg, senior associate editor, has been supportive since day one, helping craft surveys and offering prepublication ideas. Katie Crilley, editorial assistant, has double-checked every citation and figure (and there were many) to ensure that permissions had been secured. From the production editor, Laura Barrett, to the copy editor, Shannon Kelly, much care has been taken to ensure the scholarship of this book.

Last but not least, I would be remiss if I did not include the most wonderful colleagues who support and inspire me. From my home state of Illinois to my adopted state of Wisconsin, I must say that I have worked with an amazing group of educators during my career. I am also grateful to have had the opportunity to interact with such a myriad of amazing people, many of whom have become personal friends, in every corner of the United States and throughout the world.

PUBLISHER'S ACKNOWLEDGMENTS

Corwin gratefully acknowledges the contributions of the following reviewers:

Michele R. Dean, Ed.D.
Coordinator, Ventura County Indian Education Consortium
Ventura Unified School District
Ventura, CA

Miguel Fernandez, Ph.D.
Associate Professor
Chicago State University
Chicago, IL

Peggy Hickman, Ph.D.
Associate Professor
Arcadia University
Glenside, PA

Andrea Honigsfeld
Professor, Associate Dean, Director of Ed.D. Program
Molloy College
Rockville Centre, NY

Melissa Latham Keh
Assistant Professor
Bridgewater State University
Bridgewater, MA

Trish Morita-Mullaney, Ph.D.
Assistant Professor
Purdue University
Lafayette, IN

Kip Téllez
Professor
University of California, Santa Cruz
Felton, CA

About the Author

Margo Gottlieb is co-founder and lead developer for WIDA at the Wisconsin Center for Education Research, University of Wisconsin–Madison, and director, assessment and evaluation, for the Illinois Resource Center. In the last 15 years, she has spearheaded the crafting of language development standards and related resources, developed instructional assessments, designed curricular frameworks, and constructed instructional assessment systems for language learners. She started her career as an ESL and bilingual teacher for the Chicago public schools and has since worked with thousands of educators to share in professional learning with government agencies, professional organizations, publishers, school districts, states, territories, and universities. Margo has served on numerous national and state expert panels, advisory boards, technical working groups, and committees. Throughout the years she has traveled extensively to present across the United States as well as in American Samoa, Brazil, Canada, Chile, China, the Commonwealth of the Northern Mariana Islands, Finland, Guam, Indonesia, Italy, Mexico, Panama, Singapore, South Korea, Taiwan, United Arab Emirates, and the United Kingdom.

Margo's publications span over 80 articles, technical reports, monographs, chapters, and encyclopedia entries. Her most recent books include *Academic Language in Diverse Classrooms: Definitions and Contexts* (with G. Ernst-Slavit, 2014); a foundational book for the series *Promoting Content and Language Learning* (a compendium of three mathematics and three English language arts volumes co-edited with G. Ernst-Slavit, 2013, 2014); *Common Language Assessment for English Learners* (2012); *Paper to Practice: Using the TESOL's English Language Proficiency Standards in PreK-12 Classrooms* (with A. Katz & G. Ernst-Slavit, 2009); and *Assessment and Accountability in Language Education Programs: A Guide for Administrators and Teachers* (with D. Nguyen, 2007). She holds a B.A. in the teaching of Spanish, an M.A. in applied linguistics, and a Ph.D. in public policy analysis, evaluation research, and program design.

PART I

Assessment as a Context for Teaching and Learning

Bridges to Equity

True teachers are those who use themselves as bridges over which they invite their students to cross; then, having facilitated their crossing, joyfully collapse, encouraging them to create their own.

—Nikos Kazantzakis

t's official. Due to the meteoric rise of the minority student population, the rigor of the new standards with their emphasis on college and career readiness, and the importance of academic language use throughout school, we have welcomed in an age where every teacher is now a language teacher (Zwiers, 2008; Walqui & van Lier, 2010; Gottlieb & Ernst-Slavit, 2014a). This new reality that educators face comes at a time when we are challenged to make informed decisions about our students minute by minute, day by day, week by week, month by month, and year by year. To do so, we plan, gather, and analyze information for specific purposes from multiple sources so that the results, when reported in meaningful ways, inform teaching and learning. That's the core of the assessment process. If assessment is reliable, valid, and fair for all students from start to finish, then it can serve as the bridge to educational equity.

No matter how much progress we have witnessed in the last few years, discrepancies still remain when it comes to race, ethnicity, gender, national origin, linguistic background, and economic status of our students. Thus, this book is dedicated to building bridges that promote educational equity, most notably in the areas of instruction and assessment. Teachers' and school leaders' sensitivity to equitable treatment of all students, with the recognition that every one is a language learner, will hopefully pave the way to more inclusive and relevant practices and policies.

WHY FOCUS ON EQUITY?

The pursuit of educational equity has been very much part of U.S. history. Envisioned within the greater civil rights movement, its roots can be traced to the mid-twentieth century. Beginning with the 1954 U.S. Supreme Court decision in *Brown v. Board of Education* that eliminated racial segregation, successive decades have included further attempts to address social and educational inequities. In 1965 we saw the introduction of the Elementary and Secondary Education Act, which attempted to hold states, school districts, and schools more accountable for improving the academic performance of students regardless of economic status, race, ethnicity, proficiency in English, or disability. In 1974 the *Lau v. Nichols* Supreme Court case expanded the rights of English Language Learners (ELLs) by ruling in favor of Chinese students who were denied equal educational opportunities on the basis of their ethnicity and language background, thus paving the way to the endorsement of bilingual education.

The landmark 1990 Individuals with Disabilities Education Act (IDEA, Public Law No. 94-142) ensures that students with disabilities are provided free, appropriate public education in the least restricted learning environment that is tailored to their individual needs, as stated in their individualized education programs (IEPs). This law extends to ELLs from birth to age 21, stipulating that they are not to be denied language support due to a disability. A recent policy (rather than legislation or adjudication) that touches on equity of educational opportunity is state adoption of college and career readiness standards aimed at universally increasing curricular and assessment demands.

National equity assistance centers (EACs), funded by the U.S. government under the Civil Rights Act of 1964, provide assistance to public schools in the areas of race, gender, and national origin equity in order to promote equal educational opportunities. It is the contention of the centers that, if fully implemented, their six goals for educational equity will create a context that promotes equity. These goals include

- comparably high academic achievement and other positive outcomes for all students on all achievement indicators;
- equitable access and inclusion;
- equitable treatment;
- equitable resource distribution;
- equitable opportunity to learn; and
- shared accountability. (Regional Equity Assistance Centers, 2013, p. 4)

We begin laying the groundwork for assessment equity by describing the ever-increasing school-age population of linguistically and culturally diverse students. Of equal importance are the school contexts in which students interact. To that end, we identify the many educators who influence language learners and point to the necessity for linguistically and culturally responsive schools.

WHY CENTER ON LANGUAGE LEARNERS WITH SPECIAL ATTENTION TO ENGLISH LANGUAGE LEARNERS?

Language is the universal medium for meaning making and for communicating to others. Additionally, language is the primary tool for mental representation and cognitive processing. In essence, learning and cognition are interconnected as both heavily rely on language. As this notion of using language to mediate thinking and learning is not unique to any one group of students, we all can be considered language learners.

When the chain of connections between the mind and language is disrupted, such as when students do not understand the language of instruction, learning is disrupted (Kenji Hakuta, personal communication, 2014). We cannot afford this interruption; we must promote rich student discourse and sustained use of academic language across the disciplines wherever possible in the languages of our students.

During the past decade, the staggering growth in the number of students who represent our nation's myriad languages and cultures has affected teachers, school leaders, and administrators from preschool through high school and beyond. In fact, these changing demographics are transforming schools and communities (Noguera, 2014). The students in this heterogeneous mix have had very different life and educational experiences than the Anglo-centric norm; some newcomers are refugees or immigrants, while many others come from linguistic enclaves within the United States. What follows is a synopsis of some of the major changes in our student population over the past decade, with a focus on ELLs.

WHO ARE OUR ENGLISH LANGUAGE LEARNERS? FACTS AND FIGURES OF THE CHANGING DEMOGRAPHIC

The beginning of the 2014–2015 school year marked a turning point in U.S. educational history: For the first time, the minority student population escalated to the point where nationally it became the majority. While Texas has held this majority-minority student status since 2004, demographic shifts across the nation have now tipped the scales toward a greater representation of nonwhite students in many other states as well. In large part, school-age children from Hispanic and Asian/Pacific Islander backgrounds are responsible for this new wave in our student population, while non-Hispanic white students are on a decline. While there are over 150 languages spoken by ELLs, all but seven states claim Spanish as the most common one (Batalova & McHugh, 2010). With these changing student demographics trending across the country, it's time for all educators to embrace this new reality and harness the potential of every student, the hallmark of equity.

The future will see sustained growth of linguistically and culturally diverse students in the United States, especially ELLs. Whereas in 2008 ELLs—that is, students for whom English is an additional language and who qualify for language support—represented one in nine students in public schools, it is projected that by 2025 one in four students will be an ELL (McBride, Richard, & Payan, 2008). Figure I.1 shows the prekindergarten through high school (preK-12) demographic surge and decline of the largest racial/ethnic groups for 2 decades, ending in 2023 (National Center for Education Statistics, 2014).

Young children are the leading edge of this upward trend of linguistic minority representation in schools. Although most of these children have been born in the United States and are therefore citizens, in 17 states Hispanic students make up 20% of kindergarten classes (Krogstad & Fry, 2014). Let's focus for a moment on the burst of population seen among ELLs, or, as they are known in some states, English Learners (ELs).

Figure I.1 Percentage Change and Projected Change in Ethnicity in the PreK-Grade 12 Student Population Over 2 Decades

	Change From 2001 to 2011	Total %	Projections From 2012 to 2023	Total %
Hispanic	+3.6 million (+7%)	25%	+3.4 million	30%
Asian/Pacific Islander	+.8 million (+8%)	5%	+.4 million	5%
Black	−.6 million (−1%)	15%	−.2 million	15%
Non-Hispanic White	−3.1 million (−8%)	50%	−2 million	45%

Source: National Center for Education Statistics. (2014). *Racial/ethnic enrollment in public schools*. Retrieved from http://nces.ed.gov/programs/coe/indicator_cge.asp

What's in a Name?

Academic language is critical for academic success, and it has become an equalizer in the standards-driven reform movement (Francis, Rivera, Lesaux, Kieffer, & Rivera, 2006; Mota-Altman, 2006). Thus, we begin with the premise that *language learners* is a universal term descriptive of all students in prekindergarten through Grade 12, inclusive of their languages and cultural identities, and that academic language use is a vehicle that leads these students to achieve academically. That said, there are many different groups of language learners.

There is a growing variety of language learners, so let's clarify some of the school-based nomenclature associated with this intriguing group of students. School-age children exposed to cultures and languages other than English in daily interaction in their home environment are considered *linguistically and culturally diverse* students. Their linguistic and cultural roots afford these students distinct ways of seeing, thinking, interacting, and being that influence the way they learn in English medium schools.

Linguistically and culturally diverse students, who constitute approximately 20% of the K-12 student population in the United States, are tremendously heterogeneous and have a wide range of educational experiences. Some of these students may be first-generation immigrants, refugees, or even unaccompanied minors who have had little experience with English. At the other end of the spectrum, some may be *heritage language learners*. These students, generally born and raised in the United States, identify with one or more multicultural groups and may communicate in English and other languages.

Within the linguistically and culturally diverse population, there are several subgroups of students, the largest one being ELLs. Identified through screening and assessment, ELLs are students whose current levels of English language proficiency preclude them from accessing, processing, and acquiring unmodified grade-level material in English without scaffolding and instructional support. Already substantial, the numbers of these students are growing. In the 2011–2012 school year, seven of the eight states with the highest percentages of public school ELLs (over 10%) were in the western United States; ELLs constituted more than 23% of the public school enrollment in California. In addition, 14 states and the District of Columbia had percentages of ELL public school enrollment between 6.0 and 9.9%, followed by

15 states with a percentage between 3.0 and 5.9%. Rounding out the ELL count are 13 states with 3% or less (NCES, 2014).

The explosion of linguistic and cultural diversity can also be seen with our very youngest language learners, starting with toddlers. Prior to their kindergarten experience, young children who are in the process of developing two languages, whether simultaneously (the home language and English) or sequentially, are referred to as *dual language learners*. Head Start and early childhood circles use the term *dual language learners* to refer to children who communicate with family members in a home language or languages, are continuing to develop those languages, and are being exposed to English either at home and/or in child-care settings. According to Head Start program information reports, almost 30% of Head Start children come from families who speak a primary language other than English (Office of Head Start, 2008).

Once these students enter kindergarten, they may continue their dual language development by participating in a program where instruction occurs in two languages. From this point on, these students are now considered *emergent bilinguals* (a term also used to signify all ELLs by some researchers). The instructional program in which these students participate, if in fact there are opportunities for their home language to further develop alongside English, is generally known as a dual language or immersion program. Through schooling, these young children grow to become bilingual and biliterate and thus are increasingly able to communicate in two or more languages.

Other labels for language learners exist that are descriptive of some of their characteristics. Take for instance *Students With Limited or Interrupted Formal Education* (SLIFE), who are older (middle or high school) transient ELLs who attend school for a short while, return to their home country, and then often repeat the cycle, or who are highly mobile students who receive inconsistent schooling. The Unites States has also experienced some waves of undocumented and unaccompanied minors who are generally in the same age range as SLIFE. In addition to the necessity of English language development, acculturation issues, and the trauma of entry into a new country, these students must often also contend with work obligations and often feel alienated in the school community.

Long-term English Language Learners (LTELLs) are another class of older ELLs, generally with 7 or more years of language support. These students are orally proficient in English, while their academic language and literacy tend to remain around the midpoint of the language acquisition continuum. There are three subgroups of LTELLs: (a) students who have received inconsistent U.S. schooling in regards to their model of language support, (b) transnational students, who move back and forth between the United States and their families' countries of origin during the school year, and (c) students who consistently have received language support, but the support has not built on the students' home language development (Menken, Kleyn, & Chae, 2012).

Lastly, there are indigenous populations who have lived in the United States for multiple generations and wish to study, preserve, or revitalize their linguistic and cultural roots (Gottlieb, 2012a). American Indian ELLs include Native American, Alaskan Native, and Native Hawaiian students, some of whom live in tribal communities and some of whom are interspersed in the general population. Many Pacific Islanders, such as peoples from American Samoa, the Marshall Islands, the Commonwealth of the Northern Mariana Islands, and Guam, also have indigenous roots and multicultural foundations.

Educational Services

Many other terms that are associated with educational services, delivery models, or funding sources often become attached to students. Although these labels, such as Title I, bilingual, or English to Speakers of Other Languages (ESOL), might be convenient, they do not convey an accurate depiction of these students; instead, they describe the kinds of support programs or interventions the students receive. Additionally, response to intervention (RtI) and multi-tier system of supports (MTSS) are general education approaches for students, including ELLs, who may potentially qualify for special education services.

A lot of different terminology must be sorted out with regard to the description of language learners from linguistically and culturally diverse backgrounds. Resource I.1 at the close of Part I invites you to create a scheme for personal use or to reflect on the one used by your school, district, or state. In that way you will be able to consistently apply the terms throughout the book to your own setting.

The rise of the minority student population, in particular ELLs, has been accompanied by some complex societal and civil rights issues that often impact school systems, such as immigration, poverty, and inequity of educational opportunities. According to Kurt Landgrat, "We need to find new ways to reach out (to the new majority). This is not only socially conscious, but frankly in the best interest of the U.S. economy and in terms of equity of education" (quoted in McBride et al., 2008, p. 2). Equity of education is the premise on which we have built this book.

Interestingly, in the decade from 1990 to 2000, dual language programs, with proficient English speakers learning content and language side by side in two languages with their ELL peers, grew tenfold to over 2,000 in operation. These proficient English speaking students have become part of the mix of language learners, and their numbers continue to rise as the demand for dual language or immersion programs increases across the country. Growth in these numbers is attributed in part to research that has validated the mission of these dual language programs to promote biliteracy and to positive cross-cultural attitudes in our increasingly multilingual world (Wilson, 2011).

The challenge of providing equitable educational opportunities comes at a time when school leaders and teachers are focusing on implementing standards-referenced educational reforms. One solution is to make our schools more reflective of a can-do spirit and for educators to provide an equitable education by assuming an advocacy perspective (WIDA, 2012; Staehr Fenner, 2014). With increasing numbers of minority students filling our classrooms, the need for linguistically and culturally responsive education is becoming more and more apparent.

WHO ARE THE EDUCATORS OF LANGUAGE LEARNERS?

If there is in fact a "shared mission and vision within the school community that is inclusive, then the groundwork [is set] for not only establishing equality for all students but equity as well" (Dove, Honigsfeld, & Cohan, 2014, p. 1). Working as a team, every educator has a distinct yet complementary role to ensure that students have seamless access to and participate in appropriate and relevant curriculum, instruction, and assessment. Figure I.2 describes the overall responsibilities

Figure I.2 Primary Responsibilities of Teachers Who Contribute to the Education of Language Learners

Educators	Instructional and Assessment Responsibilities
Bilingual or dual language teachers	• Content-based instruction and classroom assessment in two languages • Oral language and literacy development in two languages
Content teachers (e.g., subject-area "sheltered" teachers)	• Integration of academic language and conceptual development in English • Content-specific skills and knowledge in English with support in the home language to clarify and advance conceptual understanding
Language specialists (e.g., English as a Second Language [ESL], English to Speakers of Other Languages [ESOL], English Language Acquisition [ELA], or English as Additional Language [EAL] teachers, among others)	• Language development in English • Introduction/reinforcement of content-related concepts in English • Support in home language, as applicable • Collaboration with content and general education teachers
General education teachers and teachers of the gifted and talented	• Language and literacy development in English • Academic development in English, along with assessment of content skills and knowledge • Collaboration with language specialists
Instructional coaches (e.g., data or literacy coaches)	• Model lessons with built-in instructional assessment • Support for coordinated content and language teaching • Display of language proficiency and achievement data for making decisions
Teachers of specialized subjects (e.g., technology, fine arts, physical education)	• Extension of language and skill development in English (with reinforcement in the home language, as applicable) • Development of cross-disciplinary literacy
Title I and other support teachers (e.g., intervention teachers or special education teachers if students have IEPs)	• Literacy reinforcement in the home language or in English • Reinforcement of math skills and concepts • Collaboration with content and language teachers

Source: Adapted from Gottlieb, 2006, p. 5.

of the teachers and teacher leaders who contribute to the total educational program of language learners. In addition, where available, paraprofessionals, especially those who are multilingual, provide another linguistic resource and model. At the close of this section, Resource I.2 offers you the opportunity to identify the language educators in your setting and reflect on their roles and responsibilities.

WHAT ARE LINGUISTICALLY AND CULTURALLY RESPONSIVE CLASSROOMS AND SCHOOLS?

In linguistically and culturally responsive schools, each and every student is envisioned as a learner with inherent strengths, resources, and assets. These schools set high expectations and provide scaffolds to support the academic success of all students (Bazron, Osher, & Fleischman, 2005). Within these schools, administrators advocate on behalf of their students and teachers are culturally competent; these professionals realize that the academic challenges of culturally diverse students may stem from interactions among educators and assessment measures rather than from the students themselves (Cummins, 2000).

School leadership that is socially just supports equitable educational opportunities for students who historically have been marginalized, including those who are linguistically and culturally diverse. Leadership is not necessarily limited to principals but instead is inclusive of a collective of stakeholders who have the responsibility to enact school improvement (Louis, Leithwood, Wahlstrom, & Anderson, 2010). According to the literature, the successful education of these students rests on (a) facilitating their social integration, (b) cultivating their academic language proficiency, and (c) promoting their academic achievement (Scanlan & López, 2015; Brisk, 2006).

In linguistically and culturally responsive classrooms, teachers are mediators who help students build bridges from the known to the unknown. Teaching is grounded in an understanding of the critical role of culture and language, and teachers are sensitive to the sociocultural contexts in which learning occurs. Classroom instruction and assessment are congruent with the cultural value systems of the surrounding communities and reflect their "funds of knowledge" (Bazron et al., 2005; González, Moll, & Amanti, 2005). In applying culturally responsive teaching to instructional assessment, teachers should consider

- the range and types of linguistic and cultural experiences of the students;
- the sociocultural identities students bring to classroom activities;
- the inclusion of multiple perspectives in carrying out tasks and projects;
- interpretation and reporting of data within a linguistic and cultural context; and
- student self- and peer assessment as viable sources of decision making. (Gottlieb, 2012b)

All in all, schools have to become more responsive to increasingly heterogeneous student populations and their families. Schools that have a multicultural presence or that have undergone a cultural transformation tend to

- understand how learners construct knowledge through cultural lenses;
- learn about students' experiences and cultures;
- be socioculturally conscious by being aware of the school context;
- hold affirming views about diversity;
- use appropriate instructional strategies, such as tapping the students' home language and community resources; and
- advocate on behalf of all students. (Villegas & Lucas, 2007)

Students' knowledge of their own culture and that of others is important to their performance in school and in life. "Schools can make a positive and significant difference for students when educators account for the complex interaction of language, culture, and context, and decisions are made within a coherent theoretical framework" (Miramontes, Nadeau, & Commins, 2011, p. 10).

Culturally responsive standards-based teaching combines the notion that culture permeates every classroom with the belief that teachers are responsible for ensuring the representation of the students' languages and cultures in everyday lessons. Additionally, students' resources are to be valued, enhanced, and incorporated into standards-referenced instruction (Saifer, Edwards, Ellis, Ko, & Stuczynski, 2011). If educators create a caring and nurturing environment, students will feel safe and will be more likely to take risks in their new or home language. Classroom communities that exhibit respect, personal connection, and mutual understanding based on acceptance of diversity will ultimately result in acceptance and promotion of linguistic equity in learning.

Culturally responsive teaching is about building trust with students who historically have been marginalized in schools (and society) through a learning partnership. Teachers' ability to use this earned rapport and trust of linguistically and culturally diverse students helps deepen the students' understanding. In turn, the students' increased ability to tackle more rigorous work leads to enriched learning (Hammond, 2015).

The optimal educational environment should be a dynamic school where there are opportunities for students to learn, grow, and thrive. In reality, in some school systems conditions are less than optimal. As a result, there can be underrepresentation or overrepresentation of minority students in certain high-incidence disability categories in special education, including the categories of emotional disturbance, speech pathology, and learning disabilities. In light of this dilemma, the notion of culturally competent assessment has gained traction for special education eligibility. Obtaining accurate information from assessments that contain minimal bias is not only required for validity's sake but is an ethical and equity imperative. Where is your school on the linguistically and culturally responsive scale? Refer to Resource I.3 to see where it might fall.

Today educators are focused on optimizing opportunities for the multicultural young children and/or young adults with whom they interact each day. These students have the potential to thrive academically. You too can help language learners, including ELLs and ELLs with disabilities, flourish by engaging in the equitable assessment practices introduced in the upcoming pages.

RESOURCE I.1

Describing Your Language Learners

Who are the language learners in your setting? What is the terminology that is used to describe each group of students and the kinds of support services they receive? If you would like, make a pie chart that reflects the representation of different groups of language learners or complete the table below by checking which terms are used in your setting. Share it with your colleagues and discuss student population trends nationally, in your state, your district, or your school.

Term for Language Learners	Personal or Local Definition	Used by the School	Used by the District	Used by the State
Dual language learners				
Emergent bilinguals				
English Language Learners (ELLs) or a comparable term				
ELLs with learning disabilities				
Gifted and talented ELLs				
Heritage language learners				
Linguistically and culturally diverse learners				
Long-term English Language Learners (LTELLs)				
Students With Limited or Interrupted Formal Education (SLIFE)				

RESOURCE I.2

Identifying Educators of English Language Learners

Think about all the teachers and other school personnel who are responsible for the education of ELLs. Make a diagram that serves as a metaphor for how educators work together in your school to provide comprehensive services to students. Then describe your figure and the roles and responsibilities of each educator.

Educators	Roles and Responsibilities
Bilingual or dual language teachers	
Content teachers (e.g., subject area teachers)	
Language specialists (e.g., ESL, ESOL, ELD, EL, EAL teachers)	
General education teachers	
Instructional coaches (e.g., data or literacy coaches)	
Teachers of specialized subjects (e.g., technology, fine arts, physical education)	
Title I and other support teachers	
Teachers of additional services (e.g., special education teachers or teachers of gifted and talented students)	

RESOURCE I.3

A Rating Scale of a Linguistically and Culturally Responsive School

Research has pointed to clear signs of a linguistically and culturally responsive school; these traits are identified in the rating scale below. You are welcome to use this tool as a thumbnail evaluation of where your school is situated in relation to its linguistic and cultural responsiveness. Use the following criteria in responding from 1 to 4: 1 = traces, 2 = intermittent signs, 3 = noticeable presence, and 4 = full integration of languages and cultures.

Linguistic and Cultural Responsiveness in My School	1	2	3	4
Multilingualism and multiculturalism permeate the air, from signage to murals to conversations in the halls.				
High expectations are set for all students, and language learners can reach their goals in one or more languages.				
Students' languages and cultures are valued every minute of every day.				
The linguistic and cultural resources of the community and family members are an extension of the school.				
Curriculum, instruction, and assessment invite multiple perspectives and reflect the identities of the students.				
Every adult in the school advocates on behalf of students, and special attention is paid to languages and cultures.				
Linguistic and cultural responsiveness is part of the school's and district's mission and vision.				

1

Assessment of Language Learners

The Bridge to Educational Equity

All children have preparedness, potential, curiosity and interest in constructing their learning, in engaging in social interaction and in negotiating with everything the environment brings to them.

—Lella Gandini

How do we begin to tackle the complex world of assessment and its interaction with standards and instruction? Why is context so important in framing assessment and interpreting the results, especially when English Language Learners (ELLs) are involved? What is the vision of assessment *as, for*, and *of* learning, and what are the corresponding purposes and audiences? How do we take all this information and convert it into practice? In this chapter, as we start to unweave the many intertwining threads of assessment, we focus our attention on the students, our most important stakeholders.

CONSIDERATIONS IN ASSESSING ENGLISH LANGUAGE LEARNERS

The context for assessment revolves around the characteristics of the student population, including their linguistic expertise and their multicultural resources. A careful examination of the unique features of linguistically and culturally diverse students helps teachers understand how language, culture, and prior experiences help shape the identities of this eclectic group.

A School-Based Scenario

South Side Middle School is located in a midsized city that historically has become the home of waves of immigrants. Its Latino population, consisting of many Spanishes from Mexico, Puerto Rico, and Central America, has remained stable over the past couple of decades. In response to the community's request, the school district has offered dual language immersion in Spanish and English for the last 6 years, and this first cohort of dual language students has now entered the middle school. In the past several years, South Side has seen an influx of refugees from several war-torn countries who have experienced trauma and who may be considered SLIFE since they have had inconsistent formal schooling. In addition, students represent over 20 other countries from around the globe, and some of these students have been identified as ELLs and are receiving language support. This year the school has decided it wants to gather additional data on the interests and concerns of the students and their families so that it can better serve its multilingual, multicultural community.

How can school leaders and teachers begin to understand the complexities of language learning? Figure 1.1 identifies the factors to be taken into account in the instruction and assessment of language learners, particularly ELLs.

Figure 1.1   Individual and Programmatic Variables That Influence the Academic Success of Language Learners, Particularly ELLs

Individual Student Variables
<ul><li>Age and gender</li><li>The language(s) and culture(s) of everyday interactions</li><li>The exposure to academic language inside and outside of school</li><li>Educational experiences outside of and inside the United States, starting at preK</li><li>Continuity of educational experiences (considering mobility, interruption of schooling, attendance)</li><li>Oral language proficiency and literacy in the home language</li><li>Academic achievement in the home language</li><li>Oral language proficiency and literacy in English</li><li>Academic achievement in English</li><li>A student's personality, attitude toward language and language learning, and motivation as well as other affective factors, such as trauma</li><li>Socioeconomic status of students' families in the United States, including access to resources (e.g., technology) and opportunities for grade-level learning</li><li>Identified learning disabilities</li></ul>
Programmatic Variables
<ul><li>Allotment of time per day for language support services</li><li>Amount and types of sustained language support across years—stability of the instructional program for individual students</li><li>The quality of language support over time</li><li>The correspondence between language support and the general education program</li><li>The collaboration among teachers serving language learners</li><li>The continuity of the language(s) of instructional support</li><li>Opportunities for student growth or support in the home language</li><li>Support of leadership for linguistic and culturally responsive schooling</li></ul>

Source: Adapted from Gottlieb, 2006, p. 6.

Not all data on ELLs necessary for decision making come from assessment. Information pertaining to a student's mobility, continuity in education, types of language support services, the amount of time devoted to support per week, and the language(s) of instruction over the years can be obtained through surveys as part of school registration (see Resources 1.3 and 1.4 at the end of this chapter for examples). Teachers can use this survey information in conjunction with assessment data as a starting point for planning instruction and classroom assessment.

IDENTIFICATION OF ENGLISH LANGUAGE LEARNERS

With the dawn of assessment consortia from grants awarded by the U.S. Department of Education starting in 2002 and new academic content standards or college and career readiness standards in 2010, the playing field for achievement testing has been altered considerably. One stipulation that the federal government imposed upon consortia of affiliated states and territories was to agree on a common definition of *English learner*. In other words, how can schools and districts reliably identify this growing subset of linguistically and culturally diverse students? The reasoning behind this mandate is to establish greater uniformity in procedures to (a) identify the potential pool of ELLs, (b) classify and place ELLs in instructional programs with language support according to specific criteria, (c) stipulate when ELLs meet established criteria for obtaining English language proficiency, and (d) reclassify ELLs as English proficient and monitor their performance after their transition from language support services.

As a protected class status guaranteed by a U.S. Supreme Court decision (*Lau v. Nichols*, 2004), ELLs have a right to fair and equitable educational opportunities. As soon as they walk through the school doors, assessment plays a sizeable role in determining policy and practice in regard to the education of these students. At the onset of the process is a high-stakes decision: determining which students who come from linguistically and culturally diverse backgrounds qualify as ELLs. Several researchers have spearheaded a multiyear, multiphase process involving states and stakeholders that has led to a set of recommendations regarding the common definition of *English learner* and a reconceptualization of the Language Use Survey (also known as the Home Language Survey), the primary enrollment document that identifies a student's language background (Linquanti & Bailey, 2014; Linquanti & Cook, 2013).

What are the procedures for identifying ELLs in your district or state? A Reflection will help you think through the process or ask related questions. Often found at the close of a section, the purpose of a Reflection is to offer opportunities for you, your grade-level or department team, or your professional learning community to think more deeply about a topic or apply some of the questions surrounding the instruction and assessment of language learners to your own setting. By sharing these Reflections with colleagues, whether they are just entering the teaching profession or are veterans of the craft, or simply by using them as personal opportunities to be reflective, hopefully you will gain multiple perspectives and insights on how to approach the dilemmas facing educators with regard to the assessment of language learners.

REFLECTION

Identifying English Language Learners

Investigate the process in your setting for making the initial determination of which K-12 students are ELLs or which children in prekindergarten settings are dual language learners. Who is responsible for securing the information? What questions are asked of family members or students and are they presented in a language that is understood? Are the criteria for initial identification applied uniformly? If not, what might you suggest to ensure that more reliable decisions can be made?

Although new federal guidance is on the horizon, consortia or individual states are still required to set up the initial screening process to determine the classification of students as potential ELLs or not. The flowchart in Resource 1.1 at the close of the chapter outlines one way to pursue this determination. It begins when any young child or student walks through school doors for the first time. The Language Use Survey (see Resource 1.2), often incorporated into the initial registration process, serves to differentiate monolingual English-speaking students from those who interact with other languages and cultures on a daily basis. Once students are known to come from linguistically and culturally diverse backgrounds, further screening is required. This first round of data collection and assessment after the initial Language Use Survey, which we refer to as Phase I, generally includes

- a survey of oral language use (a local option);
- a literacy survey (a local option); and
- a standards-based, reliable, and valid screening test of English language proficiency (a state requirement).

Based on results from these and other state or district mandates, teachers—or, in some cases, assessment specialists or coaches—determine if students qualify as ELLs and are eligible for language support services. Phase I measures provide an overall thumbnail sketch of students.

Phase I Measures

The Language Use Survey or Home Language Survey required by most states serves as an initial classification tool for determining whether or not students have experienced languages and cultures other than English. Given upon initial entry into school districts, the Language Use Survey should be made available in the students' and families' home languages as well as English. A YES response to any of the first questions, such as, "Does your child speak a language other than English at home?" triggers the subsequent administration of an English language proficiency screener and optional surveys (see Resources 1.3 and 1.4).

Language Use Surveys provide teachers insight into students' language and literacy practices in their home language and English. Even though caution must always be exercised in interpreting self-reported results, this information is invaluable for gaining insight into students' educational backgrounds and experiences.

School districts or schools should translate these surveys so that they are available in the languages of all students. Otherwise, paraprofessionals might be helpful in translating and obtaining the information.

An English language proficiency screener or short test adopted by a state or used by a consortium serves as the primary tool for identification of ELLs. Based on the results for listening, speaking, reading, and writing, or a combination of those language domains, students are assigned a level of English language proficiency. Those students who qualify as ELLs, as determined by state criteria, may then be further assessed with optional Phase II measures, generally a school or district choice, to best match students with the most appropriate instructional services.

Phase II Measures

By gathering more specific information on student performance, Phase II measures of the classification process complement those of Phase I. More diagnostic information can be obtained from this second round of data collection. These measures center on students' academic achievement (in English and their home language) and may include standardized tests as well as evidence collected from informal reading inventories and content-based writing samples.

Although instruction may or may not be afforded in a student's home language, there are several reasons for suggesting assessment in the home language at the time of initial identification. First, ELLs are a mix of students with different competencies, proficiencies, literacies, knowledge bases, and school experiences. It is always beneficial for teachers and school leaders to have a full portrait of any student's performance. Second, achievement in the home language is the strongest predictor of future success in other languages, most notably English (Collier & Thomas, 2002, 2009). This information is invaluable for teachers in planning instruction. Students with strong conceptual development in their home language merely need to acquire the labels for the concepts they already know; consequently, their pace of developing English language proficiency will be accelerated. Conversely, students without such a foundation may need to learn language, literacy, and content simultaneously. Instructional methodologies and the types of instructional support services vary considerably for these two broad categories of students.

Student data on academic achievement, in particular in language arts and mathematics, pinpoint instructional placement for students and provide diagnostic information for teachers. This information, coupled with that from language proficiency testing and survey results, establishes the basis for selection of an optimal program design and services. In addition, teachers have a firmer sense of how to plan sound instruction and assessment for individual students.

Whenever feasible, one of the first suggested actions after identification of an ELL is a visit to the student's home (Ernst-Slavit & Mason, 2012; Cardenas, Jones, & Lozano, 2014). Home visits are a goodwill gesture that signal an educator's interest in the student's home life and provide insight into each student's background. Obviously, when meeting family members from linguistically and culturally diverse settings, it might be beneficial to ask another adult who speaks the home language of the family to accompany you. In essence, home visits can expand the context for understanding assessment data. Although local constraints may exist, this policy should extend to all new students whenever possible.

Contextualizing Assessment

What contextual information, (e.g., prior school experiences, refugee or immigrant status, socioeconomic status) is taken into account in interpreting a student's initial assessment data in your school, district, or state? Are there any policies that impact the placement of students in specific educational programs or support services? Investigate state and local rules and regulations regarding *when* initial data are collected, *what* data are collected, *how* the data are collected, and *which* data are used for decision making.

IDENTIFICATION OF ENGLISH LANGUAGE LEARNERS WITH DISABILITIES

One of the most perplexing questions in the field of language education is how to make the determination whether a student is an ELL or an ELL with a learning disability. A recent study sheds some light on the questions that states and districts need to ask to decipher whether an ELL's academic challenges are related to developing a new language, a learning disability, or some other root cause. In reviewing the research literature, Elizabeth Burr, Eric Hass, and Karen Ferriere, in their Institute of Education Sciences (IES) study, found four key questions to help trigger this distinction:

- Is the student receiving instruction of sufficient quality to enable him or her to make the accepted levels of academic progress?
- How does the student's progress in hearing, speaking, reading, and writing English as a second language compare with the expected rate of progress for his or her age and initial level of English proficiency?
- To what extent are behaviors that might otherwise indicate a learning disability considered to be normal for the child's cultural background or to be part of the process of U.S. acculturation?
- How might additional factors—including socioeconomic status, previous education experience, fluency in his or her first language, attitude toward school, attitude toward learning English, and personality attributes—impact the student's academic progress? (2015, p. i)

In researching the policy and practices of 20 states, the research team concluded that generally two factors can be attributed to the inconsistent identification of ELLs with disabilities. First, educators are not familiar with the process of language and literacy development; overall, there is an inadequate understanding of why ELLs are not making acceptable progress in academic English. Second, referral processes are often not designed with linguistically and culturally diverse students in mind, assessment is not sensitive to linguistic and cultural differences in the student population, and services are inconsistently implemented.

What is rarely mentioned when it comes to ELLs with disabilities is the role and influence of culture on learning. Equally important is taking the time to investigate the influence of students' home language on their literacy development and the extent to which their home language instruction and assessment are extended to response to instruction (RtI) or multi-tier system of supports (MTSS) strategies (Hamayan, Marler, Sanchez-Lopez, & Damico, 2013; Klingner, Hoover, & Baca, 2008).

EDUCATIONAL POLICY AND ITS IMPACT ON ASSESSMENT

Educational policy revolves around a specific plan or a course of action for a particular issue that influences local decision making; in the United States, it often emanates from the federal government or from individual states. Much of the federal educational policy stems from iterations of the Elementary and Secondary Education Act (ESEA). For example, when the ESEA was reauthorized in 2001 as the No Child Left Behind Act, it in essence became de facto language policy as it eliminated any reference to previously established bilingual education practices. Consequently, the provision of bilingual education programs declined across the country, as did the use of languages other than English for assessment (Menken, 2008). Unfortunately, when policymakers disregard the potential of bilingualism that these students are capable of developing through rich schooling experiences, educators simply perpetuate inequities in education (García, Kleifgen, & Falchi, 2008).

It is true that our nation has not sufficiently fostered the full development of its multilingual, multicultural resources, especially within the realm of preK-12 education. However, the ESEA has pushed for greater inclusion of ELLs in standards-based instruction and assessment. Notable stipulations include insistence in each state having English language proficiency/development standards, connecting those standards to an English language proficiency assessment, as well as state content standards and requiring that state content assessment be disaggregated by student subgroups for accountability purposes.

REFLECTION

Investigating State and Local Policy Regarding English Language Learners

To what extent do your state and school district have policies that you consider equitable in identifying ELLs and ELLs with disabilities? Are there policies that honor the students' languages and cultures? If so, in what ways? How do these policies affect instruction, assessment, and referral to special education services?

The language of instruction and assessment may vary depending on state or local policy. State tests, for example, may be exclusively in English. However, in dual language or language immersion classrooms, assessment must proceed in two languages in order to reflect and measure programmatic, instructional, and student goals. To be equitable, the allocation of languages (the percentage of use of each language or the subject areas assigned to each language) for instruction should always be mirrored in assessment.

PRINCIPLES FOR ASSESSING LANGUAGE LEARNERS

Throughout its entire process—the initial planning phase, development, and implementation—assessment must be inclusive of all learners, otherwise the results will not be valid indicators of what the students can actually do. It would be unfortunate to make an inappropriate decision that carried high-stakes consequences, such as grade retention, based on misinterpreted or biased data. What can educators do? One idea is to craft a set of assessment principles at the school or district level that truly reflect universal design and the expanding role of teachers as assessment leaders.

Assessment designs need to consider

- the characteristics of the student population, including linguistic and cultural variability;
- multiple pathways for students to reach their goals;
- the complexity of language so that it does not mask the students' academic achievement;
- the language(s) of instruction;
- visual, graphic, interactive, and linguistic supports;
- potential linguistic, cultural, gender, and socioeconomic bias;
- ways in which students and teachers can receive and use feedback on content and language; and
- features such as use of color, font size, appropriateness of illustrations for specific cultural groups, and time on task.

Teachers need to engage in assessment practices that are

- fair, transparent, and equitable for all students;
- supportive of all students, including those with learning disabilities and those who are learning in two languages;
- based on realistic, grade-level goals;
- considerate of students' strengths, including their knowledge of other languages; and
- adaptive to individual students without losing sight of developmental appropriateness, including ELLs at varying levels of language proficiency, gifted and talented students, and those with learning disabilities.

REFLECTION

Exploring Assessment Principles

Does your school or district have assessment principles that form the basis for equitable practice for all students, inclusive of ELLs? Which of these principles might you adopt as a school? Might some of these principles be converted into school or district policy? If so, which ones, and why?

Before going further, we must confront and put to rest the notion of formative and summative assessment that somehow has been grossly misunderstood yet continues to plague the field.

FORMATIVE OR SUMMATIVE? WHICH ONE IS IT?

The terms *formative* and *summative* actually have been borrowed from the field of evaluation research. So labeled by Michael Scriven in 1967, formative evaluation is an internal method for judging the worth of an educational program while it is still forming or is in progress. Its intent is to foster further development and improvement of the program's activities. On the other hand, a summative evaluation is an external or independent method of judging the worth of a program at the end or summation of its activities. Summative evaluation determines the extent to which a program's goals have been met.

Moving to the assessment arena, it was Scriven's belief that all assessments have the capacity to be summative in their function, but only some have the additional capability of serving formative functions. Thus, the formative-summative distinction is really context dependent rather than a dichotomy; it depends on the purpose of the assessment and the use of the data. For example, a high-stakes test, such as an annual summative achievement measure, which gives item-level analysis of its results, is in some sense diagnostic in nature. These results could be applied to differentiating instruction for individual or groups of students—a formative application of the data. On the other hand, data from oral language samples collected within a lesson may offer formative feedback and can also be considered summative in nature as the samples measure a student's language development up to that point in time. Figure 1.2 points out some characteristics that are commonly used to distinguish formative from summative assessment practices as they occur in classrooms.

Figure 1.2 General Features of Formative and Summative Assessment Within a Classroom Context

Formative Assessment Feature	Summative Assessment Feature
Monitors student progress	Evaluates student progress
Occurs internal to instruction	Occurs toward the end of an instructional cycle or on a predetermined basis (e.g., quarterly, annually)
Provides ongoing descriptive feedback	Provides feedback that may take the form of grading
Co-occurs with learning	Demonstrates learning
Is process oriented	Is product or outcome oriented
Informs instruction	Gauges instructional effectiveness

REFLECTION

Distinguishing Between Formative and Summative Purposes for Assessment

Robert Stake, an evaluation researcher, once said, "When the cook tastes the soup, that's formative; when the guests taste the soup, that's summative" (quoted in Scriven, 1991, p. 169). How might this analogy apply to assessment? Think of a grade-level example and share it with your colleagues or make a poster highlighting the differences between the two.

Varying interpretations of formative assessment can be found today; Figure 1.3 outlines its most common definitions. Even though a range of perspectives exists, all attempt to frame formative assessment in a positive light, claiming it serves as a tool for informing and improving teaching and learning rather than functioning as a list of student shortcomings. Even so, there is no general consensus as to its features or uses.

Figure 1.3 Different Conceptualizations of Formative Assessment

Differing Perspectives of Formative Assessment	Literature Support for the Perspective
It's a test or a series of tests.	Products of testing companies and publishers of instructional materials
It's a set of practices.	Stiggins, 2005
It's a reflective process.	Heritage, 2010; Moss & Brookhart, 2009; Popham, 2008
It's a system.	Fisher & Frey, 2014; Marzano, 2010

REFLECTION

Assessing for Formative and Summative Purposes

We realize that not everyone will be convinced to reconsider how to apply formative and summative data to assessment. If, in fact, you were to retain the terms *formative* and *summative*, how can you use them more succinctly for your specific purposes? With your professional learning team, sketch out various definitions and come to agreement as to how to move forward with these concepts for your grade, department, or school. Make sure you include school leadership to obtain support for your ideas.

INTRODUCING ASSESSMENT *AS, FOR,* AND *OF* LEARNING

Assessment is often defined by how consumers use the data—in fact, the primary use of assessment is to gather information to help us make decisions that benefit stakeholders (Bachman & Palmer, 2010; Chatterji, 2003). All assessment should have clear descriptions of the intended learning and afford students opportunities to demonstrate their competencies. Assessment should be referenced to standards or criteria for success. However, there are different approaches to assessment that highlight various users of assessment information.

The model we introduce and use throughout this book is assessment *as, for,* and *of* learning (see Chapters 5, 6, and 7 for detailed descriptions). Figure 1.4 displays the defining traits of this model. By widening the scope of assessment to encompass multiple perspectives and voices, we hope to make the assessment experience engaging and meaningful for all audiences. By inviting multiple stakeholders, starting with students, to be part of the conversation, we hope to bring balance and equity to the field of education.

Figure 1.4 Features of Assessment *as, for,* and *of* Learning

Assessment as Learning	Assessment for Learning	Assessment of Learning
Generates data used to foster students' metacognitive and metalinguistic awareness	Generates data used for formative purposes	Generates data used for summative purposes
Occurs on an ongoing basis, facilitated by teachers until self-regulated by students	Occurs on an ongoing, continuous basis between teachers and students	Occurs at designated time intervals, as in the same month each year (such as annual state testing)
Is internal to student learning	Is internal to instruction and teacher learning	Is associated with the culmination of an instructional cycle or year and accrued learning
Is individualized for students	Is individualized for classrooms and, at times, across classrooms	Is standardized or standard in administration (for example, teachers follow the same set of directions and procedures) for schools, districts, or states
Encourages co-construction by students and teachers of criteria for success	Encourages teachers to create tasks and determine shared criteria for success with students	Encourages departments, programs, districts, or states to create or select measures
Uses original student work as data sources	Uses student work coupled with a variety of instructional methods and response formats as data sources	Uses testing as the primary data source, with multiple-choice, short-answer questions or constructed-response formats
Is intrinsically motivated	Is instructionally bound	Is accountability driven
Relies on students as assessors, based on jointly constructed criteria for success	Relies on immediate feedback to students	Relies on a quick turnaround of scores

Together, assessment *as, for,* and *of* learning forms a balanced assessment system, a unique application of the BASIC model to today's context (Gottlieb & Nguyen, 2007). It acknowledges that each approach to assessment offers a valued contribution to understanding student performance in school. Assessment *as* learning is most personalized as it recognizes students as an important data source. Assessment *for* learning embraces the role of teachers in making everyday decisions from instructionally embedded data. Assessment *of* learning affords administrators a sense of their school's or district's position in relation to standards-referenced data.

As education is all about learning, students should be the primary consumers and should take center stage in this process. When students are able to make personal goals that are fortified by standards and provide evidence for meeting those outcomes through self- and peer assessment, then assessment and learning become blended. The recognition and encouragement of student voice and student agency in framing and using data help shape assessment *as* learning.

Just as important as students are the teachers who plan and use assessment data to guide and improve instruction. Teachers provide timely descriptive feedback to students, make minute-by-minute adjustments to their instructional plans, and ensure a scaffolding of learning for their students on a continuous basis. When assessment within and across classrooms affords teachers opportunities to make instructional decisions, teachers are engaged in assessment *for* learning (Stiggins, 2005).

Supported by district and state administrators, large-scale assessment requires the use of standard conditions across multiple classrooms and include schools, districts, or states in the planning, gathering, analyzing, and reporting of student data. Standardized norm-referenced or criterion-referenced tests are large-scale measures. They involve a development process over several years that entails trying out items in cognitive labs on individual students, pilot testing on a small sample of students, and field testing on a large number of students before selecting items or tasks that perform the best to create a final test form. Assessment *of* learning, when administered on an annual basis, is generally high stakes in nature, with consequences attached to results. Data generated from assessment *of* learning generally contribute to pivotal decisions for both students and teachers.

REFLECTION

Assessing *as*, *for*, and *of* Learning

Assessment *of* learning is administrator supported, assessment *for* learning is teacher guided, and assessment *as* learning is student centered. What are the pros and cons of using this tri-part scheme to describe different approaches to assessment? For instance, does it help clarify user roles for assessment? Is it more descriptive than the process currently in place in your setting? Why or why not?

Think of the myriad terms that have become associated with assessment—*formative, interim, summative, common, benchmark, formal, informal, standardized, large scale, classroom, criterion referenced, norm referenced, diagnostic,* and *performance,* to name a few. These terms are shown in Figure 1.5 alongside their definitions. For those of you not familiar with the field of assessment, consider making strips of the terms and their definitions. Match the terms with their definitions and then think of or investigate to find an example. For those of you who feel comfortable with the assessment terms, categorize them to represent examples of assessment *as, for,* and *of* learning.

Insight into the purposes for assessment is also useful in matching stakeholders—students, teachers, and administrators—with their corresponding level of implementation, whether that is the classroom, school, district, or state.

PURPOSES FOR ASSESSING ENGLISH LANGUAGE LEARNERS

Unless educators know *why* we assess ELLs, there is bound to be misinterpretation of the resulting data. Figure 1.6 on page 26 outlines six major purposes for assessment at the classroom, school, district, and state level. At the classroom level, students are engaged in self- and peer assessment, while teachers are directly involved in the ongoing monitoring of student performance and in improving their day-to-day instructional practice. The other purposes of assessment, although they operate at a district or state level, should ultimately inform instruction and promote student

Figure 1.5 Assessment Terms and Their Definitions

Assessment Term	Definition
Assessment	The process of planning, gathering, analyzing, and interpreting data for decision making
Benchmark	A measure generally used to predict performance on an annual high-stakes test
Classroom	Collection of data as part of the instructional routine (may also be considered instructional assessment)
Common	A measure that is crafted based on mutually agreed-upon decisions by educators for uniform use across multiple classrooms
Criterion-Referenced	A measure whose results are reported in reference to established criteria, such as standards, rather than by ranking student performance
Diagnostic	A measure whose results pinpoint the extent of mastery of specific skills
Formal	Data collected with a set plan in mind
Formative	A process internal to instruction that offers results in a timely fashion that inform and improve instruction and are used for giving descriptive feedback to students
High-Stakes	A test with results that have consequences for students, teachers, schools, or districts
Informal	Data collected without any specific planning
Instructional	Data collected within the instructional cycle (also referred to as classroom assessment)
Interim	A measure used to monitor student progress at predetermined junctures throughout the school year
Large scale	A test given to large numbers of students within and across districts and states
Norm-Referenced	A test that compares scores of a selected group of students who have taken the test and are typically of the same age or grade with those of the test taker
Performance	Authentic, hands-on tasks where students produce original work that is generally interpreted with a rubric, checklist, or rating scale
Standardized	A test with results given as standard or scale scores so that performance of individual or groups of students can be compared
Summative	The sum of evidence for learning gathered at the culmination of a designated point in time, such as at the end of a unit or on an annual basis

learning. To personalize the purposes for assessment in your setting, you may wish to refer to Resource 1.5.

Teachers working with ELLs need to have a sense of the students' baseline or starting point for both language proficiency and academic achievement (in English and their home language) in order to document progress over time. After establishing baseline data, teachers can then monitor students' growth throughout the school year. Classroom assessment mirrors ongoing instructional practices in each day's lesson. Common assessment across classrooms, such as at a grade or department level, offers information from unit to unit. Student portfolios, in which original student work is collected and analyzed, are another form of evidence of student performance over time and may be utilized on a quarterly or semester basis.

Figure 1.6   The Primary Purposes for Assessing English Language Learners and Their Associated Types of Measures

Purpose for Assessment in K-12 Settings	Types of Measures Compatible With the Purpose for Assessment
Screening and classifying students to determine eligibility for language support services and to assist in placement decisions	• Language Use Surveys • Additional language/literacy surveys and school records (e.g., transcripts) • English language proficiency screener • Measures of literacy and academic achievement in the home language and English
Monitoring progress of students' language development and academic achievement	• Classroom assessment that reflects the language(s) of instruction • Common assessment across classrooms • Student portfolios, including self-reflection • District- or school-level interim or benchmark measures
Enhancing teaching and learning	• Instructionally embedded assessment • Student self- and peer assessment
Fulfilling federal, state, and local accountability requirements for academic achievement and English language development	• State/consortium test of academic achievement • State/consortium English language proficiency test • District assessment of academic achievement in English and other languages, as appropriate • District assessment of language proficiency in English and other languages, as appropriate
Reclassifying students within or transitioning from (language) support services	• State and district accountability measures • Teacher recommendations based on classroom assessment and other data (e.g., GPAs)
Evaluating educational programs to ascertain effectiveness of instructional support services	• Contextual variables (e.g., demographics, types of support services, teacher qualifications) • Accountability measures • Student portfolios, including data from common assessment • Focus groups and interviews of students, teachers, and school leaders

Source: Adapted from Gottlieb, 2006, p. 9.

REFLECTION

Charting the Purposes for Assessment

What are the specific measures used in your classroom, school, district, and state to assess ELLs' language proficiency and achievement that are matched to the purposes in Figure 1.6? How are the data used to make accountability, programmatic, and instructional decisions? Do you feel that there is a full complement of measures, too many measures, or too few valid measures to obtain a fair and accurate account of your students' performance? What suggestions might you make to have a more balanced assessment system for language learners? What specific provisions need to be made for non-ELLs in dual language programs to monitor their academic achievement and language development?

Measuring Academic Language
Proficiency and Academic Achievement

Assessment of ELLs who receive language support services is a more complex undertaking than assessment of proficient English-speaking students because it involves the documentation of both language proficiency and academic achievement. Language proficiency is an expression of a student's processing and use of language within and across four language domains or modalities: listening, speaking, reading, and writing. Language proficiency assessment reveals the extent of a student's language development, generally expressed as a language proficiency level.

Accountability reform efforts beginning in the early 2000s have pushed measurement of language proficiency into academic contexts (Bailey & Wolf, 2012). In addition, language development standards, the anchor for language proficiency assessment, have emphasized the language of the content areas required for students to succeed academically (WIDA, 2004, 2007, 2012). Thus, in the last decade, assessment of academic language proficiency has expanded in scope to measure the language of school—that is, the language specific to each discipline or content area.

In contrast to language proficiency, academic achievement reflects the extent of a student's subject matter knowledge, skills, and concepts for the core content areas (in particular, in English language arts and mathematics) for his or her grade or age. It is a mark of conceptual learning directly tied to school-based curriculum and state academic content standards (Gottlieb, 2003).

With the new generation of assessments initiated in 2014–2015, measuring academic achievement as an educational outcome has become intertwined with academic language use. This creates a conundrum for ELLs who may have the conceptual base in their home language but have not yet developed the academic language in English to express and apply it.

It might be convenient for teachers and school leaders to have an overall assessment map to plot language proficiency and academic achievement measures for ELLs at each level of implementation: state/province, district county, school, campus, grade, and classroom. School leaders and teachers could then complete the applicable portions to ascertain the amount and range of assessment for ELLs. Figure 1.7 provides a sampling of hypothetical measures from the classroom to state levels.

REFLECTION

Mapping Assessment for English Language Learners by Levels of Implementation

Using Resource 1.6 brainstorm and list assessment measures at your state/province, district, school, grade/department, and classroom levels given to ELLs. Then classify the measures into those that represent language proficiency and those that are measures of academic achievement. You may wish to further delineate those measures in English and the home language of the students. Is there a balanced representation of academic achievement and language proficiency at each level of implementation? If not, what suggestions might you make to equalize the two?

Figure 1.7   A Range of Assessment for English Language Learners at Each Level of Implementation

Construct	Measuring Language Proficiency				Measuring Academic Achievement			
Measurement at the:	Listening	Speaking	Reading	Writing	Language Arts	Math	Science	Social Studies
State level	State test of English language proficiency				State tests of academic achievement			
District level	Common/interim language proficiency measures in English (and another language for students in dual language programs)				Common/interim or benchmark/end-of-course achievement tests in English (or the student's home language for subjects where instruction is in the home language)			
Grade/ department or school level	• Interdisciplinary, thematic projects with standards-referenced rubrics for language proficiency and academic achievement • Common performances, projects, or products with integrated rubrics							
Classroom level	• Observation of use of words/expressions with multiple meanings in context • Academic conversations with feedback • Interviews or student-led conferences • Content-based writing samples				• Informal reading inventories • Math-related charts and graphs • Science investigations and reports • Timelines of historical events			

Source: Adapted from Gottlieb, 2006, p. 10.

Planning Ahead: An Assessment Schedule

Teachers and school leaders should have a plan to deal with all the tests and assessments that occur outside their individual classrooms during the school year. Figure 1.8, a sample schedule for assessment of ELLs, provides a hypothetical month-by-month account of state and district measures. Ideally, it should be color coded so it is easy to see the distribution of different types of measures or student groups at a glance. (A blank schedule can be found in Resource 1.7, or you may wish to use an Excel spreadsheet to create your own.)

Extra rows can be added to document school- and grade-level measures. In fact, it might be helpful for teachers to jointly complete a schedule to avoid overburdening students with assessment. Collectively, a teacher team can decide which data are most useful for reporting student performance on a quarterly, trimester, or semester basis, depending on when report cards are issued.

Multiple measures of the oral language, literacy, and conceptual development of ELLs and dual language learners should be collected throughout the year. If there is more than one language used for instruction, the schedule could also serve as a cross-check to ensure a match of instruction with the language of assessment.

Figure 1.8   A Hypothetical Calendar for Assessment *of* Learning for English Language Learners and Dual Language Learners at District and State Levels

	August	September	October	November	December
District measures	Reading and math placement tests	Computer-based reading and math tests	Interim language proficiency measure in one or multiple languages	Content-based writing sample in one or multiple languages	
State measures	Initial input data and screening tools	Early years observation tool		Interim achievement test of language arts and math	

	January	February	March	April	May	June
District measures	Computer-based reading and math tests		Content-based writing sample in one or multiple languages		Interim language proficiency measure in one or multiple languages	Student writing portfolios
State measures	English-language proficiency test		Early years observation tool; Interim achievement test in one or more languages	Assessment of academic achievement in language arts, mathematics, and science		Early years observation tool

Source: Adapted from Gottlieb, 2006, p. 13.

REFLECTION

Scheduling Assessment *of* Learning

Assessment has become so pervasive it is hard to keep track of it all! There is no reason to systematically record assessment *for* and *as* learning since it is internal and integral to what happens in classrooms every day. But it is important to have a sense of when assessment *of* learning is going to occur. With your grade-level team, take time to complete a calendar for assessment, such as that suggested in Figure 1.8, so it becomes an extension of teaching rather than a distraction from it. You may wish to add common assessment for your grade or department.

ACADEMIC LANGUAGE USE AND ASSESSMENT

One important contributor to educational equity is the conscious integration of and attention to content and academic language. Academic language, the language of textbooks, classrooms, assessment, and school, is different in register, structure, and vocabulary from the language of social interaction (Gottlieb & Ernst-Slavit, 2014a). Being academically proficient in a language means knowing and using general and content-specific vocabulary in conjunction with complex grammatical structures, language functions, and discourses; the purpose behind academic language use is to acquire new knowledge, interact with that knowledge, and impart that knowledge to others (Bailey, 2007).

Lev Vygotsky, the eminent Russian psychologist, claimed that social interaction, a cultural trait, plays a critical role in cognitive development. In fact, development cannot be separated from its social context (Lucas & Corpuz, 2007). Academic language learning always occurs within a sociocultural context, as do standards, instruction, and assessment. A sociocultural approach to learning takes students' social and cultural experiences into account in their acquisition, organization, and use of language (Gauvain, 2005). For ELLs, one of the first tasks of academic learning is to interpret the sociocultural context of schooling and that of the classroom; this may be challenging as it is not reflective of the students' social, familial, linguistic, and ethnically related practices through which they see the world (Garcia & Ortiz, 2006).

Given the significance of academic language use as a marker of school success, assessment must reflect this new norm. Assessment of academic language use that focuses on its three dimensions—discourse, sentences, and word/phrases—should simulate the more rigorous kinds of grade-level language tasks students are expected to be able to do in their classrooms. In essence, the presence of academic language has been the impetus for teachers to raise the bar in terms of student engagement in higher-order thinking, asking them, for example, to evaluate text, create an argument, and defend a stance by providing claims and evidence. In response to this added academic demand comes a more sophisticated and targeted use of language and content. Gone are the days when teachers rely on multiple-choice responses as the sole data source for decision making; today's assessments must reflect the performance of students who are busy making meaning by designing models, conducting experiments, and producing multimedia projects.

REFLECTION

Applying Academic Language Use to Assessment

In response to college and career readiness standards, is academic language use more visible in curriculum, instruction, and assessment in your district and school? Give an example or two of changes that have taken place over the last several years. How have you responded to more intentional use of academic language in your classroom assessment practices? If you have not focused much attention on this topic, no worries, we will be exploring it more in depth in the next chapter.

REACTION AND REFLECTION

The growing presence of ELLs in our classrooms and the increasing focus on school, district, and state accountability give us reason to reexamine our assessment practices. In doing so, teachers and school leaders must become familiar with the rationale for the different types of assessments, their purposes, and their audiences. They also should consider the impact of college and career readiness standards and their academic language demand on reshaping their thinking toward assessment. Ultimately, by viewing assessment as three complementary approaches— assessment *as* learning, assessment *for* learning, and assessment *of* learning—we begin to bring more equitable systems into our classrooms.

Thinking back on this chapter, is your school or district following the trend of increased numbers of ELLs? If so, it might be interesting to track the demographic data of different subgroups of students over the last years. How is your school or district making use of its additional linguistic and cultural resources? As you reflect with your colleagues, here are some additional questions you might wish to ponder:

- Resource 1.7 lists measures and assessment-related policies that are appropriate for language learners, particularly ELLs. How might you use this list for students' initial entry into a school district or at the beginning of each school year?
- How might using the assessment approaches *as, for,* and *of* learning help unify assessment practices for a school or school district? What steps might your grade/department or professional learning community take to jump-start their implementation?
- Think about the purposes for assessment and the corresponding measures that are currently in place in your school and district. Does each measure match its intended purpose? If not, it is not valid and the data cannot be trusted. To what extent do you trust the data used for decision making for the students in your school and district?
- Where would you place your school, your district, and your state on the bridge to educational equity for ELLs? What might be your goal at the end of this school year? You and your grade-level team or entire school might think about a 3-year plan for designing and implementing a plan for improving assessment equity.

Assessment must be inclusive, fair, relevant, comprehensive, valid, and yield meaningful information for multiple stakeholders. Teachers must understand the power of assessment data in helping provide evidence that students are growing, learning, and making academic progress. Ultimately, it is our responsibility to create a bridge connecting the characteristics of our students with sound assessment to ensure educational equity of all learners.

RESOURCE 1.1

A Decision Tree for the Identification and Placement of English Language Learners

Newly enrolled student in a state or school district

↓

• Administer Language Use Survey

↓

Linguistically and culturally diverse student? YES*

↓

Proceed with Phase I measures

• Administer Oral Language Use and Literacy Surveys (optional)

• Administer an English Language Proficiency Screener (usually within first weeks of registration)

↓

English language learner? YES

↓

Proceed with Phase II measures

• Administer Measures of Language Proficiency and Academic Achievement in the Home Language (L1)**

• Administer Measures of Academic Achievement in English (L2)

↓

Eligible for collaborative support services? YES

Place student in an educational program with provision for language support according to survey data and results from the screener

---

Source: Adapted from Gottlieb, 2006, p. 15.

* At any point when the answer to the question in the flowchart is NO, students are to be placed in classrooms without additional support for English language development and monitored for at least a quarter. In making placement decisions, there should be additional consideration for linguistically and culturally diverse students with individual education programs (IEPs).

** Measures in the students' home languages are recommended as part of initial entry for all students identified as ELLs in order to collect necessary baseline data on their literacy and academic achievement. These measures should be required for ELLs who are instructed in their home language.

RESOURCE 1.2

A Sample Language Use Survey for Newly Enrolled Students

Help us know about you. Tell us about the languages you use. Please answer these questions.

1. Is a language other than English spoken in your home?

   YES   NO

   If yes, which language or languages? _____

2. Do you speak a language other than English with someone in your home?

   YES   NO

   If yes, which language or languages? _____

3. Do you speak a language other than English **every day** at home?

   YES   NO

4. Put an X in the box on the top line to show the grades you went to school here in the United States. (If applicable), put an X on the bottom line for the grades where you went to school in another country. Put a circle around the year(s) or grades you did not go to school.

Which Grades?															
Schools in the United States. How many have you attended? PreK	K	1	2	3	4	5	6	7	8	9	10	11	12		
Schools outside the United States. How many have you attended? PreK	K	1	2	3	4	5	6	7	8	9	10	11	12		

Source: Adapted from Gottlieb, 2006, p. 16.

RESOURCE 1.3

A Sample Oral Language Use Survey for English Language Learners

Directions: Which language or languages do you use around your home, neighborhood, and school? Tell me if use your home language, English, or both languages with the people and places that I name. *As the student responds, mark the designated box.*

Which Languages Do You Speak	My Home Language	English	Both Languages	Not Applicable
With your parents or guardians				
With your grandparents				
With your brothers and sisters				
With other relatives who live with you				
With your caregivers (if any)				
With your neighbors				
With your friends				
Around Your Neighborhood				
At the store				
At the clinic or doctor's office				
Outside, as in a park				
At a market or fast food place				
Around Your School				
On the playground or outside				
In the lunchroom				
In the halls				
During free time				

Source: Adapted from Gottlieb, 2006, p. 17.

RESOURCE 1.4

A Sample Literacy Use Survey for English Language Learners

Directions: Which kinds of materials do you read and write outside of school? Mark the box to show whether you use your home language, _____, English, or both languages when you read and write. *Not applicable* means that you do not use those materials for reading or writing.

Before or After School . . .	*In My Home Language*	*In My Additional Language, English*	*In Both Languages*	*Not Applicable*
I Read . . .				
Street signs and names				
Maps or directions				
Schedules (e.g., school, bus, or train)				
Web sites				
Magazines or e-articles				
Notes from friends (e.g., e-mails or texts)				
Information from the Internet				
Brochures/pamphlets				
Short stories				
Poetry				
Books				
I Write . . .				
Information on forms				
To-do lists				
Notes in my classes				
E-mails or texts				
Responses to questions				
Short stories				
Poetry or songs				

Source: Adapted from Gottlieb, 2006, p. 18.

RESOURCE 1.5

Purposes for Classroom Assessment, Types of Measures, and Language(s) of Assessment

In this table there is a list of possible types of measures associated with a purpose for classroom assessment of ELLs (those that do not fit are marked with an X). Based on your personal knowledge, or that of other teachers in your school, write the names of the measures that are used in the designated box. Then discuss with other teachers how you use the information obtained from assessment.

Purpose for Assessment: To Determine a Student's . . .	Types of Measures				Not Applicable
	Language Proficiency— Languages of Administration		Academic Achievement— Languages of Administration		
	Home Language	English	Home Language	English	
Relative language proficiency (performance in one language in relation to another one)			×	×	
Overall growth in English language development	×		×		
Pre-referral for evaluation for special education					
Diagnosis within a specific language domain (e.g., reading comprehension)					
Eligibility for additional support services					
Depth of knowledge on a topic within a content area	×	×			

Source: Adapted from Gottlieb, 2006, p. 19.

RESOURCE 1.6

A Hypothetical Calendar for Assessment *of* Learning for English Language Learners

State and District Levels

Mark the months in which required state and district assessments occur for ELLs, including assessments of both academic achievement and language proficiency. Optionally name the measures. You may wish to replicate this calendar for each grade or grade-level cluster.

	August	September	October	November	December
District measures					
State measures					

	January	February	March	April	May	June
District measures						
State measures						

Source: Adapted from Gottlieb, 2006, p. 21.

RESOURCE 1.7

An Inventory of Initial Measures and Assessment Policies for English Language Learners

Here is a list of measures and assessment-related policies that your state, school district, or school may currently use with its ELLs upon their entry into a school system or at the beginning of each school year. Put an X in the circles alongside the measures and policies that are used in your setting.

Suggested Measures Upon Initial Entry in a School District

○ A Language Use Survey (or the equivalent, such as a Home Language Survey)

○ A survey (or interview) of oral language use

○ A (multi) literacy survey

○ An English language proficiency screener

○ A content-based writing sample in English and the home language

○ A measure of academic achievement in a student's home language (if feasible)

○ An informal reading inventory (if literate in English or Spanish)

Policies

Here is a partial list of potential policies that your state, school district, or school may have in place for its ELLs. Put an X in the circles alongside the policies present in your setting.

○ A policy regarding accessibility and accommodations for state and district achievement tests (provisions that may enhance student performance but that do not affect the test's validity)

○ A policy regarding accommodations for state and district language proficiency tests for ELLs with disabilities (provisions, such as extended time, that may enhance student performance but that do not affect the test's validity)

○ A policy regarding district assessment for local accountability, including measures of achievement and language proficiency (e.g., interim or benchmark tests)

○ A policy regarding the language(s) of assessment and their match to instruction

○ A policy regarding the assessment of ELLs according to their levels of language proficiency (e.g., allowing additional supports for ELLs at the beginning stages of English language development)

Source: Adapted from Gottlieb, 2006, p. 22.

2

Assessment of Academic Language Through Standards

The Bridge to Systemic Equity

Fairness does not mean everyone gets the same. Fairness means everyone gets what they need.

—Rick Riordan

Standards can serve as a cornerstone of systemic equity for classrooms, schools, districts, and states. From their inception at the close of the twentieth century, the influence of standards on educational practice has been undeniable. Today, a range of student standards covers different curricular and assessment foci, namely (a) prominent content areas and language development; (b) different age groups, from students in K-12 settings to children in early learning contexts; and (c) different languages, particularly Spanish-speaking communities. Standards are pivotal in designing a coordinated assessment system that builds on strong curriculum and instruction.

Content standards of each discipline or subject area are the starting point and reference for teaching and learning. Language proficiency development standards connect to content standards and specify grade-level language expectations for each level of language proficiency. Bridges from academic language proficiency to student achievement allow teachers and language learners to seamlessly integrate language development within the content areas through standards.

This chapter explores academic language use in standards-driven systems for language learners as the anchor for assessment. While each set of standards is treated independently, together they serve complementary purposes and uses. We begin our journey into the world of standards with grade-level content expectations, their affiliated assessments, and the demands on ELLs. Then we explore how academic language use ties content and language standards and address its applicability to instruction and assessment. Finally, we reveal how language proficiency development standards provide the scaffolds for language learning that can transfer over to assessment.

Revisiting the School-Based Scenario

This past year South Side Middle School has focused its professional learning on academic language use across the curriculum. Each grade-level team has dissected the state's college and career readiness standards and has matched them to their language development standards. From there, the teams have analyzed the academic language of their textbooks and other instructional materials. Next, the teachers have generated ideas of community resources or student experiences that might facilitate ELLs' deeper understanding of some of the genres emphasized in their grade. For example, a group of students from American Samoa is very concerned about the ongoing conflict regarding the banning of shark fishing—a topic ripe for debate (see Lam, Low, & Tauiliili-Mahuka, 2014, for a more detailed account). Another contingent of Spanish speakers is wrapped up in mysteries and has taken character traits from "El Chupacabra" ("the Goat Sucker"), a familiar oral gothic legend, and have applied them to Edgar Allen Poe's *The Cask of Amontillado*, a written gothic tale (see Minaya-Rowe, 2014, for a more detailed account). In both instances, teachers have been able to apply content standards and language standards to challenging grade-level academic language in planning their units of learning.

Teachers and school leaders that have an inclusive mission and vision for all students realize that this is the grounding for equity (Dove, Honigsfeld, & Cohan, 2014; Miramontes, Nadeau, & Commins, 2011). Since diverse learners are integral to a school's infrastructure, the interweaving of content standards and language standards provides language learners full and fitting access to grade-level curriculum and, ultimately, to more socially just assessment.

COLLEGE AND CAREER READINESS STANDARDS, OTHER CONTENT STANDARDS, AND RELATED ASSESSMENT

Since the late 1980s, national organizations, beginning with the National Council of Teachers of Mathematics (1989), have developed content standards to describe what students should know and should be able to do as the result of schooling. By the early 1990s, other professional organizations had followed suit, including the National Council of Teachers of English (NCTE), the International Literacy Association (formerly the International Reading Association), the National Research Council (which produced the National Science Education Standards), and the National Center for History in the Schools. This groundbreaking work set in motion a national standards movement that continues to this day.

Student standards have played a prominent role in federal legislation—namely, their association with the Elementary and Secondary Education Act (ESEA). First, the Improving America's Schools Act of 1994 required state academic content standards. Subsequently, the 2001 reauthorization of the ESEA, also known as the No Child Left Behind Act, mandated English language proficiency/development standards and compulsory disaggregation of assessment data. As a result, ELLs emerged as a viable student subgroup with focused attention on their achievement.

College and career readiness standards were launched in 2010 with the Common Core State Standards (CCSS) for English language arts and mathematics; the Next Generation Science Standards, based on *A Framework for K-12 Science Education* (2012), closely followed. In 2013 social studies joined the rank of standards documents with *The College, Career, and Civic Life (C3) Framework for Social Studies State Standards: Guidance for Enhancing the Rigor of K-12 Civics, Economics, Geography, and History.* In 2014 the National Core Arts Standards for dance, media arts, music, theatre, and visual arts were instituted.

Although the nationalization of standards has been fraught with controversy, the positive potential of these standards on a statewide basis can be realized if state and local policymakers, education leaders, and practitioners view equity as a means to and an essential outcome of their implementation. So let's examine some practices associated with these standards and their implications for ELLs.

REFLECTION

Examining Content Standards

What does your state call college and career readiness standards? Some states, such as Virginia, Alaska, Nebraska, and Texas, never adopted the CCSS. Others initially did but over time changed the name or revised some of the standards, either due to political motives or because they preferred to have content standards specific for their state. No matter what the label, however, this generation of content standards is considered more academically and linguistically demanding, with an emphasis on higher-order thinking. Do you agree? Find some grade-level examples that are particularly challenging for ELLs in your state and share them with your colleagues.

GETTING ORGANIZED FOR STANDARDS-REFERENCED ASSESSMENT OF ACADEMIC LANGUAGE USE

Sound instructional and assessment practices that undergird educational systems stem from standards. The figure below, which is a broad outline of this chapter, enables educators to visualize the relationship among standards, academic language use, and related assessment.

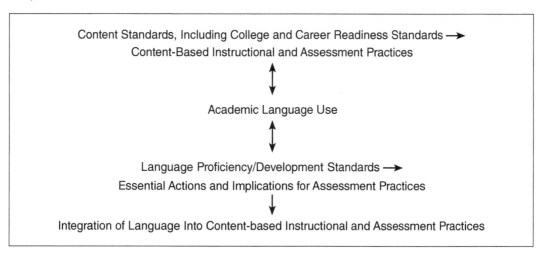

Content Standards, Including College and Career Readiness Standards →
Content-Based Instructional and Assessment Practices

↕

Academic Language Use

↕

Language Proficiency/Development Standards →
Essential Actions and Implications for Assessment Practices

↓

Integration of Language Into Content-based Instructional and Assessment Practices

While standards are the anchor for curriculum, instruction, and assessment, academic language is the unifying thread and crosswalk among them.

ACADEMIC LANGUAGE: THE BRIDGE CONNECTING CONTENT STANDARDS AND LANGUAGE PROFICIENCY DEVELOPMENT STANDARDS

Teachers are keenly aware of the importance of academic achievement for all students, but they may not realize that academic language development is the stepping-stone to achievement. To be successful in school, all students must be able to process and interact in academic language as they learn content. In essence, academic language allows students access to content across school settings (Echevarria, Vogt, & Short, 2012). Thus, academic language is the glue that cements content and language learning.

Academic language development refers to the course of acquiring and using different genres across the content areas (e.g., the language of scientific inquiry or the language of mysteries), and, within those discourses, possessing the necessary language structures, words, and expressions required to process, understand, interpret, and communicate curriculum-based content. Academic language centers on the delivery or understanding of ideas or messages through one or more language domains (listening, speaking, reading, or writing), and it consists of three dimensions:

- Discourse: Linguistic complexity (length and variety of sentences), register (formality), organization, and cohesion of oral interaction or writing expressed in varied genres
- Sentences: The grammatical structures (syntax) that shape the the meaning (semantics) of language in context
- Words and expressions: General academic, specialized academic, and technical academic vocabulary, phrases and expressions that are associated with content-related topics or themes. (Gottlieb & Ernst-Slavit, 2013; WIDA, 2012; Saunders, Goldenberg, & Marcelletti, 2013; Bailey & Butler, 2003)

REFLECTION

Analyzing Academic Language Use in Standards

Take some time in grade-level teams or as professional learning communities to examine the academic language use in your state college and career readiness standards and language proficiency/development standards. Compare the two to see the extent of their correspondence. What are the implications of this analysis for curriculum, instruction, and assessment for your ELLs?

College and career readiness standards visibly interweave content and academic language use. With greater academic and linguistic expectations at every grade level has come a greater awareness of academic language and its increased presence in assessment. Figure 2.1 underscores the role of academic language in standards before

Figure 2.1 Perceptions of Academic Language Before and After the Introduction of the College and Career Readiness Standards

Prior to College and Career Readiness Standards	After College and Career Readiness Standards
Academic language is implicit in standards.	Academic language is more explicit in standards.
Academic language is considered secondary to key concepts and skills of content standards.	Academic language is embedded in and a focus of standards.
Academic language demands of content standards are variable from state to state.	Academic language demands of standards are more uniform across states.
Academic language is primarily associated with English language proficiency/development standards.	Academic language is shared between English language proficiency/development and content standards.
Academic language is largely perceived as vocabulary.	Academic language is extended to include sentence and discourse features.
Academic language is generally confined to English language arts.	Academic language is associated with every school discipline.
Academic language is often taught in isolation or frontloaded prior to a lesson.	Academic language is taught in context within and across lessons.
Academic language is the purview of language teachers.	Academic language is the responsibility of all teachers.

Source: Adapted from Gottlieb & Ernst-Slavit, 2014a, p. 57.

and after 2010, when college and career readiness standards gained prominence. The recognition of academic language as a twenty-first-century skill for all students to ideally possess has indeed raised its standing in the educational community.

With the introduction of college and career readiness standards has come a series of curricular and instructional shifts that appear in the new generation of state- and consortia-led achievement testing. One of the major changes in English language arts requires regular practice with complex text and its academic language. What might teachers do to ensure opportunities for meaningful participation of ELLs? Here are some suggestions:

- Analyze complex text, making connections to the students, and engage ELLs in identifying its features and using them in context.
- Pay specific attention to words with multiple meanings, idiomatic expressions, and sociocultural contexts unfamiliar to students.
- Couple students' oral language with their literacy development when dealing with complex texts across the content areas.
- Collaborate with other teachers to coordinate content-based instruction centered on academic language.
- Promote cross-linguistic transfer by having students become aware of cognates and other language-related strategies that capitalize on their home language resources.

Source: Adapted from Teachers of English to Speakers of Other Languages International Association 2013, p. 5.

REFLECTION

Focusing on Academic Language Use for English Language Learners

What are you or your school currently doing so that your students have plenty of practice time to dive into grade-level academic language in oral or written discourse? Which strategies do you find the most effective in dealing with complex text and which ones might you tackle next? Having identified academic language in instructional materials, where might you begin to think about assessing its use for your heterogeneous mix of ELLs?

Teachers often collaborate to combine multiple standards in creating thematic units of study. To illustrate how language proficiency/development standards reinforce academic language use, Figure 2.2 shows the complementary features of content and language learning.

Figure 2.2   Complementing Content and Language Learning

Content Learning Through Language, the Basis for College and Career Readiness Standards	Language Learning Through Content, the Basis for Language Development Standards
The focus is on attainment of content-related skills and conceptual understandings.	The focus is on communication, centering on the interaction among the four language domains within and across the content areas.
Language is the medium of instruction for content-area disciplines.	Content-area disciplines provide the contexts for language learning.
Students demonstrate mastery of content-related skills and concepts.	Students demonstrate processing and production of language within content-related contexts.
Students' accuracy and precision in showing their content-related knowledge and skills are paramount.	Students' consistency of academic language use within and across the content areas is of utmost importance.
Assessment measures student achievement.	Assessment measures students' language proficiency.

Source: Adapted from Gottlieb & Ernst-Slavit, 2014a, p. 62.

REFLECTION

Integrating Standards Into Assessment for Local Accountability

Think about the common or interim assessments in your school or district. To what extent are both content standards and language proficiency/development standards being systemically represented? Are they unified around a central theme or content topic? If students are instructed in languages other than English, does local accountability extend to assessments of and in those languages? Do scores or score reports consider ELLs' language proficiency in relation to their achievement?

Building pathways between language development and academic achievement enhances language learners' learning opportunities by providing accessibility to content. The creation and implementation of comprehensive language proficiency/ development standards facilitate this journey. By systematically defining the language of schooling associated with social and academic language development, ELLs with sound instruction can more readily learn or transfer their knowledge of the concepts and skills of grade-level content standards. Academic language functions, the specific uses of language to accomplish communicative purposes, offer an equitable route to that end.

Academic Language Functions in Standards

Language development refers to the process by which individuals accrue age-appropriate competencies for communicating within and across the language domains or modalities of listening, speaking, reading, and writing. There are two defining features to the language development process: the use of language for specific purposes, situations, and audiences; and the role of language functions to express what to do with language, its intent, or its message (Finocchiaro & Brumfit, 1983; Halliday, 1976).

Language functions are ways in which we use language or communicate for social and academic purposes, often to carry out an action. When language functions are associated with social action, there is generally an implicit, underlying interaction with another person. Salutations, apologies, complaints, and requests, for example, represent social language behaviors. On the other hand, language functions can be descriptive of academic proficiency, such as when we explain, interpret, and justify. For example, if we are asked to "compare two characters, two scientific inventions, or two historical events," the language function *compare* begs the use of certain sentence structures that indicate relationships between the two entities, such as "is more violent than," or "is less aggressive than."

Language learners must be exposed to and practice multiple and varied language functions throughout the school day. Teachers have to remember that functional language for newcomers must simultaneously relate to how students can acclimate socially, acculturate to their school climate, and progress academically. We cannot forget that some ELLs, such as LTELLs and SLIFE, are challenged in achieving grade-level standards and expectations required of the academic registers at school. These students simply are at different points along a continuum of language and literacy practices. Teachers must build broad academic discourses using the students' linguistic resources at hand, including their home language and English (Menken & Kleyn, 2015).

In today's classrooms there must be a correspondence between standards so that there is equity in achievement expectations of all students. With students having the same academic goals, built-in opportunities exist for teachers to collaborate to provide continuity of educational experiences. Figure 2.3 gives examples of academic language functions that are present in both college and career readiness standards and language proficiency/development standards. Thus, for all students, academic language functions can readily be reinforced through standards-referenced curriculum, instruction, and assessment. For ELLs, however, differentiation of language according to their language proficiency (without diminishing their cognitive engagement) is necessary when designing tasks around these functions.

Figure 2.3   A Sampling of the Cross-Referencing of Academic Language Functions Present in Content Standards and Language Development Standards

Academic Language Functions in College and Career Readiness Standards, Including Common Core and Next Generation Science Standards	Academic Language Functions in Representations of WIDA Language Development Standards (2012)
Defend a position or stance	Defend choices made in the design process
Compare and contrast ideas, people, or events	Compare and contrast narrative points of view
Sequence processes, procedures, or operations	Sequence sentences to solve problems
Debate issues or ideas	Critique (debate) the impact of significant individuals or events on society
Summarize conflicts, story lines, or results of investigations	Summarize questions and conclusions
Construct an argument with evidence	Construct models based on extended oral discourse
Recount information	Recount and reflect on information
Explain processes, how authors use reason, why strategies work	Explain outcomes; explain step-by-step processes or strategies

Source: Adapted from Gottlieb & Ernst-Slavit, 2014a, pp. 66 & 73.

REFLECTION

Using Academic Language Functions as the Basis for Assessment and Instruction

The similarities between academic language functions in content and language standards are striking. Given their likenesses, tying them to common performance tasks for assessment should be relatively easy. How might you, your grade-level team, or your professional learning community incorporate some of these language functions into a grade-level performance assessment and subsequent instruction of oral or written language, based on that topic?

While the language functions in Figure 2.3 are applicable across multiple disciplines, there are also language functions that are associated with specific content areas. Figure 2.4 provides examples of language functions found within college and career readiness standards, the Next Generation of Science Standards, and the C3 Framework for Social Studies State Standards.

Figure 2.4 Select Academic Language Functions in English Language Arts, Mathematics, Science, and Social Studies Standards

Academic Language Functions in English Language Arts Standards	*Academic Language Functions in Mathematics Standards*	*Academic Language Functions in Science Standards*	*Academic Language Functions in the C3 Framework for State Social Studies Standards*
• Ask and answer questions • Recount information; recount the key details • Tell stories • Describe characters, settings and major events, the structure of stories, and relationships • Compare and contrast themes, two versions of the same story, texts in the same and different genres, important points and details, and structure of two texts • Explain processes and how authors use reason using evidence • Identify words and phrases in stories and main topics • Explain differences between books • Summarize points of a speaker • Interpret information from diverse media	• Interpret equations, multiplication as scaling • Compare two-digit numbers, two decimals, and properties of two functions • Describe the relationship between two quantities • Explain addition and subtraction strategies • Summarize numerical data sets • Explain patterns in the number of zeros of the product when multiplying a number by powers of 10 • Identify parts of an expression using mathematical terms	• Compare the effects of different strengths or different directions, or life in different habitats • Describe patterns or different kinds of materials • Construct an argument with evidence • Ask questions to obtain information • Determine cause and effect relationships • Define design problems • Evaluate the evidence for the role of group behavior on individual and species' chances to survive and reproduce	• Explain how a question represents key ideas in the field • Explain how groups of people make rules to create responsibilities and protect freedoms • Describe the roles of political, civil, and economic organizations in shaping people's lives • Compare the benefits and costs of individual choices • Discuss theories, methodologies, and empirical findings necessary to plan, conduct, and especially interpret research results

Sources:

The Next Generation Science Standards (2013). Retrieved from http://www.nextgenscience.org/next-generation-science-standards.

College, career & civic life (C3) framework for social studies state standards: Guidance for enhancing the rigor of K–12 civics, economics, geography, and history. (2013). Silver Spring, MD: National Council for the Social Studies.

Using Academic Language Functions for Content-Area Assessment

With a grade-level team or professional learning community, choose several prominent language functions of your content-area instruction. Then create classroom activities with embedded assessment to ensure that the students are comprehending and producing the language of the content area and its concepts. For example, when young language learners are asked to *compare* modes of transportation by their speed, knowing the relative speed of each mode is conceptually based. However, knowing how to use comparatives to express understanding of speed—that is, a car goes *fast*, an airplane goes *faster*, and a rocket goes the *fastest*—depends on the children's academic language use.

Academic language functions, in essence, represent the linguistic focus of standards. While functional language is interspersed in college and career readiness standards, it is systematically woven into language proficiency/development standards. Let's take a look.

THE FOUNDATION FOR LANGUAGE "PROFICIENCY" ASSESSMENT: LANGUAGE PROFICIENCY/DEVELOPMENT STANDARDS

English language proficiency/development standards historically have been crafted exclusively for ELLs. However, with the introduction of college and career readiness standards and an increased emphasis on their academic language use, now all students can benefit from knowing the language expectations related to content. Think about it. Although accountability for the language development of ELLs rests with language proficiency assessment, the language proficiency/development standards themselves might be useful for those students who may benefit from an oral academic language or a literacy boost.

Considering the Audience for Language Proficiency/Development Standards

Examine the language proficiency/development standards or language progressions for your state. Now mentally identify those students who would profit from language support. Do you agree with the statement that these standards might be of value for language learners outside the subset of ELLs? If so, what suggestions might you make to classroom teachers and school leaders as to which students they might benefit from their use and how?

Performance Definitions

Performance definitions overarch language proficiency/development standards and provide an umbrella descriptive of the range of student performance. For language proficiency/development standards, criteria are set for listening/reading and speaking/writing across designated levels. As part of a multistage process to define and classify ELLs, an attempt has been made to create a common English-proficient performance definition for states (Cook & MacDonald, 2014). The descriptors set forth in the report represent ELL performance in English at the end of each of three proficiency levels (low, moderate, and high) for receptive and productive language. It is further presented by oral and text-based language across the three dimensions of academic language: discourse, sentence, and word/phrase. Figure 2.5 summarizes receptive and productive descriptors reflective of performance definitions across five levels of language proficiency—the number that typifies the developmental sequence that most states use.

Figure 2.5   Abbreviated Performance Definitions for Receptive and Productive Language

At their given level of language proficiency, ELLs will . . .		
	Comprehend (through listening and reading)	Produce (through speaking and writing)
Language proficiency level 5	A broad range of academic vocabulary in a variety of sentences of varying language complexity in extended discourse of each content area	Cohesive, organized, and fluent language that includes multiple registers and genres, varied sentence structures related to content-area topics, purpose, and audience, along with precise vocabulary
Language proficiency level 4	Specialized academic and technical vocabulary in sentences of varying language complexity within discourses across content areas with some instructional supports	Organized language that flows and includes several registers and genres that contain a variety of sentences structures and a range of specialized academic vocabulary related to content-area topics
Language proficiency level 3	General academic and some specialized vocabulary related to the content areas presented in a variety of expanded sentences within discourses that rely on visual, graphic, and interactive supports	Language that includes a sense of register and genre with some sentence variety and length, along with specialized academic vocabulary related to content
Language proficiency level 2	General academic language related to the content areas presented in simple and compound sentences within discourses that rely on visual, graphic, and interactive supports	Words and expressions presented in short, often repetitive sentences that relay a generalized meaning of the communication within a genre
Language proficiency level 1	Some phrases and short, simple sentences that rely on visual, graphic, and interactive supports	Pictorial and graphic representation of language with sporadic words, phrases, and memorized chunks of language

Source: Adapted from Gottlieb, 2006, p. 28.

REFLECTION

Using Performance Definitions for Language Differentiation

Figure 2.5 presents a thumbnail sketch of criteria associated with levels of language proficiency. Using this information as a starting point, how might you group your ELLs according to their receptive and productive language? You may wish to use Resource 2.1 and add names of your students to each cell to help form different groups for language instruction.

The criteria in performance definitions are useful for teachers in communicating with one another about a student's overall language development, grouping ELLs, and planning for differentiated language instruction and assessment.

Generally, students' receptive language (listening and reading) is more advanced than their productive language (speaking and writing), and within the productive domains, writing is generally the last to be fully developed (Gottlieb & Hamayan, 2007; Spolsky, 1989). That is, although ELLs may speak English quite fluently, they still may be challenged with the academic language needed to communicate content through writing at the same level of proficiency. Additionally, ELLs may be connecting with content of one subject-area class through listening and reading, but in another class they feel more comfortable expressing content through speaking and writing.

Language Proficiency/Development Standards

English language proficiency/development standards, grounded in and corresponding to academic content standards, serve as the blueprint for planning, designing, implementing, and evaluating curriculum, instruction, and assessment for language learning.

With the reauthorization of the ESEA in 2001 came the dawn of assessment consortia dedicated to standards and assessment for ELLs. Since its inception, World-Class Instructional Design and Assessment (WIDA), the first of the ELL assessment consortia, has maintained five English language development standards. What has evolved over the years has been a more sophisticated, research-based representation of how academic language relates to content teaching and learning (WIDA, 2004, 2007, 2012). These language development standards center on social instructional language in conjunction with the language of the content areas—namely, the language of language arts, mathematics, science, and social studies. However, the language of other curricular areas is also recognized, such as the language of technology and engineering, music and fine arts, health and physical education, music and performing arts, and visual arts as integral to schooling.

The English Language Proficiency Assessment for the 21st Century (ELPA21) consortium has crafted 10 English language proficiency standards (CCSSO, 2014). Other states with sizable ELL populations who are not members of either consortium—California, Texas, and Arizona—have designed their own English language proficiency/development standards or, in the case of New York, new language arts progressions. Resource 2.2 lists the language standards from the two ELL consortia: WIDA language development standards in English, Spanish, and for early years, and the ELPA21 English language proficiency standards.

Language proficiency/development standards, like content standards, spiral vertically from grade to grade in their developmental expectations. What is unique to language standards is that there is also a horizontal progression across the levels of language proficiency. That is, within a grade or grade-level span, there is a scaffolding of language expectations from beginning levels to the most advanced ones. As teachers may have ELLs with a range of language proficiency levels in one classroom, thought must be given to differentiation of instruction and assessment by language, in addition to content. Figure 2.6 notes the complementary features of language and content standards.

Figure 2.6 A Comparison of the Features of Language and Content Standards

Language Proficiency/Development Standards	Content Standards, Including College and Career Readiness Standards
• Designed for ELLs • Largely based on linguistic theory • Focused on the language of social interaction and language of the content areas • Grounded in academic content or college and career readiness standards • Centered on the four language domains: listening, speaking, reading, and writing • Matched to the development progression in acquiring language • Based on the language development process with scaffolded levels of language proficiency • Considered dynamic with components that may be adjusted to meet student and classroom needs • Anchored in language proficiency testing	• Designed for all students • Largely based on cognitive theory • Focused on grade-level concepts, knowledge, and skills • Informed by language proficiency/development standards • Centered on the core content areas: language arts, mathematics, science, and social studies • Matched to the benchmarks in acquiring content • Based on a single set of content expectations or outcomes • Considered fixed and unalterable • Anchored in testing of academic achievement

Source: Adapted from Gottlieb, 2006, p. 31.

English Language Learners pass through a series of developmental progressions or levels of proficiency as they acquire a new language, but their pace varies. Students who are literate in their home language and those with continuous schooling will move through the language proficiency levels more rapidly than those who do not have such a strong foundation or whose education has been limited or interrupted. Other factors include a student's personality attributes, such as motivation, attitudes, perseverance, and maturation. Finally, there are also educational influences that impact movement across the language development continuum, such as types of instructional support, continuity of language support, and classroom experiences, including access to language associated with grade-level content.

Additionally, students start at different points along the continuum of language development. Some ELLs may have had previous exposure to English as a foreign language outside the United States and have gained some literacy skills. Within this country, some ELLs have preschool experiences; others have siblings or other family members who interact in two or more languages. Still others, typically at beginning levels of language proficiency, have not been previously exposed to English whether newcomers to our shores or native born.

Spanish Language Development Standards/Home Language Arts Progressions

There are Spanish language development standards for kindergarten through Grade 12 classrooms where Spanish is the language of content instruction and early Spanish language development standards for ages 2.5 to 5.5 (WIDA, 2013, 2015).

The audience for these standards includes all students in Spanish dual language programs, Spanish speakers in bilingual education settings or, in the case of young children, dual language learners in a variety of school and community settings. These standards make explicit connections to college and career readiness standards, other state content standards, and content standards from Puerto Rico, Mexico, and Chile while reflecting authentic Spanish language development within a U.S. context. The early Spanish language development standards directly connect to state early learning standards. During the 2014–2015 school year, the state of New York launched Home Language Arts Progressions for kindergarten through Grade 12. The progressions have five levels of literacy and performance indicators for each modality that parallel their new language arts progressions and lead to college and career readiness standards.

More standards, you say. And why are there Spanish language development standards when there are literally hundreds of languages spoken by students? First, the prototypes for English and Spanish language development standards can serve most all languages. You just need a team of dedicated professionals, time, and a review process that validates the work, although a bit of funding also helps. Second, it is difficult to create an aligned system without having standards as the anchor—what would be the basis for assessment and what would be the criteria of success in classrooms where languages other than English are the medium of instruction? Finally, standards offer legitimacy to educational programs, and with the exponential increase of dual language instructional models across most every state, it is only equitable that there are standards that reflect the pathways to language development.

REFLECTION

Exploring Language Proficiency/Development Standards

Individually, in grade-level teams, or as a professional learning committee, devote some time to reading the front matter of your state's language proficiency/development standards and early language development standards (if applicable). What is the theoretical rationale for the standards? How are they organized? What is the purpose for each component? How might you explain these standards to other classroom teachers?

Standards alone will not make a difference in educational reform. For ELLs, instructional supports either should be built in or readily available so students can more easily tackle grade-level challenging content.

Supports for Instruction and Assessment

Supports are resources, strategies, and practices to enable students to have equal opportunities for success at school by promoting their engagement in learning. All students can benefit in constructing meaning from instructional supports. The purpose behind instructional supports during language development is to scaffold language learning. In today's classrooms, scaffolding extends to peer interactions, in which students support one another; software tools; and other forms of instructional support afforded students to help them learn successfully.

ELLs—especially those at the early levels of language proficiency—need multiple supports to optimize their opportunities to access, participate in, and achieve grade-level content in English. Likewise, other language learners participating in dual language programs who are proficient in English need supports in their other language of instruction. There are various types of instructional support: (a) linguistic, such as use of a student's home language; (b) graphic, such as the use of tables or graphic organizers; (c) sensory, such as real-life objects or any concrete referent; and (d) interactive, such as opportunities to interact with other language models. Figure 2.7 provides examples of these types of support for instruction and assessment.

Regardless of an ELL's stage of language development, with sensory, graphic, linguistic, and interactive support, students can engage in higher-level thinking in English. For example, ELLs at the intermediate grade levels can readily compare and contrast characters, scientific objects, quantities, or historical time periods using a variety of graphic organizers. Older ELLs, who may be considered SLIFE and have not had the benefits of schooling, may show their conceptual understanding by constructing scientific models, graphs, charts, or timelines based on data or information in lieu of writing lengthy essays or reports. As ELLs accrue more language and move through the language development continuum, instructional supports are gradually reduced depending on the students' age, grade level, and context.

Figure 2.7 Types and Examples of Instructional Support for Language Learners

Linguistic Support	Graphic Support	Sensory Support	Interactive Support
• Use of home language • Definition of key terms within sentences (e.g., "What are your plans this weekend? Tell me what you are going to do on Saturday and Sunday.") • Modification of sentence patterns (e.g., avoiding passive voice) • Use of redundancy or rephrasing for emphasis • Use or integration of multimodalities	• Charts (e.g., pie, T) • Tables (e.g., histogram, data) • Timelines and number lines • Graphs (e.g., line, whisker plot) • Graphic organizers (e.g., Venn diagrams, semantic webs)	• Real objects (e.g., maps, coins, rocks) • Manipulatives (e.g., cubes, Cuisenaire rods) • Gestures • Photographs, pictures, illustrations • Diagrams • Models (e.g., displays) • Magazines, newspapers • Videos • Multimedia, including Internet, podcasts	• In pairs • In small groups • With mentors • With tutors • With technology • With other language models (e.g., teachers, peers)

Source: Adapted from Gottlieb, 2006, p. 29.

IMPLEMENTING A STANDARDS FRAMEWORK THROUGH ESSENTIAL ACTIONS

Analogous to instructional practices that stem from college and career readiness standards, WIDA has identified 15 essential actions that jumpstart the implementation of its standards framework. Each action is tied to evidence-based strategies for educators to apply in enacting standards-referenced, language-rich education. Figure 2.8 names the WIDA essential actions and describes applicable assessment practices.

Figure 2.8   Matching *Essential Actions* for ELLs to Assessment Practices

Essential Action	Implications for Assessment Practices
Capitalize on the resources and experiences that ELLs bring to school to build and enrich their academic language	Utilize the students' "funds of knowledge" in planning relevant and engaging assessment
Analyze the academic language demands involved in grade-level teaching and learning	Specify language targets for a unit of learning that center on academic language use and match the targets to performance assessment, along with an accompanying rubric
Apply the background knowledge of ELLs, including their language portraits, in planning differentiated language teaching	Differentiate language assessment according to the students' levels of language proficiency without altering grade-level concepts or skills
Connect language and content to make learning relevant and meaningful for ELLs	Extend the integration of language and content learning to assessment, yet be sensitive to the contribution of each when reporting results
Focus on the developmental nature of language learning within grade-level curriculum	Plan grade-level, developmentally appropriate assessment for ELLs at all levels of language proficiency
Reference content standards and language development standards in planning for language learning	Craft assessment around content standards and language development standards and reference both sets of standards in reporting results or giving feedback from assessment
Design language teaching and learning with attention to the sociocultural context	Be aware of how ELLs relate to the context for assessment and the assumptions made as part of the assessment experience
Provide opportunities for all ELLs to engage in higher-order thinking	Extend higher-order thinking instructional tasks to assessment
Create language-rich classroom environments with ample time for language practice and use	Incorporate the academic language of the content areas into meaningful assessment tasks and projects that encourage student engagement and voice
Identify the language needed for functional use in teaching and learning	Use the dimensions of academic language—discourse, sentences, and words/phrases—to help organize language assessment around a communicative purpose
Plan for language teaching and learning around discipline-specific topics.	Make sure assessment of language is contextualized within meaningful content related topics or themes
Use instructional supports to help scaffold language learning	Embed supports used during instruction into assessment
Integrate language domains to provide rich, authentic instruction	Interweave language domains in assessment *as* and *for* learning and encourage students to use multimodalities and multiliteracies to demonstrate their learning
Coordinate and collaborate in planning for language and content teaching and learning	Plan common assessment for units of learning that address both language and content in grade-level, school, or district professional learning teams
Share responsibility so that all teachers are language teachers and support one another within communities of practice	Agree upon how to use results from assessment *of* learning for grading (if applicable) and local accountability

INTEGRATION OF STANDARDS AND ASSESSMENT IN AN EDUCATIONAL SYSTEM

Standards are the watchdog of educational reform, and assessment is often a driver of educational systems. When these systems involve ELLs, there must be parallel content and language components. One such system for language learners is illustrated in Figure 2.9. The paired components of this system can be considered gears that work in an interlocking, coordinated fashion.

In this particular system, language development standards pair with academic content standards. Large-scale tests (assessment *of* learning) and classroom practices (assessment *for* and *as* learning) form the second pair. Curriculum and instruction within language education and general education programs serve as the third set of gears. Academic language use is the thread that weaves these major components together and sustains equity within an educational system.

Figure 2.9   Academic Language Use Within Sociocultural Contexts for Learning

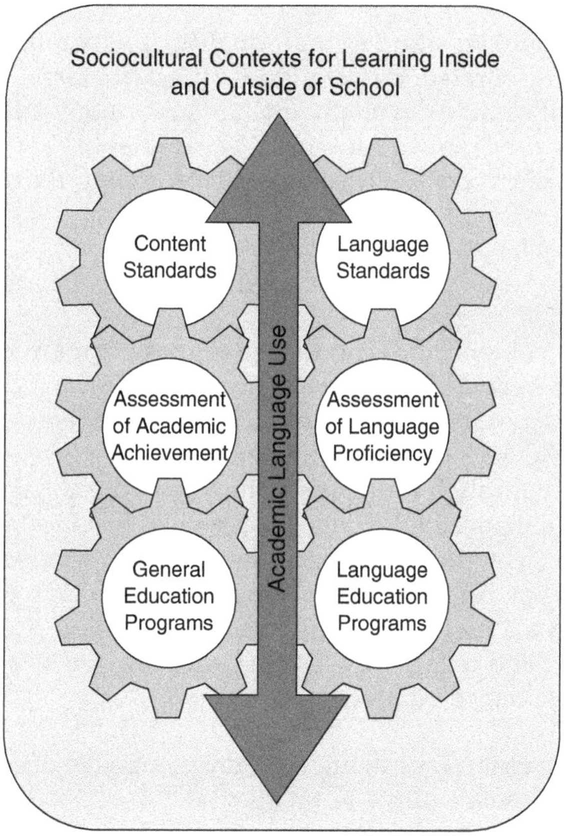

Source: Adapted from Gottlieb & Ernst-Slavit, 2014a, p. 81.

REACTION AND REFLECTION

According to Schmidt and Burroughs, American schools exhibit "pervasive inequality. A bold claim, but that's the inescapable conclusion of 20 years of examining mathematics and science standards, student achievement, textbooks, standardized tests, and classroom content coverage" (2013, p. 2). Across states and school districts, inequities in content coverage deny students equal learning opportunities. "The U.S. educational system has patently failed to ensure equal access for all to the essential knowledge, skills, problem-solving abilities, and reasoning abilities that are necessary to succeed" (Schmidt & Burroughs, 2013, p. 2). So you can imagine what it must be like for linguistic and culturally diverse students who historically have been marginalized from grade-level academic content. Teachers and school leaders who implement standards-referenced curriculum, instruction, and assessment with fidelity and are sensitive to the needs of ELLs can start chipping away at some of these inequalities.

Language development and academic achievement are partners in the education of ELLs, and standards are the guideposts for their implementation. Teachers who are aware of their students' academic language proficiency (in English and their home language) as well as their academic achievement are better prepared to provide a systematic, continuous, and appropriate content-grounded education. It is academic language use that unifies and fortifies the integration of language and content in their respective standards as the basis for curriculum, instruction, and assessment.

Every student should be afforded high-quality opportunities to learn, and consequently be assessed, in relation to standards (Carr & Harris, 2001). The value of having language proficiency/development standards alongside college and career readiness standards for language learners is irrefutable. Both sets of standards benefit language learners and their teachers by providing the groundwork for

- assessment *as, for,* and *of* learning;
- integrated grade-level curriculum design, minimally in language arts/reading, mathematics, and science;
- differentiated content and language instruction for the varying levels of language proficiency; and
- a coordinated set of instructional services for students.

In bridging equity through standards within an educational system, we are able to provide students enhanced educational opportunities and help tackle academic challenges. We have created the stepping stones for ELLs to reach academic parity with their proficient English peers. Most importantly, we have energized the educational community to act on behalf of our students. As you react to the ideas presented in this chapter and reflect on what they mean to you as an educator, here are some additional questions to ponder:

- How do you envision leveraging academic language use by all students as a means to educational equity?
- How might you pair college and career readiness standards and language proficiency/development standards and maintain their presence throughout a cycle of instruction and assessment?
- What can schools do to promote a systemic and fair approach to standards-referenced assessment?
- Where would you place your school, district, or state on the bridge to systemic equity?

RESOURCE 2.1

Grouping English Language Learners by Levels of Language Proficiency

Using the performance definitions in Figure 2.5 and scores from their latest English language proficiency test (if available), how might you group your ELLs according to their receptive (listening and reading) and expressive (oral and written) language? What kinds of instructional decisions can you make based on this classification scheme?

	At their given level of language proficiency (LP), ELLs will . . .	
	Comprehend (through listening and reading)	*Produce (through speaking and writing)*
LP Level 5		
LP Level 4		
LP Level 3		
LP Level 2		
LP Level 1		

Source: Adapted from Gottlieb, 2006, p. 39.

RESOURCE 2.2

Language Proficiency/Development Standards

The WIDA English Language Development Standards

	Standard	Abbreviation
ELD Standard 1	English language learners **communicate** for **Social and Instructional** purposes within the school setting.	Social and Instructional language
ELD Standard 2	English language learners **communicate** information, ideas, and concepts necessary for academic success in the area of **Language Arts**.	The language of Language Arts
ELD Standard 3	English language learners **communicate** information, ideas, and concepts necessary for academic success in the area of **Mathematics**.	The language of Mathematics
ELD Standard 4	English language learners **communicate** information, ideas, and concepts necessary for academic success in the area of **Science**.	The language of Science
ELD Standard 5	English language learners **communicate** information, ideas, and concepts necessary for academic success in the area of **Social Studies**.	The language of Social Studies

Source: WIDA, 2004, 2007, 2012. © Board of Regents of the University of Wisconsin System, on behalf of the WIDA Consortium. www.wida.us.

The WIDA Spanish Language Development Standards
Estándares del desarrollo del lenguaje español, Kínder-Grado 12

Estándar		*Abreviatura*
Estándar 1 DLE	Los bilingües emergentes se **comunican** con fines **sociales y de instrucción** dentro de entorno escolar.	El lenguaje social y de instrucción
Estándar 2 DLE	Los bilingües emergentes **comunican** información, ideas, y conceptos necesarios para el éxito académico en el área de las **artes de lenguaje**.	El lenguaje de las artes de lenguaje
Estándar 3 DLE	Los bilingües emergentes **comunican** información, ideas, y conceptos para el éxito académico en el área de las **matemáticas**.	El lenguaje de las matemáticas
Estándar 4 DLE	Los bilingües emergentes **comunican** información, ideas, y conceptos para el éxito académico en el área de las **ciencias naturales**.	El lenguaje de las ciencias naturales
Estándar 5 DLE	Los bilingües emergentes **comunican** información, ideas, y conceptos para el éxito académico en el área de las **ciencias sociales**.	El lenguaje de las ciencias sociales

Source: WIDA, 2013. © Board of Regents of the University of Wisconsin System, on behalf of the WIDA Consortium. www.wida.us.

The WIDA Early English Language Development Standards, Ages 2.5-5.5

	Standard	*Abbreviation*
E-ELD Standard 1	Dual language learners **communicate** information, ideas, and concepts necessary for success in the area of **Social and Emotional Development.**	The **language** of Social and Emotional Development
E-ELD Standard 2	Dual language learners **communicate** information, ideas, and concepts necessary for success in the area of **Early Language Development and Literacy.**	The **language** of Early Language Development and Literacy
E-ELD Standard 3	Dual language learners **communicate** information, ideas, and concepts necessary for success in the area of **Mathematics.**	The **language** of Mathematics
E-ELD Standard 4	Dual language learners **communicate** information, ideas, and concepts necessary for success in the area of **Science.**	The **language** of Science
E-ELD Standard 5	Dual language learners **communicate** information, ideas, and concepts necessary for success in the area of **Social Studies.**	The **language** of Social Studies
E-ELD Standard 6	Dual language learners **communicate** information, ideas, and concepts necessary for success in the area of **Physical Development.**	The **language** of Physical Development

Source: WIDA, 2014. © Board of Regents of the University of Wisconsin System, on behalf of the WIDA Consortium. www .wida.us.

ELPA21 English Language Proficiency Standards with Correspondences to K–12 Practices and Common Core State Standards

1	Construct meaning from oral presentations and literary and informational text through grade-appropriate listening, reading, and viewing
2	Participate in grade-appropriate oral and written exchanges of information, ideas, and analyses, responding to peer, audience, or reader comments and questions
3	Speak and write about grade-appropriate complex literary and informational texts and topics
4	Construct grade-appropriate oral and written claims and support them with reasoning and evidence
5	Conduct research and evaluate and communicate findings to answer questions or solve problems
6	Analyze and critique the arguments of others orally and in writing
7	Adapt language choices to purpose, task, and audience when speaking and writing
8	Determine the meaning of words and phrases in oral presentations and literary and informational text
9	Create clear and coherent grade-appropriate speech and text
10	Make accurate use of standard English to communicate in grade-appropriate speech and writing

Source: Council of Chief State School Officers, 2014. © Council of Chief State School Officers.

3

Assessment of the Language of the Content Areas

The Bridge to Academic Equity

The child begins to perceive the world not only through his eyes but also through his speech.

—Lev Vygotsky

Ultimately, accountability for learning rests on students' academic performance; their content area achievement, in large part, is a marker of success in school. For ELLs, although language development is a vehicle toward reaching that goal, it often becomes entangled with content in getting there. It is only when teachers and school leaders come to understand the impact of language on achievement and account for this relationship in assessment that we will be able to move schools closer to academic equity. The following **school-based scenario** illustrates the interweaving of content-area concepts and compatible language functions to maximize students' opportunities to participate in learning experiences.

South Side Middle School is on a mission. The faculty has decided to devote 3 weeks to implementing a schoolwide multidisciplinary theme on space exploration. It is built around an interesting proposition that situates the backdrop for learning: "One day humans may have to leave the Earth and travel to another planet to settle down and live." Teacher teams have worked diligently over the past year during their protected co-planning time to design this curricular unit with input and feedback from students. Its outcomes will reflect the integration of content and language learning from the following subject areas as students.

> Language arts—compare biographies of astronauts, risk takers, and explorers
>
> Geography—describe the location and features of the planets, with attention paid to the possibility that any of them could support intelligent life
>
> Science—evaluate sources of energy, effects of gravity, potential for agriculture, sustainability of life
>
> Government—discuss the proposed laws or a constitution and a governance structure
>
> Physical education—ask and answer questions on fitness requirements for the mission or for survival on the other planets
>
> Mathematics, technology, and engineering—explain how to use tools created for exploration or how to design robots to help carry out the mission
>
> Art—justify their plan for a spaceship, a space station, or a land vehicle

Teachers feel confident that all students, working in small, heterogeneous groups, will have opportunities to participate in the unit's activities. Encouraging the use of multiliteracies will motivate students to pursue one of the pathways to a final product. For example, newcomers and SLIFE, alongside gifted and talented ELLs, will be able to work together to demonstrate their conceptual understanding by creating models that would be adaptable and sustainable on a new planet. Other linguistically and culturally diverse students might examine governments from around the world and conduct a comparative analysis to help inform the drafting of a constitution for their new habitat. Still others might rely on technology to research aspects of their project in multiple languages in order to produce video clips of imagined terrain or show a specialized vehicle moving about the planet.

You might wish to keep this scenario in mind as you read through Chapters 3 and 4. All the while, you might think about your students and how to intertwine content-area concepts with their language and literacy development during instruction and how the students will demonstrate their new learning during assessment.

This chapter reminds us of the co-existence of content and language in classrooms. It addresses language specific to mathematics, language arts, science, and social studies requisite to navigate school and how this language might be assessed. We introduce four key uses of academic language that serve as a means of establishing common ground for standards and anchors for learning targets that, in turn, are the basis for assessment and instruction.

PLANNING FOR STANDARDS-REFERENCED ASSESSMENT

Content or college and career readiness standards simultaneously serve as guideposts and goalposts for assessment of both language proficiency and academic achievement. Figure 3.1 on the next page depicts the companionship of content and language throughout the planning process for designing curriculum, assessment, and instruction.

If we are to follow the figure, planning for assessment begins with students, as they are the heart of our educational endeavor and the most important participants in the process. In thinking about assessment for each content area, we select pairs of standards to ground corresponding content targets and language targets for a unit of learning. These form the basis for common assessment. Later, differentiated content objectives and differentiated language objectives guide individual or related lesson activities in which instructional assessment is inserted (you may wish to refer to Gottlieb & Ernst-Slavit, 2014a & b and 2013, for further explanation and classroom-based examples).

REFLECTION

Placing Academic Language in the Center of Curricular Planning

Schools and school districts generally work from a curricular design that is content focused without consideration of the academic language that is necessary for language learners to access and achieve that content. Based on your experience, do you agree with this statement? If not, how does your school or school district equalize content and language learning as part of curriculum and assessment planning? How does it highlight content and language integration and how do teachers work together to ensure the representation of both?

Learning the language of language arts, mathematics, science, and social studies has to correspond with learning the concepts and skills of those content areas. By integrating the two, language and content reinforce each other and become stronger. However, when it comes time for assessment, sometimes we have to tease language and content apart. In language proficiency assessment, we focus on language, while content provides the context for communicating the message. In the assessment of academic achievement, the converse is true; the skills and concepts associated with content take precedence over the language demands.

Research has confirmed that academic English is indeed a distinct register with explicit discourse and grammatical and lexical features, only some of which are shared across content areas (Frantz, Starr, & Bailey, 2015). Research also points out that ELLs who have mastered the content-area concepts in their home language can readily transfer those skills and knowledge from one language to the next—in fact, the home language is useful for promoting academic development and biliteracy (Goldenberg, 2013). For other students without a firm foundation in literacy or academic language, simultaneous language and content learning is a much more complicated and lengthy process.

Figure 3.1   Steps for Synchronizing the Integration of Content and Language Within Curriculum, Assessment, and Instruction

1. Collect information on students' linguistic, cultural, and experiential backgrounds, conceptual base, literacies, and language development.

2. Select content or college and career readiness standards and pair them with language proficiency/development standards that are based on a theme or topic of interest to the students.

3. Create overall learning targets for content and for language referenced to their respective standards for each unit.

4. Analyze the use of academic language in the standards, community resources, and instructional materials.

5. Design with teacher teams or co-construct with students end-of-unit products, projects, or performances that reflect the learning targets as the basis for common assessment.

6. Create differentiated content and language objectives with or to share with students based on the learning targets for the activities of each lesson or across a cluster of lessons.

7. Embed differentiated content and language assessment within instruction, allowing for student voice.

8. Use day-to-day and end of unit data to inform content and language teaching and learning.

In planning assessment at a classroom, grade/department, or school level, teachers have to consider both language and content instruction. Check out Resource 3.1 at the close of the chapter. It lists instructional assessment features of language and content vertically and displays the core content areas horizontally. This matrix may be used as a guide for crafting assessment, adapting assessment, mapping curriculum, and creating lessons.

GETTING ORGANIZED FOR ASSESSMENT

In preparing for assessment, this chapter follows Figure 3.1; it centers on steps 2 (introduced in Chapter 2), 3, and 4. These steps, together with step 1, knowing your students (outlined in Chapter 1, Figure 1.1) are geared to gaining a firm understanding of the foundation of standards-based assessment. The flowchart below provides a graphic of the internal functioning of language alongside content.

Before we get started exploring the language of each content area, let's remember that learning is strengthened when students are able to analyze the messages in oral and written language and transpose that information into other forms, such as charts or graphs. By reducing their dependence on print, students, especially ELLs, are able to process information more readily and demonstrate their understanding. Figure 3.2 on the following page offers some widely used graphic organizers and content-area examples that reinforce content and language learning.

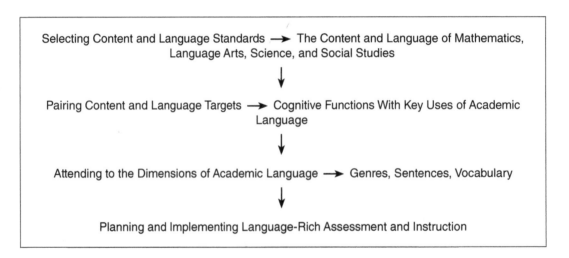

The new generation of standards, along with high-stakes assessment *of* learning, has influenced the instruction and classroom assessment *for* and *as* learning. Let's visit each of the major disciplines with an eye on its language in relation to content within the context of instruction and assessment.

THE LANGUAGE OF MATHEMATICS

When thinking mathematically, there are several discourses, or the ways in which language is organized, that are tied to how we use academic language. Discourses

Figure 3.2   Examples of Graphic Supports for Instruction and Assessment Across the Content Areas

Graphic Support	Language Arts	Mathematics	Science	Social Studies
Venn diagrams: comparing two or more ideas or entities	• Two (or more) texts • Different genres • Different characters	• Different pathways for problem-solving • Different operations • Different geometric figures	• Different forms of technology • Different body systems or organs • Different ecosystems	• Different historical eras • Different geographic regions • Different forms of transportation
T-charts: classifying ideas or objects	• Claims/evidence • Main ideas/details • Facts/opinions	• Metric/nonmetric measurement • Fractions/decimals • Addition/subtraction	• Hypotheses/findings • Acids/bases • Vertebrates/invertebrates	• Wants/needs • Characteristics of political parties • Conflict/resolution
Cycles: connecting a series of events or processes	• Informational texts on different cycles • Biographies • Plots revolving around different time periods	• Repeated patterns • Trends in data • Seasonal temperature/precipitation cycles	• Water cycles • Life cycles of plants and animals • Astronomical cycles	• Business/economic cycles • Election cycles • Cycle of abuse
Cause and effect: defining a relationship	• Technology and creation of new genres • Action/reaction of characters • Events and consequences in narrative and informational text	• Geometric theorems • Solving algebraic equations • Addition to multiplication	• Impact of weather patterns on life styles • Chemical/physical reactions • Adaptations to the environment	• Global democratization • Economic and demographic trends • Social issues and potential resolutions
Semantic web: identifying related ideas to a theme or concept	• Multicultural resources related to genres • Word/morphological families • Multiple meanings of words/expressions	• Applications of problems to the real world • Math operations for solving problems • Money/prices around the world	• Influences of technology • Ingredients in foods • Habitats around the world	• Cultural contributions to historical periods • Community resources • Human rights

Source: Adapted from Gottlieb, 2006, p. 135.

may also be expressed as key uses of academic language or the overarching purposes for engaging in and communicating with others within and across content areas. Four key uses used throughout this chapter—discuss, explain, argue, and recount—represent a distillation of the academic language encountered in college and career readiness standards, language development standards, and current literature (WIDA, 2015). By focusing on key uses, educators can more readily identify their associated grade-level language expectations. Figure 3.3 presents some ways of organizing the language of mathematics around these key uses, along with an example of each.

Figure 3.3 Engaging in Mathematical Discourse Using Key Uses of Academic Language

Type of Discourse: Key Use of Academic Language	Example Student Oral or Written Expectations in the Content Area of Mathematics
Discussion	Elaborate the choice of potential purchases with set amounts of money
Explanation	Describe different pathways for how to arrive at a solution to mathematical problems
Argumentation	Defend how to solve geometric theorems using numerical representations to support claims
Recount	Give step-by-step directions using thinking aloud (metalinguistic) strategies in solving mathematical problems

REFLECTION

Planning Instruction and Assessment Around Key Uses of Academic Language

How might the four key uses introduced in Figure 3.3 be helpful as a planning tool for grade-level instruction and assessment? With your grade-level team, generate a list or make a chart of related ways to seamlessly assess each key use during classroom observation.

Judit Moschkovich recommends "improving mathematics learning through language (where) instruction provides opportunities for students to actively use mathematical language to communicate about and negotiate meaning for mathematical situations" (2012). If curriculum and instruction are organized into units of learning, then the learning targets become the standards-referenced focal points for language assessment and related sets of lessons. Here you see a sample content target and an associated language target based on college and career readiness mathematics standards.

Common Core State Standards (CCSS) for Mathematics, Grade 3, Operations and Algebraic Thinking	
Academic Achievement: Content target for a Grade 3 unit of instruction	*Academic Language Proficiency: Language target for a Grade 3 unit of instruction*
Analyze story problems that involve everyday situations to determine the correct mathematical operations to perform	Discuss the language of story problems that involve everyday situations around the options for various mathematical operations

---

REFLECTION

Comparing Content and Language Targets

The notion of learning targets for a unit of learning may be new to you, or your school or district may use a different term. What is the benefit of having both content and language targets and how might they work together? How might they guide assessment of the unit as a whole for all students?

You may note that there is a distinction between a content target and a language target. In large part, the knowledge base that centers on cognitive functions from Bloom's revised taxonomy—remembering, understanding, applying, analyzing, evaluating, and creating—heads up the content target. In contrast, language functions or the communicative purposes associated with key uses of academic language spearhead the language target.

The Dimensions of Academic Language: Implications for Assessment and Instruction

Having a sense of key uses of academic language helps pinpoint the communicative intent of a unit of learning, but that does not go far enough. The three dimensions of academic language further delineate what students need to do linguistically. Figure 3.4 provides an example of each dimension of the academic language of mathematics that is applicable to both assessment and instruction.

Taking the use of words and phrases within sentences a bit deeper, we arrive at the language of math operations. Not only do all students need to gain automaticity in math operations, they have to be aware of the words and phrases that are associated with each operation.

The Language and Culture of Mathematics Operations

Language and culture go hand in hand; for mathematics, as for all content areas, there are cultural links to learning. Not only are there cultural views of learning mathematics, there are also culturally relevant ways of teaching it (Kersaint, Thompson, & Petkova, 2009).

Figure 3.4   Highlighting the Dimensions of Academic Language of Mathematics

Dimension of Academic Language	Implications for Instruction and Assessment
Discourse features: genres	• Recount steps in solving problems involving mathematics (e.g., geometric theorems) using sequential language • Explain how to arrive at answers to math problems using reasoning
Sentence structures: syntax	• Use different prepositions and prepositional phrases in sentences (e.g., The temperature dropped *by, from, to* 50 degrees.) • Use complex noun phrases (e.g., least common denominator; mixed whole numbers)
Use of words/ phrases: vocabulary	• Use synonyms for math operations (see Figure 3.5). • Use numerical adjectives (e.g., a half a meter, four-fifths of a circle, six tens) in speaking or writing mathematically

For ELLs, there are cultural interpretations of how mathematics operations work around the world; such is the case of how to perform long division. Mathematical symbols may also differ, such as the use of the comma in some countries to designate the separation of whole numbers from their decimal parts. In addition, all students must learn the technical language specific to mathematics. However, in English we tend to interchange numerous terms or expressions to signify one mathematical concept. Figure 3.5 provides a list of the multiple words that trigger different calculations for math operations.

Because ELLs have had limited practice in manipulating the syntax, or word order, of sentences in English, they cannot recognize how the same mathematical operation can be signaled in numerous ways (Crandall, 1987). Spanish speakers may recognize *sum* because the cognate resembles the word in their home language (*suma*), but *in all, altogether,* and *total,* all of which infer addition, are expressed only as *total* in Spanish. These words and expressions are not automatically acquired and internalized by students; teachers should introduce and reinforce each one independently within mathematics problem solving.

Figure 3.5   Vocabulary Associated With the Four Basic Math Operations

Addition	Subtraction	Multiplication	Division
And	Take away	Group by	Goes into
Plus	Take from	Times	Divided by
More	Minus	Multiple	Divide
More than	Less (than)	Double, triple, quadruple	Divisor
Altogether	Diminished by (deduct)	Multiplier	Dividend
Increased by	Are left	Product	Quotient
Sum	Remain	Set	Remainder
In all	Fewer than	By	Per
Total	Not as much as	Of	Out of
Combine	Difference	Factor	Split into
Add	Subtract	Twice	Halve
Put together	Decreased by	Groups of	Shared equally among

Source: Adapted from Gottlieb, 2006, p. 67.

During instruction, teachers often interchange math sentences using varying grammatical structures, words, and expressions. The next Reflection illustrates this point.

REFLECTION

Exploring the Language of Mathematics

Assume you are a fourth-grade teacher. Think about and jot down possible sentences typically used to relate the mathematical operations of addition, subtraction, multiplication, and division. Have students pair up and generate their own mathematical statements, commands, and questions using Figure 3.5. If applicable, have them search for cognates, such as *groups* and *grupos* in Spanish. Together you and your class can create a giant sentence wall for the four operations.

As shown in the language of mathematical operations (a term that itself carries multiple meanings), ELLs may be confused by mathematical terms that are also everyday objects. The word *table*, for example, is specific not only to mathematics (times table, data table) but has distinct meanings in social studies (table top or plateau), science (periodic table, water table), and language arts (table of contents, table the discussion) as well as being a common household object. Not only is the English language full of multiple meanings, it has nuances that are difficult for language learners to comprehend. When a teacher asks, "How many are left?" the reference is mathematical; with a subtle conversion to a prepositional phrase, "How many to the left?" the question now applies to directionality.

Word combinations in English often make mathematics conceptually compact, as in the phrase "least common denominator" or "two-thirds the base price." Even a phrase such as "percent off" where, in this instance, *off* means *reduction,* is confusing to ELLs who are more familiar with social language usage, as in, "Turn *off* the light," or, "Get *off* of my chair." Teachers must understand that for ELLs, acquiring the academic language of mathematics is as important as applying their mathematical knowledge for problem solving.

Below is a writing sample from an ELL who states the steps to finding the area of a rectangle. In terms of academic language use, notice the sequential language of the step-by-step process, a feature of the discourse of recount or explanation. The use of pronouns is not consistent, but technical language, such as formula, height, and length, are all applied in the mathematical context.

> First they are mesureing the length. The second thing that they do is mesuring the height. Now I have to use the formula to find the area of the rectangle. The length X height = 7 in. X 4 in. so the area would be 28 in.[2]

Measuring the Language of Mathematics

Students can benefit from learning through multiple modes and modalities. English language learners' use of concrete referents helps them attach meaning to language and concepts. Besides linguistic, interactive, visual, or graphic supports, each content area has specific tools of its trade, so to speak. The following display lists some helpful math supports that go hand in hand with instruction and assessment.

Manipulatives for Mathematics

- Blocks, cubes
- Clocks (digital and analog), sundials, and other timekeepers
- Counters (including coins, abacus)
- Data graphs
- Geometric figures
- Number lines
- Geoboards
- Rulers, yardsticks, nonmetric measures (e.g., paper clips, hands)
- Compasses
- Calculators
- Protractors
- Scales, balances
- Interactive math software

To ascertain whether ELLs understand the language of mathematics, have them manipulate real objects such as Unifix cubes, Cuisenaire rods, or whatever is age appropriate, matches the content and language objectives of the lesson, and represents content and language standards. Through a series of oral commands, teachers can observe whether students respond correctly, either nonverbally or verbally. Older students may listen to a teacher relate situations with embedded math problems. To demonstrate their comprehension of the language, the students may produce equations or construct graphs, charts, or tables according to oral input or written text.

Achievement in mathematics centers on the concepts and skills required for problem solving. This underlying knowledge forms the basis for the manipulation of numbers to derive solutions to problems. Unlike language proficiency, when addressing achievement teachers ask whether students know their number facts, can prove theorems, or can apply the correct formulas. However, what is often not considered is that the linguistic complexity of math story problems, especially on high-stakes tests, negatively impacts ELLs' math achievement (Martiniello, 2008). By maximizing opportunities for ELLs to make meaning from the content, the results from assessment will be more valid indicators of the students' subject matter knowledge and the language they use to express it.

THE LANGUAGE OF LANGUAGE ARTS

Whether we are referring to language arts or the language of language arts, it's all about language. While the constructs of language proficiency and academic achievement differ, when examining English language arts standards in relation to the language in English language proficiency/development standards, there is some degree of blurring. Both sets of standards

- emphasize language, in particular, grade-level academic language;
- identify language associated with the content area;
- use language functions as a means of relating the purpose for language use;
- address the four language domains or interaction among the modalities of listening, speaking, reading, and writing;

- represent multiple literacies by including technology and multimedia as expressions of language; and
- encourage academic conversations between and among students.

To illustrate the differences between the knowledge and skills of language arts, here is a Common Core reading standard followed by a content target and a corresponding language target.

Common Core State Standards, English Language Arts, Reading, Grade 5
RL.5.1 & RI.5.1. Quote accurately from a text when explaining what a text says explicitly and when drawing inferences from the text.

Academic Achievement: Content target for a unit of instruction	*Academic Language Proficiency: Language target for a unit of instruction*
Analyze the characteristics of gothic literature using text-based evidence	Argue orally or in writing why gothic literature is a legitimate genre based on its characteristics using text-based evidence

Academic content standards identify what students should know and be able to do at the completion of each grade. Figure 3.6 breaks down the fifth-grade reading standard into its key concepts and related skills that all students are expected to master.

Figure 3.6   Concepts and Skills in College and Career Readiness Reading Standard 5.1 for English Language Arts

Language Arts Concepts Embedded in the Standard	*Associated Skills*
• Types of textual evidence • Implicit information • Explicit information • Use of quotation from text	• Classify types of textual evidence • Identify characteristics of implicit and explicit information • Distinguish between implicit and explicit information • Apply conventions to quotations

REFLECTION

Deconstructing Language Arts Content Standards

Think about one of your English language arts classes. What are the major concepts and skills of the grade-level reading, writing, or speaking/listening standards? How might you or your grade level team deconstruct the content standards following the model in Figure 3.6?

Figure 3.7 is a strand of model performance indicators representing the language development standard for language arts; note how it exemplifies a developmental progression of language learning. In it, language scaffolds across the levels of English language proficiency and is aided by instructional supports through level 4. In that way even ELLs at the beginning of the language continuum are exposed to grade-level content while simultaneously building the academic language they need to progress to the next language proficiency level.

The English language arts standard shown above connects with the strand from English language development standard 2, the language of language arts, Grade 5 in the language domain of reading (WIDA, 2012). Both deal with the topic of types of evidence (e.g., explicit v. inferential). By keeping the students' levels of language proficiency in mind, instruction and assessment can subsequently be differentiated to become a valid representation of what ELLs can do.

Figure 3.7   A Fifth-Grade English Language Development Standard Representing the Language of Language Arts

Level 1	Level 2	Level 3	Level 4	Level 5
Identify character traits based on evidence from oral text, along with visual cues, physical movement, and tone of voice	Identify details related to character traits based on evidence from oral text, along with visual cues and tone of voice	Identify character traits based on evidence from oral text using visual and graphic support	Make predictions from character traits based on evidence from oral text using visual and graphic support	Infer character traits based on evidence from oral text

Source: WIDA, 2012, p. 77. © Board of Regents of the University of Wisconsin System, on behalf of the WIDA Consortium. www.wida.us.

Just as in mathematics, certain key uses of academic language overarch the language of language arts. In the fifth-grade example, students need to relate evidence for explicit information, such as, "It says that _____," or, "On page ____, it states that _____." Those expressions are distinct from the language used to relate implicit information, which may be signaled by the phrases "It seems that _____," or, "Based on the evidence, I think that ____." Figure 3.8 provides some additional means of engaging in the discourse of language arts.

Now let's dig a little deeper. Each key use has its own way of arranging written or oral text. By analyzing a key use by the dimensions of academic language, we gain insight into how it works. Figure 3.9 describes the features of *argumentation* according to discourse, sentences, and words/phrases.

Figure 3.8 Engaging in Language Arts Discourse Using Key Uses of Academic Language

Type of Discourse: Key Use of Academic Language	Example Student Expectations
Discussion	Compare the personality traits of the two main characters
Explanation	Describe how the protagonist evolves throughout the book
Argumentation	Justify the motives for the murder using claims and evidence
Recount	Tell the story of the three little pigs from different cultural perspectives

Figure 3.9 Dimensions of Academic Language for Argumentation

Discourse: *How text is organized to communicate meaning*	• Argumentative text begins with a thesis statement or a statement of position to present the claim with background information on the issue. • Arguments are then stated to justify a claim, along with supporting evidence. • At the conclusion there is a resolution, reaffirmation, or summary of a claim, with sometimes a call for action.
Sentences: *How phrases and clauses work to construct meaning*	• Nominalization, or changing actions into nouns, makes arguments more objective. For example, changing from *Everyone will "starve" to death.* to *There will be widespread "starvation."* • Tenses: Present tense is used to state claims and arguments, past tense is used to present historical background information, and future tense is used to make predictions for argumentation. • Connectives and phrases serve different purposes; for example, *however* to rebut a point, *moreover* to add or explain, and *likewise* to connect.
Words/expressions: *How word choices affect meaning*	• Nouns: Specialized vocabulary associated with argumentation includes *opinion, claim, argument, reason, evidence*; technical and abstract vocabulary relate to the specific issue. • Verbs: Modal verbs show emotions: *should, shall, will*; verbs indicate own and others' judgment, such as *assume* to imply disagreement, *prove* to imply agreement, and *suggest* to change direction or to show possible qualified argument/claim; and verbs make abstractions and generalizations, as in *indicate, reflect, show, influence, cause, lead to, consider.* • Emotive expressions such as *"It is important . . ."* and *"Above all . . ."* emphasize a point.

Source: Adapted from Lam, Low, & Tauiliili-Mahuka, 2014, pp. 56–57.

REFLECTION

Applying the Key Use of Argumentation to Instruction and Assessment

Figure 3.9 breaks down the key use of argumentation into the three dimensions of academic language. How might you use this information for instruction and assessment? Might you convert it into a checklist to be used for planning an essay or as a means for examining the language of an essay? Think about how both teachers and students might benefit from this analysis.

Having crafted examples of key uses of academic language for a content area, it becomes much easier to think about how to incorporate the dimensions of academic language into instruction and assessment.

Revisiting the Dimensions of Academic Language: Implications for Instruction and Assessment

The dimensions of academic language apply across all content areas. In Figure 3.10 you will see how genres, syntax, and vocabulary might be a stimulus for instruction and assessment of language arts.

Figure 3.10 Highlighting the Dimensions of Academic Language of Language Arts

Dimension of Academic Language	Implications for Instruction and Assessment
Discourse features: genres	• Explain the differences of the language of multiple genres (e.g., folktales v. fairytales, biographies v. autobiographies) • Discuss how to use rhetorical markers
Sentence structures: syntax	• Indicate time through the use of tense markers: past, present, and future tense • Become aware of and use noun referents
Use of words/phrases: vocabulary	• Become aware of and use words/phrases associated with onomatopia—for example, *hyperbole* • Identify and use words with multiple meanings

As with every discipline, there are certain supports that lend themselves to bolstering instruction; here are some associated with language arts that may be useful for ELLs and ELLs with disabilities.

Instructional Supports for Language Arts

- Sequenced pictures or cartoons
- (Illustrated) sentence strips
- Word/phrase/sentence or learning walls
- Graphic organizers
- Educational gaming through technology
- Interactive apps (e.g., voice recognition software)
- Student-generated posters
- Stories on tape, podcasts, videos, or streaming content
- Use of home language, as appropriate

Measuring the Language of Language Arts

For a unit of learning, students might design a product, perform in a drama, or be involved in a project that is directly aligned to college and career readiness language arts standards. In order to do so, however, there is academic language that the students must navigate. Figure 3.11 is taken from a seventh-grade unit on research; it gives some ideas of what students can do linguistically to demonstrate their oral language and literacy development.

Figure 3.11 Ideas for Assessing the Academic Language of Language Arts

Academic Language Within Language Arts	Assessment of Academic Language
Oral language (listening and speaking) Students will: • Restate research questions generated by other students • Paraphrase oral text • Compare attributes of different Web sites	Students will: • Make oral presentations based on research questions • Summarize text orally with a partner • Evaluate Web sites based on a set of attributes and share with a small group
Literacy (reading and writing) Students will: • Process questions generated during literature circles • List attributes of different Web sites • Analyze content of Web sites	Students will: • Produce individual journal entries • Answer questions on a Web site evaluation form • Organize text on individual white boards

Source: Adapted from Walsh & Staehr Fenner, 2014, p. 130.

Assessing the language of language arts deals with the organization of genres and how sentences and words/phrases within those sentences carry distinct meanings. Some of the ways teachers may wish to explore the language of language arts is by having ELLs distinguish the use of

- stock phrases associated with genres (e.g., "Once upon a time" introduces a narrative fairy tale, while "The moral of the story" ends a legend);
- prepositions phrases (e.g., *in* time v. *on* time);
- articles (e.g., "I am going in the store" v. "What's in store for me?");
- multiple meanings (e.g., "*Scale* the fish and then put it on the *scale*");
- idiomatic expressions (e.g., "Day in, day out"); and
- collocations, a combination of words that generally co-occur (e.g., "strong tea," but "a powerful computer").

REFLECTION

Explaining Multiple Meanings and Idiomatic Expressions

It seems that so many words in English have multiple meanings. Take for instance exterior body parts—from your face to your toes. If there is an extra 5 minutes at a faculty meeting, assign a body part to small groups of teachers and see which group can generate the most examples of multiple meanings. Then think about how this information might be helpful for classroom instruction and assessment for ELLs.

Whenever there are linguistically and culturally diverse students who have more than one language in common, translinguistic transfer or translanguaging, the intentional interexchange between languages, is bound to occur. Using their full linguistic repertoire, students are able to maximize their understanding and communication by drawing from their resources from both languages.

Cognates, words in languages from the same root, offer another way in which teachers can facilitate vocabulary development for these emergent bilinguals who are simultaneously using two languages.

Opportunities for Crosslinguistic Transfer Through Cognates

Methods of teaching language learners strategies to increase their vocabulary that draw from multiple languages, such as using word parts (morphology) and cognates, help open a window onto the world. Students who are able to use this expanded bank of resources from two or more languages strengthen their metalinguistic awareness as well as their vocabulary. Since research points to vocabulary in one or more languages as an index for content knowledge and skill development (Graves, August, & Mancilla-Martinez, 2012), students can take more responsibility for their own learning and become independent word learners.

When prefixes and suffixes are congruent between languages, students, when directed, can readily make that crosslinguistic transfer. Many affixes are cognates—that is, the words carry the same meaning and form from one language to another language. For example, in English and Spanish there are specific spelling patterns that denote parts of speech, such as tion = ción in nouns, -ous = -oso/a in adjectives, -ate = -ar in verbs, and/or -ly = mente in adverbs. Figure 3.12 presents the correspondence between select word endings in English and in Spanish that appear in an eighth-grade literature piece. Intentionally teaching this metalinguistic skill can readily boost student achievement in two languages.

Having a keener sense of the academic language use within language arts, let's continue the discussion with the language of science.

THE LANGUAGE OF SCIENCE

Although there are similarities among content areas, each has its own special discourse. Science is no exception. According to Carrasquillo and Rodríguez, "Science, itself, is a language and each different science is a separate language" (2002, p. 132).

Figure 3.12 Transferable Patterns in English and Spanish for Different Parts of Speech

Nouns	Adjectives	Verbs	Adverbs
-tion = -ción	**-ous = -oso/a**	**-ate = -ar**	**-ly = mente**
retribution/retribución	furious/furioso/a	contemplate/ contemplar	really/realmente
attention/atención	spacious/espacioso/a	celebrate/celebrar	immediately/ inmediatamente
satisfaction/satisfacción	curious/curioso/a	illustrate/ilustrar	seriously/seriamente

Source: Adapted from Minaya-Rowe, 2014, p. 150.

Therefore, we must prepare language learners for the challenge of learning the language of this discipline.

Learning science necessitates learning the language of science; the two are inseparable (Lemke, 1990; Lee & Quinn, 2012). No doubt about it, students' language and concepts are expanded through the exploration and interpretation of scientific phenomena. While active science is endorsed for all students (Hein & Price, 1994), "learning by doing" promotes language and conceptual development simultaneously (Miller & MacDonald, 2015; Mohan, 1986).

The Next Generation of Science Standards, guided by the Framework for K-12 Science Education, introduces scientific learning as the interaction among three dimensions: science and engineering practices, disciplinary core ideas, and crosscutting concepts. As language is essential for successful engagement in the scientific practices, teachers need to foster authentic discourse among students. Thus, by focusing on these practices, students have opportunities to develop content along with language. One of the eight science and engineering practices is that students will "engage in argument from evidence." Here are some examples of learning targets based on a third-grade science standard that exemplifies this practice.

Next Generation Science Standards, Grade 3, 3-LS4-3. Construct an argument with evidence that in a particular habitat some organisms can survive well, some survive less well, and some cannot survive at all.

Academic Achievement: Content target for a unit of instruction	*Academic Language Proficiency: Language target for a unit of instruction*
Analyze the habitats in an ecosystem according to set characteristics to determine the relative chance of survival of their organisms	Argue in favor of the organism that has the greatest chance of survival in a particular habitat

Teachers must keep in mind that even in science, culture influences our perceptions of the world and it is our responsibility to honor our students' heritage. For example, Native Americans may categorize plants and animals according to their function, whereas formal science uses structure as a classification scheme (Smith, 1986). Through comparison and contrast of cultures, both students and teachers are able to broaden their experiential bases and cross-cultural understanding.

Darian (2003) discusses how the structure, style, and presentation of scientific information—in other words, its discourse—can present challenges to ELLs. Therefore, we might consider starting with the key uses of academic language, as shown in Figure 3.13.

Figure 3.13   Engaging in Scientific Discourse Using Key Uses of Academic Language

Type of Discourse: Key Use of Academic Language	Example Student Expectations
Discussion	Describe the impact of pollution on animal life
Explanation	Distinguish how natural disasters have differential effects
Argumentation	Persuade the local government or organizations to adopt your green architectural plans
Recount	Reenact phases of life cycles

Let's examine what fifth graders might encounter in a science text. The following excerpt speaks to coral reefs as ecosystems. Think about how you might begin to deconstruct this informational text in terms of its dimensions of academic language, starting with discourse.

> Dazzling living jewels fill the warm, shallow seas of the tropics. In the clear sunlit waters, large colonies of animals called corals have built underwater walls and platforms known as reefs. The reefs are made from the hard bony skeletons of the corals. As some corals die, others grow on top of them until spectacular underwater "cities" are formed. Coral reefs are among the world's oldest ecosystems. (Collard, 1998, as quoted in McCloskey & New Levine, 2014, p. 138)

REFLECTION

Examining the Academic Language of Science

What might be specific challenges of the sentence structures to ELLs in this informational paragraph? For instance, there are multiple examples of definitional language and an instance of passive voice ("are formed") within a complex sentence. Where do you see metaphorical language? Discuss how this passage might be applied to classroom assessment of content and language.

The Dimensions of Academic Language: Implications for Instruction and Assessment

You might begin to decipher the academic language of science by comparing the examples of the key uses in terms of their uniqueness to the scientific discipline and their similarities to other content areas. Case in point, complex noun phrases (for example, "cardiac transplant patient") are very much a part of every discipline (including education, such as "career readiness standards"), while the language of scientific research is distinct from other branches of research (e.g., null hypothesis v. research questions). Figure 3.14 provides examples of key uses of academic language for science.

Figure 3.14   Highlighting the Dimensions of Academic Language of Science

Dimension of Academic Language: Key Use of Academic Language	Implications for Instruction and Assessment
Discourse features: genres	• Discuss the language of scientific research • Explain how to produce a lab report
Sentence structures: syntax	• Use complex noun phrases (e.g., "a kidney transplant patient's donor") in scientific contexts • Formulate research questions
Words/phrases: vocabulary	• Use nominalizations (e.g., explain/explanation, distribute/distribution) • Become aware of Greek and Latin roots of scientific terms: photo/photo-electron, photogenic, photography

Measuring the Language of Science

Authentic or real-life materials to help students understand the language and content of science are generally available in schools. For ELLs, these materials help make connections from the concepts the students may already know in their home language to English or provide visual support for learning. The following list outlines some of the typical kinds of science resources.

Science Materials

- Instruments (thermometers, scales, telescopes)
- Physical models (human body, solar system, atoms)
- Natural materials (animals, plants, sponges)
- Actual substances (water, salt, elements)
- Illustrations or graphics of cycles and scientific processes
- Software simulations

For instructional assessment of science, students have the advantage of being able to interact with real-world materials. Students can observe scientific phenomena, illustrate what they see, and draw conclusions either orally or in written form. For young students, the most typical examples include witnessing change by watching seedlings transform into plants; growing mold on bread; making and describing collections of items, such as leaves, insects, or rocks; or making comparisons over time through observation.

In addition to actual scientific equipment and materials, videos and other forms of multimedia that combine audio and visual input can be useful instructional assessment tools for language learners. For example, after viewing clips or videos on natural disasters, students might evaluate the different types of disasters, either orally or in writing, in terms of the impact of their potential devastation. Over a unit of learning, however, how do you capture whether students have met its language expectations? Figure 3.15 provides an example of students' functional use of academic language throughout a unit of learning on ecosystems.

Figure 3.15 An Example of an Academic Language Checklist for a Science Unit

The student has met the academic language expectations of the science unit on ecosystems by . . .	Yes	No	Evidence or Documentation of Use
1. **Identifying** characteristics of various ecosystems			e.g., Students match descriptive words and phrases with animals and their habitats, such as "white bears—the polar region."
2. **Describing** animal and plant adaptations to various ecosystems			
3. **Comparing** animal and plant adaptations in various ecosystems			
4. **Explaining** how animals and plants adapt to various ecosystems			
5. **Evaluating** the consequences of changes in various ecosystems			

How might ELLs demonstrate that they have met the academic language expectations regarding ecosystems? The following writing sample from a dual language student shows his understanding of cause and effect on his native ecosystem in Argentina; in it, he pleads not to cut down trees as the plants and animals will not have oxygen and they all will die. And in addition, the implication is that the landscape will be impacted.

No Cortes

No cortes los árboles porque en Argentina no hay muchos árboles más y no van a tener oxígeno puro y los animales van a morir y todas las plantas mueren. Y no va a ver muy brillante.

(Don't cut the trees down because in Argentina there are not many trees left and they are not going to have pure oxygen and the animals are going to die and all the plants die. And it isn't going to seem very sparkly.)

Source: Add.a.lingua, http://addalingua.com.

Here is an older student, a middle school ELL, who writes a persuasive paragraph on a similar topic, the use of trees as energy. As you read it, compare the academic language use by the two ELLs.

Don't Cut the Trees

The disadvantages of having to use trees as a thermal energy are that that's a waiste of trees. We shouldn't have to cut trees which gives us oxygen for heat. I mean we can instead use heaters and use its steam. We would have to provide gas but that's all the choices we have. The advantages of solar energy is that by using the sun light we wont waiste electricity. The sun keeps us warm. An exclusively when you wash clothes you can just put it to dry by the sun light.

Source: WIDA, 2005.

At the high school level, students may use materials for physical science to, for instance, harness solar power, design circuits, or build weight-bearing bridges. To maximize language and grade-level content learning, ELLs should maintain logs with illustrations and written text to document what they do as scientists and to reflect on their personal progress toward meeting their goals.

As in all classes, teachers must be sensitive to cultural connections and be attuned to students' backgrounds; some ELLs may have experienced diseases (e.g., malaria) and disasters (e.g., typhoons, tsunamis) less likely to strike in the United States. If given opportunities to express their experiences, feelings, and reactions, students will be more readily able to use their prior knowledge and apply it to new situations. This strategy is especially helpful when ELLs enter the world of social studies.

THE LANGUAGE OF SOCIAL STUDIES

The College, Career and Civic Life (3C) Framework for State Social Studies Standards is centered on an Inquiry Arc—a set of interlocking and mutually supportive ideas that frame the ways students learn social studies content. By focusing on inquiry, the framework emphasizes the disciplinary concepts and practices that support students as they develop the capacity to know, analyze, explain, and argue about interdisciplinary challenges in our social world. (National Council for the Social Studies, 2013, p. 6)

It is quite evident from this statement that language is central to exploring and understanding social studies content. In fact, the document goes on to say how literacy defined in college and career readiness anchor standards is foundational to social studies inquiry.

The identification of dates, places, people, and events that students encounter in social studies directly relate to content. The description, explanation, and comparison of these entities are some of the academic language functions needed to access that content. The following example illustrates distinct language and content targets in the area of history.

C3 Framework Dimension 2: Change, Continuity, and Context

D2.His.3.3-5. By the end of Grade 5, individually and with others, students:

Generate questions about individuals and groups who

have shaped significant historical changes and continuities (p. 46).

Academic Achievement: Content target for a unit of instruction	Academic Language Proficiency: Language target for a unit of instruction
Evaluate the significance of the leaders of the civil rights movement based on critical events	Discuss biographies of the leaders of the civil rights movement based on their significance

For ELLs, especially students with limited or interrupted education, the content area of social studies is often fraught with challenges because many of its concepts, historical events, and famous figures fall outside the students' experiential realm. In addition, many themes that thread through U.S. curriculum are abstract in nature or pertain only to the U.S. context. How do you explain *democracy, justice, freedom,* or *equity* to a refugee child who hasn't had even remote contact with these basic precepts of American history?

As in all learning, we must begin with an ELL's world base—connect with prior knowledge, language, and culture and expand on what he or she knows. Do teachers realize that the Vietnam War to a Vietnamese student is the American War? Instead of presenting information from a single perspective, seize the teachable moment to probe deeper. In this instance, teachers may ask the students, "Why do you think the war has two names?" or, "How might you compare the war from two different perspectives?" As we have elaborated with the other content areas, Figure 3.16 provides some examples of key uses of academic language applicable to social studies.

The Dimensions of Academic Language: Implications for Instruction and Assessment

Academic language use of social studies has some traits in common with other disciplines, but it has some features that are unique to the content area. Figure 3.17 gives a glimpse into a few examples based on the dimensions of academic language.

There are instructional strategies, supports, and methods that facilitate ELLs' language development and conceptual understanding. To promote academic talk between and among students, Zwiers, O'Hara, and Pritchard (2014) suggest the use of academic language development strategies as scaffolds. A number of these tools are described within the context of social studies.

Figure 3.16 Engaging in Social Studies Discourse Using Key Uses of Academic Language

Type of Discourse: Key Use of Academic Language	Example Student Expectations
Discussion	Compare and contrast the value of democratic elections
Explanation	Elaborate why community workers are important
Argumentation	Critique the economic impact of significant global events
Recount	Trace the demographic shift from majority to minority in the K-12 student population in the United States from 1965 to the present

Figure 3.17 Highlighting the Dimensions of Academic Language of Social Studies

Dimension of Academic Language	Implications for Instruction and Assessment
Discourse features: genres	• Argue using claims and evidence in historical debates • Discuss the language associated with the disciplines that constitute to social studies: economics, history, geography, political science
Sentence structures: syntax	• Become aware of and use passive voice (e.g., Florida *was discovered by* Spanish explorers) • Become aware of and use historical present (e.g., "As Kennedy says, 'Ask not . . .'")
Use of words/phrases: vocabulary	• Identify and use cognates (e.g., ocean/océano, north/norte) • Understand and use abstract concepts (e.g., justice, democracy, liberty)

Using Cooperative Learning Strategies to Promote Oral Interaction

The new generation of standards emphasizes communication and collaboration. For instance, we expect students to "participate in collaborative conversations with diverse partners about grade-level topics and texts with peers and adults in small and larger groups" (Common Core State Standards Initiative, 2010). These oral language expectations spiral throughout the grades through rich conversations that foster critical thinking and content understanding. The question at hand is, how can teachers implement these standards to ensure all students have opportunities to practice holding academic conversations?

Academic talk must be intentionally planned so that all students can develop the academic discourse within and across content areas. With more focused attention on oral language development comes accountable talk and specific strategies that promote student engagement in academic conversations in more authentic ways (Soto, 2014; Zwiers & Crawford, 2011; Fisher, Frey, & Rothenberg, 2008).

Several tried and true collaborative strategies have been successful over the years that readily promote academic language development alongside content, in addition to social and cognitive development. One such set of strategies is cooperative learning structures that organize social interaction in the classroom (Kagan, 1989). Cooperative learning promotes academic conversations among students, increases their metacognitive awareness, and encourages friendships. Incorporated into the classroom routine, these strategies are useful for instruction and assessment across the curriculum and have broad applicability.

Cooperative learning may not be familiar for ELLs who have been schooled outside of the United States. Instruction and assessment that incorporates cooperative structures should begin with the social and sociocultural skills required of the tasks, such as taking turns, sharing information, and respecting student responses. It also provides ample opportunities for students to engage in self- and peer assessment within a natural setting. Below are several examples of cooperative learning strategies for the language of social studies.

For *two-way tasks*, students are paired and each is given different information. Through oral interchange, students question each other to figure out or complete their missing information. In the lower grades, for instance, one student may have a map with a school, post office, and library, while his or her partner has the identical map showing other places in the community, such as the police station, hospital, and fire station. Students instruct each other how to locate the places on their specific map. For instance, one student might say to his or her partner, "Go up Main Street to Third Avenue. The police station is on the corner of Main and Third." Self-assessment is built into this type of activity as students receive immediate feedback by examining each other's maps throughout the activity.

Think-pair-share is similar to brainstorming in that there isn't just one correct answer. Teachers ask probing questions that embed academic language, such as, "What does democracy mean to you?" or, "What is your favorite type of transportation and why?" and then allow students thinking time. Students might be paired purposefully (such as a shy student with a risk taker, a newly arrived dual language student with another from the same language background, or an ELL with a proficient English speaker) or just randomly. Students share their ideas with each other and then with the class as the teacher writes the responses on the board or takes anecdotal notes.

In *numbered heads together*, students work in teams (usually of three or four members) where each is assigned a number. The teacher throws out a question, issue, or problem—for example, "How would you change the boundaries of the Middle East so people would live peacefully?" Team members discuss the topic and propose possible solutions. When the teacher calls a number, the designated students share their team's information or ideas with the class.

Round robin is another type of cooperative strategy in which students work in teams or small groups. Here, teachers pose questions that have multiple possible answers, such as, "What are some reasons for prejudice and discrimination?" or, "What are the advantages and disadvantages of living in the United States?" Students take turns within their groups either giving oral responses or writing them down and passing around a piece of paper to teammates until all members of the team have had opportunities to provide original thoughts.

Figure 3.18 gives examples of the language and content of social studies tasks that may be useful with different types of cooperative strategies. It is important that teachers inform students of both the language and content expectation before the activity begins. Student feedback should reflect the specific language or content being assessed. As cooperative learning is an instructional practice, when assessment is naturally interwoven, the two blend into instructional assessment. *Instructional assessment* signals the assessment occurring during instruction.

Figure 3.18   Using Cooperative Learning Structures for Instructional Assessment of Social Studies Content and Language

Cooperative Learning Strategy	Example Use With the Content of Social Studies	Example Use With the Language of Social Studies
Two-way tasks (in pairs)	Locate specific locales of conflict	Compare two areas of conflict based on location
Think-pair-(write)-share (with a partner)	Name and rank the rights from the Bill of Rights in terms of importance	Defend an important right in the Bill of Rights
Numbered heads together (in teams)	Give dates and reasons for immigration	Elaborate advantages and disadvantages of immigration
Round robin (in small groups)	Identify features of major historical eras of the past century	Describe major historical eras of the past century

Source: Adapted from: Gottlieb, 2006, p. 77.

REFLECTION

Using Interactive Supports for Instruction and Assessment

The cooperative learning structures are just a sampling of interactive supports that engage language learners and encourage them to exchange information and thinking with one another in one or more languages. What if you were to add technology to the mix, allowing students to use white boards, hand-held devices, or computers as the medium of delivery? How might you extend these student-student interactions to other content areas?

Using of Graphic and Visual Supports for Instruction and Assessment

Graphic and visual representations are invaluable for acquiring the language and content of social studies. By incorporating these forms of support into instruction and assessment, teachers can readily facilitate their students' oral language and literacy development. Here is a sampling of graphic and visual supports typically associated with social studies.

Manipulatives for Social Studies

- Maps
- Globes
- Arial and satellite photographs
- Timelines
- Atlases
- Compasses
- Multicultural artifacts
- Global Positioning Systems (GPS)
- Gaming through technology
- Video clips

Because graphic and visual supports provide avenues to meaning making for language learners they need to be incorporated into instructional assessment. ELLs, for example, may not be able to produce an essay on current economic or population trends, but they could readily relate the same concepts by constructing or interpreting a series of demographic graphs. They may not be able to distill the foreign policies of different presidents in written discourse, but they could make comparisons on a semantic web or Venn diagram.

Measuring the Language of Social Studies

As language learners progress through the grades, especially in middle and high school, it is inevitable that they will encounter text without much graphic or visual support. Consequently, assessment of achievement of social studies content becomes more literacy dependent. Such is the case of the use of cloze, a literacy-related technique where words are deleted within a passage. One type of cloze assessment is mechanical, where every nth (let's say 7th) word is deleted after the first sentence; in this instance, the assessment would be one of reading comprehension. Another type is rational cloze, where teachers decide ahead of time what specifically is to be measured, such as vocabulary related to the topic, or perhaps idiomatic expressions.

The following middle school social studies excerpt illustrates how cloze might be applied to text to measure one facet of language development. Note that the prepositions have been deleted to assess how ELLs deal with prepositional phrases within historical discourse. A preposition bank, included below, helps students narrow their possible selections.

Alexander the Great: World Conqueror

Growing up, Alexander was fascinated by Homer's *Iliad*. It was the character _____ Achilles —the hero of the story and the exemplar of all manly virtues—that especially attracted him. Sometime _____ his early formative years he decided to model himself _____ Achilles.

Emulating the famous hero was apparently encouraged _____ his teacher, the great philosopher Aristotle. According to the Roman historian Plutarch, Aristotle personally annotated a copy of the Iliad for Alexander. Alexander kept it with him _____ all his later travels, even sleeping with it _____ his pillow.

Alexander's mother, Olympias, clearly encouraged him. This woman couldn't have been more meddling and ambitious _____ Alexander if she herself were a scheming goddess _____ Mount Olympus. In fact, she may have consorted _____ the gods. Or, at least, that's the rumor she spread.

Olympias informed her son that he was actually a *descendent* of Achilles. And probably Hercules, too. And so, _____ keeping with his family tradition and the great expectations of his mother, Alexander looked for any opportunity to demonstrate his heroic strength and courage.

Preposition Word Bank

after   by   for   in   of

on   throughout   under   with

Source: http://www.interesting.com/stories/alexander/#story.

In measuring academic achievement, teachers should allow for multiple forms of expression of subject matter knowledge. For example, if the content objective for a series of lessons is for students to summarize the features of historical periods or geopolitical regions, students may present the information as a series of bullets, produce an outline, or digitally record their ideas rather than produce an historical essay. If, on the other hand, the purpose is to assess language proficiency, and language learners are to compile research from various sources, then teachers may wish to focus on the students' use of certain sentence patterns, such as use of time markers and topic-related vocabulary in context, rather than on the historical accuracy of their presentation. In the following writing sample from a sixth grader, it is clear that this ELL has a firm understanding of voting rights in a democracy (indicative of achievement), yet she uses general rather than specific vocabulary (e.g., *rules* instead of *laws*) and unconventional sentence structures (illustrative of language proficiency).

Vote!

I think wen you are in a free country you have to vote. Some people think is not important. But I will tell you why is important.

First because if you don't vote for your ideas about your country will not count. And you will be unhappy because you want other rules.

Second if you don't vote the president can be bad. And he can put bad rules and you will had to do it.

Some peoples from other country can vote. But some of they don't do it. Then if the president is mean he could said only white people from United States can live hear. And the people from other country will be sorry for not vote.

This is why I think is important to vote. And I hope you can vote.

Source: Adapted from Gottlieb, 2006, p. 81.

REFLECTION

Promoting Collaboration for Assessment of Content and Language

As content and language are integrated for instruction, so too are they integrated for assessment. This integration relies on content teachers partnering with language teachers to create a powerful duo of expertise. Using the writing sample "Vote," how might teachers work together to understand this student's language proficiency in relation to her academic achievement? What recommendations would you make as a team for furthering this student's conceptual development alongside her language development?

The Language of Other Content Areas

Language is everywhere, in every classroom, including the gym, the music room, the computer lab, and the performing arts stage. Twenty-first-century skills stress financial literacy, digital literacy, and even assessment literacy so that students can be well equipped to enter the world of work. Although schools may not have the luxury of having these affordances, it is important to remember that whenever students are exposed to such content, language is always its partner (Gottlieb & Ernst-Slavit, 2014a).

The National Coalition Core Arts Standards, released in October 2014, offer instructional guidelines for dance, music, theater and visual arts, and media arts; in addition, the standards encompass animation, computer design, film and gaming. Having students delve into the concepts and language of music and fine arts, performing arts, and visual arts helps shape their cultural development and identity. The language and skills associated with a healthy lifestyle, physical development, and the rules of game activities associated with physical education classes assist students in interacting with the world around them. Ultimately, for students to cross the bridge to academic equity, each and every one must have opportunities to develop to his or her fullest potential in every class every day.

REACTION AND REFLECTION

English is a powerful language that often is the only medium of instruction and assessment for ELLs. When ELLs don't have the opportunity to express what they know and are able to do in their home language, their English language proficiency can confound their content-area learning. To achieve academic equity, it is incumbent upon all teachers to be able to differentiate between the language and content of each discipline.

Being aware of the language of mathematics, language arts, science, and social studies is one step forward. Identifying key uses and dimensions of academic language, along with instructional supports, can lead to valid assessment. Thus, the daunting task of preparing ELLs for state assessment may be offset, in part, by collecting a body of evidence that exemplifies the students' academic language proficiency in conjunction with their academic achievement. Multiple data sources collected over time provide a more complete and accurate picture of students' growth and performance in school. In order for teachers or professional learning teams to practice key uses of academic language—recount, explain, discuss, and argue—within the context of the ideas presented in this chapter, here are some questions for reflection and to spark conversation.

- How would you explain to a colleague or your professional learning team the difference between the academic language and the concepts of a particular content area?
- What have you noticed to be the similarities and differences of the academic language use within and across content areas? If you are an elementary teacher, it should be readily apparent as you address most subject areas, but middle and high school teachers may have to explore class by class or across different departments.
- Which instructional assessment strategies do you find most helpful in addressing both language and content? How might you apply them to your context? Prepare to share an example or two with your colleagues.
- How might you begin to design instructional assessment around key uses of academic language for one of the subject areas? How would you consider the dimensions of academic language?
- Where would you place your school, district, or state on the bridge to academic equity?

RESOURCE 3.1

Features Associated With Assessment of Content and Language Across the Curriculum

You may use this resource as a checklist of features for instructional assessment or as a chart to help plan units of learning within or across content areas. The features in the upper half are language centered, and the features in the lower half are content focused.

	Feature	Mathematics	Language Arts	Science	Social Studies	The Arts
Language	Language target					
	Discourse markers					
	Language functions					
	Language patterns or structures					
	Use of specialized or technical language					
	Cross-cultural connections					
	Differentiated language objectives					
	Language proficiency/ development standards					
Content	Content target					
	Key concepts					
	Related skills					
	Differentiated content objectives					
	College and career readiness standards					

Source: Adapted from Gottlieb, 2006, p. 81.

4

Assessment of Oral Language and Literacy Development

The Bridge to Linguistic Equity

The major language right we possess is the right to learn and use our own language, but this right is often forgotten.

—Carmen Pinilla Padilla

There are more than 6,500 languages in the world, yet in his or her lifetime, each individual becomes the master of only a few at best. Language is a human phenomenon in which people interact through gestures, signs, sounds, and symbols as a means of communicating their thoughts with others. Although the onset of language occurs during the early years, academic language development is generally attributed to time at school.

The language of school revolves around students collaborating with one another, actively engaging in learning, and pursuing inquiry that spurs higher-order thinking. In essence, language is the motivation and the means for language learners to interact with one another and to express themselves through multiple modalities. Ultimately, students' academic oral language and literacy development in meaningful, culturally relevant contexts becomes the stimulus for linguistic parity.

In this chapter we investigate how language unfolds and how to attach it to effective instructional assessment. First we examine the more traditional view of comprehending and using language within and across the language domains of listening, speaking, reading, and writing. Then language learning and assessment is extended to multiliteracies that embrace other representations of meaning making, such as through digital literacy and multimedia. We also explore the interaction between languages as a linguistic resource descriptive of bilingual discourse (Celic & Seltzer, 2011). Interspersed throughout the chapter we introduce performance tasks tied to key uses of academic language so that teachers can glean ideas of how to approach language-focused assessment.

Assessment must match instructional practice, reflect the characteristics of the students, and yield useful information. To reap educational benefits, teachers and students alike must contribute to the conversation on what constitutes fair assessment that yields useful data. In honoring the language resources of each and every student and incorporating them into assessment practices, teachers will be able to move classrooms and schools to greater linguistic equity.

GETTING READY FOR STANDARDS-REFERENCED ASSESSMENT

Gibbons (2009, citing Newmann et al.) relates three significant research findings that speak to the relationship between the quality of cognitive engagement in tasks and students' academic achievement:

- Students from all backgrounds are more engaged when classroom work is cognitively challenging;
- all students, regardless of social or ethnic background, achieve at higher levels when they participate in an intellectually challenging curriculum; and
- equity gaps diminish as a result of engagement in such curricula. (p. 1)

These findings are equally relevant to assessment as instruction; students' true performance can only be measured if we are able to tap their intellect, spark their enthusiasm, and support their efforts in learning.

Keeping this sage advice in mind, we continue down the pathway that interweaves content and language. We examine the multifaceted aspects of language development that are always shaped by sociocultural context, as shown below by the many interconnecting circles. These interrelated domains of language are the impetus for the design of standards-referenced performance tasks that are the source for everyday instructional assessment within and across the content areas.

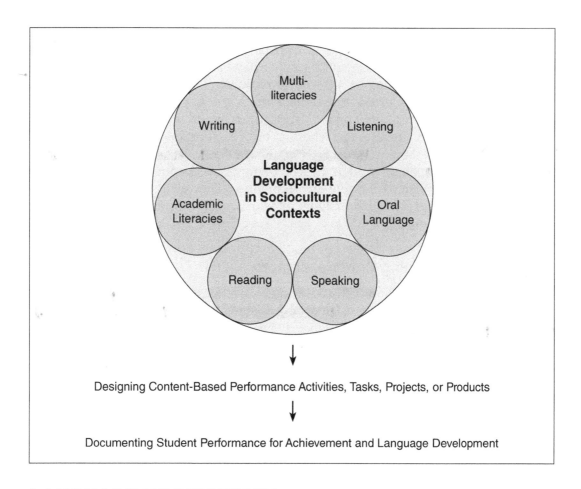

Designing Content-Based Performance Activities, Tasks, Projects, or Products

Documenting Student Performance for Achievement and Language Development

LANGUAGE PROFICIENCY ASSESSMENT: ORAL LANGUAGE

Every content-area classroom should be abuzz with rich academic conversations between and among students. College and career readiness standards have elevated the status of instructional discourse, making language central to all content areas. Academic conversations—purposeful and sustained dialogue about school-related topics—are the cornerstone for building literacy and learning (Zwiers & Crawford, 2011). To promote classroom discourse, students must have opportunities to talk to each other, take turns speaking, and engage in cooperative activities to explore learning together. Unfortunately, academic talk is often absent in classrooms with large numbers of linguistically and culturally diverse students (Zwiers & Crawford, 2011).

For ELLs, oral language development most likely proceeds in two languages. Even while enrolled in school, ELLs continue to be exposed to their home language in settings frequented by family members. Reinforcement of students' home language in school, whether informally through peer interaction or formally through instruction, is a school, district, or state policy. Nevertheless, it remains the responsibility of teachers to capitalize on the linguistic and cultural resources of their students by making continuous connections with their prior experiences.

ELLs' interaction in their home language in conjunction with English is integral to their oral language development. The extent to which the home language is an instructional aid or tool should be reflected in instructional assessment practices. Younger students might seek language assistance from paraprofessionals or other adults. Older students might consult a peer or have access to content in their home language through online support. Whichever resources are afforded ELLs for instruction should automatically extend to assessment.

Although having real-life contexts for language interaction is a mainstay of instruction, in some instances teachers must be able to isolate the language domains during assessment. Listening comprehension is generally the first step in acquiring language. Since students most likely have greater comprehension or receptive language than expressive or productive language, it is advantageous for teachers to have a grasp of the extent to which their students can process and understand oral language.

The Nature of Listening Comprehension

Literature suggests that listening comprehension is a cornerstone of early language learning since it is vital to achieving verbal expression and communicative competence. In essence, high-level speech production presupposes highly developed listening comprehension (Mordaunt & Olson, 2010). When listening, ELLs have to actively process and understand all the dimensions of academic language—vocabulary and grammatical structures, and the stress, tone, and cohesion of discourse. Simultaneously, they must be interpreting what they hear within a sociocultural context (Vandergrift, 2012).

Active listening is part of the academic discourse of today's classroom (Soto, 2014). Listening involves the interaction of students' knowledge of the topic at hand, understanding of how information being related is organized, and interpretation of any cultural inferences of the message. Students should know the purpose of a listening task so that they are aware of specific information or the amount of detail required for the response.

Listening entails auditory processing of language where the listener uses both prior contextual and linguistic knowledge to comprehend the message. For ELLs, listening comprehension in their second or third language, English, may be impacted by

- not being acclimated to the linguistic system;
- unfamiliarity with the sociocultural context of the message (such as the register or situation);
- differing background knowledge or topical knowledge;
- unique expressions, such as idiomatic expressions, collocations or double entendres; and
- influence of their home language. (Adapted from Buck, 2001)

There are various purposes for assessing listening of language learners. Discrete-point testing, in which the elements of language are isolated and decontextualized, may be appropriate for diagnosing some specific linguistic aspects of listening. Phonemic discrimination tasks are examples of this approach and include

- recognizing minimal pairs (where the sole distinction between words is a sound or phoneme), as in chip and ship, pat and pet, or, in Spanish, mesa and masa, papa and papá, cama and quema);

- grouping words into families (such as make, take, cake v. stop, drop, crop, or, in Spanish, as in boca, loca, foca v. ama, fama, cama); and
- identifying cognates in English and another language (for example, using Spanish, nouns such as product/producto; verbs such as manufacture/manifacturar; and adjectives such as rapid/rápido.

Communicative purposes, on the other hand, tend to emphasize the intent of the message or how language is used in a particular situation or context rather than knowledge of the language per se. The emphasis is on the broader communication, or listening comprehension, rather than on listening as a subskill (Madsen, 1983). In other words, listening comprehension as a component of language proficiency is an expression of communicative competence (Hymes, 1972). The overriding characteristic of communicative assessment is the use of real-world or authentic text or materials that portray realistic situations and prompt natural interaction among students. This approach has greatest applicability and utility to classrooms with ELLs (Cohen, 1994).

REFLECTION

Matching Listening Assessment to a Purpose

Think of reasons why you may wish to choose multiple purposes for assessing listening. A discrete-point diagnostic tool may be appropriate, for example, if you detect that a student has an articulation issue not related to the language development process and might benefit from the services of a speech and language pathologist. Within instructional practices, on the other hand, you may wish to assess listening comprehension to monitor ELL growth in receptive language. For example, consider keeping a running tab of students' nonverbal responses to everyday commands or instructions.

Instructional Assessment of Listening Comprehension

At the classroom level, teachers can promote the oral language development of their ELLs through a variety of activities that stem from a standards-referenced curriculum. ELLs should always be instructed just above their current language proficiency level (I +1), as stated in the input hypothesis (Krashen, 1992). However, assessment of listening should be geared to what the students can demonstrate nonverbally.

Teachers and peers are often the primary language models for ELLs. Throughout the school day, additional sources of oral input may help promote students' listening comprehension, including tapes, videos, and Internet streaming content as well as face-to-face interaction with school personnel, adult volunteers, paraprofessionals, and older students.

ELLs may demonstrate their listening comprehension in a variety of ways. Those students at the beginning stages of language development may simply point to the main characters, places, or objects in an illustrated book in response to questions or commands. Younger students may listen to a story while viewing its illustrations and then role play or reenact key events. Older students might compare the traits of two characters from a teacher's oral reading by selecting words or phrases from a bank (read orally) and placing them on a Venn diagram or another type of graphic organizer. Another option would have students classify the words that signal reference to time before and after a pivotal event in history, science, or a narrative.

ELLs in dual language classrooms can use their home language as leverage to demonstrate their understanding in English. For example, in one kindergarten classroom where students were learning the characteristics of living versus nonliving things, students were asked to draw a picture and write a sentence that described their illustration. One child wrote, "Un carro no es un ser vivo" ("A car is not a living being"). Obviously, this kindergartner thoroughly comprehends the concept and the directions of how to demonstrate his understanding.

Students demonstrate their understanding of what is said by actively engaging in performance tasks. Figure 4.1 offers several classroom examples of instructional assessment activities that center on listening comprehension.

Figure 4.1   Sample Performance Activities for Instructional Assessment of Listening Comprehension

Given oral input, English Language Learners individually, in pairs, or in small groups can process language to:
Construct/complete models, maps, timelines, or figures from oral directions
Identify symbols, icons, dates, numerals, and locations from models, maps, timelines, and figures
Categorize or sort pictures, photographs, or realia (real-life objects)
Reenact or dramatize scenes from narrative text read orally
Sequence illustrations, cartoons, or order diagrams
Follow directions using gestures and other physical response
Design charts, graphs, or tables and organize information or data
Analyze and evaluate information on charts, graphs, and tables

Source: Adapted from Gottlieb, 2006, p. 44.

REFLECTION

Assessing Listening Comprehension

How might you assess students' listening comprehension using grade-level materials? Which of the sample activities might be effective in your setting and how might you apply them? How might peer assessment, such as in a paired activity, be a powerful way to assess students' listening? What are some ways to document listening comprehension?

Documenting Instructional Assessment of Listening

Teachers, individually or in grade-level teams, must incorporate listening objectives into their lessons or language targets for their unit planning to help determine how to document students' listening comprehension. There are several ways of recording student progress at the classroom level, including

- anecdotal evidence from classroom interaction;
- checklists based on performance indicators or descriptors for listening;
- tallies of student performance based on oral input; and
- standards-referenced rating scales.

To collect anecdotal information on ELLs, for example, teachers can select individual students to observe throughout a week using performance indicators for listening from language proficiency/development standards. Figure 4.2 illustrates a middle school language progression for listening on expectations for processing learning strategies across five levels of language proficiency.

Figure 4.2   A Sample Strand of Model Performance Indicators for Listening, Grade 8, ELD Standard 3, the Language of Mathematics

Level 1	Level 2	Level 3	Level 4	Level 5
Adjust the position of figures based on simple oral commands using visual supports with a partner	Adjust the position of figures based on oral descriptions using visual supports with a partner	Adjust the position of figures based on detailed oral descriptions using visual supports with a partner	Adjust the position of figures based on a series of multistep oral instructions using visual supports	Adjust the position of figures based on information from complex oral discourse

Source: WIDA, 2012, p. 96. © Board of Regents of the University of Wisconsin System, on behalf of the WIDA Consortium. www.wida.us.

Teachers could use or modify these performance indicators to help guide instruction and then, during assessment, mark a student's demonstrated language proficiency level with the date based on his or her overall performance on a series of topic-related tasks. Another approach would be to create a checklist from differentiated language objectives from a series of lessons. Teachers can then tick whether ELLs meet the language demands of instruction or not. Figure 4.3 on the next page takes the different types of listening activities and converts them into a generic checklist for use across the core content areas.

Lastly, by crafting rubrics, such as the one shown in Figure 4.4 on page 101, teachers can designate the language proficiency level that bests describes student performance, based on observed evidence. When used throughout the school year, all these assessment techniques yield rich information on the progress of ELLs in the area of listening comprehension.

You can't have listening comprehension without oral input, so let's examine that productive language next.

The Nature of Speaking

Speaking generally involves two-way communication with the interactive role switching between the speaker, who conveys a message, and the listener, who interprets and responds to it (Underhill, 1987). The negotiation of meaning between two or more persons is always related to the context in which it occurs. Oral language is thus a purposeful, communicative action with emphasis on carrying out a specific language use or language function.

The development of oral language is complex as language consists of many facets—its phonology (the sound system of language), vocabulary (the lexicon),

Figure 4.3   An Assessment Checklist for Listening Comprehension Across the Core Content Areas

Based on oral input and the student's level of listening proficiency, check YES or NO or write the date in the appropriate box. You may also choose to write the name of the unit of instruction or provide more specific information on the type of content-based activity.

Student's Name: _____ Date _____ Listening Proficiency Level: _____

The language learner can process oral language to:	*Within the context of:*							
	Language arts		*Mathematics*		*Science*		*Social studies*	
	Yes	*No*	*Yes*	*No*	*Yes*	*No*	*Yes*	*No*
Construct or complete models, maps, timelines, and figures based on directions with sequential steps								
Identify or locate symbols, icons, dates, numerals, places, words, or phrases based on descriptions								
Classify pictures or match pictures/words/phrases based on explanations								
Reenact or dramatize scenes or issues								
Sequence illustrations or order diagrams (e.g., cycles or processes) based on temporal markers								
Respond nonverbally to commands or follow directions								
Design charts, graphs, tables, or other representations based on demonstrations								
Compare information on charts, graphs, and tables								

Source: Adapted from Gottlieb, 2006, p. 46.

syntax (the language structure), discourse (the organization and coherence of language), semantics (the meaning attached to language), and pragmatics (the social uses of language)—all of which work together to convey meaning. The instructional assessment activities in the next section tend to focus on the communicative or message-bearing nature of language and are designed for a language-rich classroom.

Instructional Assessment of Speaking

Listening and speaking are interwoven and occur naturally in conversation. While in school, it is essential that ELLs, regardless of their levels of language proficiency, have ample opportunities to engage in academic conversations that are

Figure 4.4 A Holistic Listening Comprehension Rubric

Language Proficiency Level	Level 1	Level 2	Level 3	Level 4	Level 5
Overall listening compre-hension: The student demonstrates	Sporadic understanding of academic language of the content areas when repeated and heavily supported in context	Some understanding of academic language of the content areas when supported in context	General understanding of the academic language of the content areas when supported in context	Overall to complete understanding of the academic language of the content areas when supported in context	Full understanding of the academic language of the content areas in varying contexts
Evidence of processing content area language	Date:	Date:	Date:	Date:	Date:
	Content area:	Content area:	Content area:	Content area:	Content area:
	Task:	Task:	Task:	Task:	Task:

relevant and motivating and that stimulate interaction. In fact, instructional assessment of student-student conversations should revolve around tasks that

- require both partners to talk;
- insist on critical and creative thinking;
- take on controversial issues;
- encourage taking on varying perspectives or positions;
- offer opportunities for student transfer of knowledge and skills;
- have many potential pathways or answers; and
- provide student choice and ownership. (Adapted from Zwiers & Crawford, 2011, p. 59)

While academic conversations may be geared toward content-based activities, such as those enumerated in Figure 4.5, it is equally important to recognize how students are communicating that content. Here then are some typical classroom speaking activities, tasks, and projects that occur in classrooms as part of instructional assessment and are tied to a key language use that is the primary focus for a unit of learning.

Figure 4.5 Sample Activities for Instructional Assessment of Speaking and Their Key Use of Academic Language

Example Speaking Activities for English Language Learners	Key Use of Academic Language
Book talks that include the story grammar (characters, setting, events)	Recount
Debates on school-related topics or current issues	Argue

(Continued)

Figure 4.5 (Continued)

Example Speaking Activities for English Language Learners	Key Use of Academic Language
Dialogues between students on social or culturally related topics	Discuss
Interviews between students or between students and adults	Discuss
Presentations/reports on content-related research	Explain or argue
Role plays/dramatizations of historical or current events or issues	Recount
Speeches based on topics of interest	Recount, explain, argue, or discuss
Task analyses or demonstrations on how to do specific activities, processes, or procedures	Explain
Story (re)telling from illustrations or personal experiences	Recount
Student-led conferences on original work or their portfolio collection	Explain
Think-alouds (personal reactions to reading) on articles, stories, or literature	Recount or explain
Two-way tasks involving maps or missing information	Discuss
Critiques of videos, games, or movies	Argue

REFLECTION

Pairing Language Assessment With Key Uses of Academic Language

The key uses of academic language help teachers organize language around specific purposes or genres. Do you think it is helpful to identify a key use for instructional assessment activities, tasks, and projects? How might the key use connect to college and career readiness standards? How might it aid in documenting students' oral language development over time?

Assessment of academic conversations should at times center on language use rather than content knowledge. Teachers may record student conversations, ideally with a hand-held device, and store them digitally, or, for more high-stakes decisions, such as consideration of a student for special education, they may transcribe the language samples. Subsequently, student samples can be catalogued according to language objectives, language targets, or language development/proficiency standards to create a student portfolio. Over time teachers will accrue detailed information on the students' academic language use.

Hopefully students will also have opportunities to ask and answer questions with each other to document their oral language development. For example, as part of a classroom routine, students could learn to pose questions that deal with the key uses of academic language as shown in Figure 4.6; alternatively, these questions (or others) could be put on laminated cards for discussion by student pairs or incorporated into a question wall. If these types of academic conversations are recorded around the key uses every quarter, students will readily see their oral language growth over time.

Figure 4.6   Organizing Academic Conversations Around Key Uses of Language

Key Use of Academic Language	Sample Questions to Elicit or Enhance Student Conversations
Discuss	Can you present a different perspective? How does this (idea) compare with that one?
Explain	Can you elaborate on that idea by telling me how you thought of it? Can you describe that in more detail, telling me how it works?
Argue	What is the evidence that goes with your claim? What is your opinion on this issue?
Recount	Can you tell me that (response) in another way? Can you tell me that using sequence words?

The conscious coupling of content and language teaching yields rich activities and tasks that intentionally have a dual focus. When it comes time for assessment, although the activities remain the same, the language expectations vary according to ELLs' language proficiency levels. Thus, all students can benefit from instruction in general education classrooms when language is scaffolded. For SLIFE or beginner language learners, the language expectations for interactive oral activities are appropriate when these students are paired with more proficient partners who can serve as models and supports for both the home language and English.

Let's take two-way tasks as an example of an activity that promotes both language and conceptual development. In these tasks, each partner has half the information, such as location of places on a graphic organizer, landmarks on a map, or data on a chart. Through a series of oral commands or directions from his or her partner, each student attempts to obtain the missing half of the information. More proficient students can engage in the same activity, but they would be expected to use probing and more detailed questions and answers to accomplish the same end. At the conclusion of the activity, time is given for students to compare their respective responses and decide the extent to which they understood or misinterpreted each other.

Task analyses are another type of instructional assessment activity for relative newcomers to English that involves explanation through the use of a series of descriptions. Demonstrations can revolve around everyday social language, such as recounting how to tie a shoelace or how to play a favorite video game, or they can focus on academic language of the content areas, such as describing how plants grow from seeds or explaining how cells undergo mitosis.

Certain language frames can accompany think-aloud activities in which students become aware of language use through metalinguistic strategies. In assessing oral language, teachers should listen for phrases that denote how language learners are processing and conveying the information rather than relating specific facts related to the content. Phrases students may use in the content area of language arts include the following:

- "I see . . ."
- "The title tells me that . . ."
- "The bold print is important because it . . ."
- "The pictures help me . . ."
- "I think that the story is about . . ."

- "From what I read, I can predict that . . ."
- "The story reminds me of . . ."

Teachers need to explicitly instruct ELLs how to express themselves in a variety of ways. Students who are at the beginning of the language proficiency continuum will rely on the most concrete referents and will use the more simple phrases, such as "I see..." As ELLs acquire more academic language, they can begin to build complex sentence structures and become less reliant on sensory or graphic support.

Documenting Instructional Assessment of Speaking

Documenting the oral production of ELLs may occur through direct observation or recording of speaking events. Data from teacher or district-level checklists or rating scales, derived from language proficiency/development standards, offer evidence that ELLs are progressing in their new language. Figure 4.7 shows a series of performance indicators for speaking for an English language development standard involving the language of third-grade science. Using this developmental progression as a documentation tool, by swapping out "outcomes of experiments on electricity" with other relevant topics in other content areas, teachers can mark the language proficiency level of their ELLs throughout the year based on classroom assessment.

Figure 4.7   A Sample Strand of Model Performance Indicators for Speaking, ELD Standard 4, the Language of Science, Grade 3

Level 1	Level 2	Level 3	Level 4	Level 5
State reasons for outcomes of experiments on electricity using illustrations or realia and teacher guidance	State reasons for outcomes of experiments on electricity using illustrations or realia, oral sentence starters, and teacher guidance	Explain outcomes of experiments on electricity using illustrations or realia and oral sentence frames	Explain in detail outcomes of experiments on electricity using illustrations or realia and word/ phrase banks	Explain in detail outcomes of experiments on electricity using illustrations or realia

Source: WIDA, 2012, p. 67. © Board of Regents of the University of Wisconsin System, on behalf of the WIDA Consortium. www.wida.us.

Teachers need to become familiar with the rubric or scoring guide of the state's English language proficiency test. If, for example, speaking is assessed on the students' fluency, sentence structures, and vocabulary use, as in Figure 4.8, teachers should incorporate those components in instruction and classroom assessment. Expectations are to be shared with students, along with oral language samples as models, so they are aware of their level of oral language proficiency.

Measuring oral language development is only half the equation. The next sections examine aspects of reading and writing, digital literacy, and linguistic transfer, along with suggestions for assessment. But to give you a sense of the ease of extending oral language into literacy, check out how students might integrate the modalities in different projects in Figure 4.9.

Figure 4.8   An Analytic Speaking Rubric With Five Levels of Language Proficiency for Classroom Use

	Oral Language Proficiency Level				
Component	Level 1	Level 2	Level 3	Level 4	Level 5
Fluency	Fragmentary speech	Hesitant, telegraphic speech often with long lapses	Conversant speech with some search for words and expressions	Generally fluent with strategies to compensate for challenging vocabulary or structures	Fluid, flowing, effortless speech
Sentence structures	Syntactic structures consisting of chunks of language	Simple, short, often repetitive sentences	Simple and compound sentences	Simple, compound, and complex sentences	A variety of sentence structures and uses specific to the context
Vocabulary use	Isolated words and memorized expressions	Everyday words and phrases with some academic words	Everyday language sprinkled with academic words and phrases	Use of idioms, multiple meanings, and academic language in oral discourse	Use of age-appropriate nuances and academic language in specific oral discourse

Source: Adapted from Gottlieb, 2006, p. 50.

Figure 4.9   Connecting Oral Language to Literacy in Instructional Assessment

Ideas for Measuring Oral Language	Extending to Instructional Assessment of Literacy
Book talks	Create illustrated PowerPoint presentations about the author's or other perspectives using multiple sources
Debates	Research a topic, take a stance, and defend that stance with evidence in writing or compare evidence using graphic organizers
Demonstrations	Explain in writing how to use a product or describe a process based on streaming videos
Dialogues	Discuss a topic between two people and share the text on which it is based with peers
Presentations	Make illustrated posters outlining or summarizing the major points of the issue or topic
Dramatizations	Produce scripts, lyrics, or short plays in small groups
Story retellings or predicting the conclusion of narratives	Rewrite stories from different points of view or change the endings of narrative text

Source: Adapted from Gottlieb, 2006, p. 59.

Assessing Oral Language and Literacy

There are numerous ways to extend oral language development to literacy development, or the converse. For each activity or task within a unit of learning, think about how you might assess multiple language domains or two or more modalities.

LANGUAGE PROFICIENCY ASSESSMENT: LITERACY

As with oral language development, literacy is often viewed along a developmental continuum where ELLs pass through a series of predictable stages in one or more languages. Their pace is determined by their oral language proficiency in English, their literacy experiences in their home language, and their exposure to explicit literacy instruction. Research points to a relationship between ELLs' oral language and literacy development, as oracy and literacy naturally intertwine during language development. Additionally, there is a crosslinguistic relationship involved in literacy development of students with two or more languages (August & Shanahan, 2006; Riches & Genesee, 2006).

When assessment taps both oral language and literacy, there should be strategies to facilitate the bridging of the two constructs. In blending these language domains, teachers can

- engage students as active listeners, readers, speakers, and writers within and across languages through a variety of strategies;
- guide students to identify and compare literary elements as they read aloud, listen to, and discuss text together;
- help students understand and make connections between oral language and literacy, such as through daily oral sharing of literacy-related activities or assignments;
- encourage students to share insights from their reading with each other in pairs or small groups;
- explain to students using examples of text-to-self, text-to-text, and text-to-world connections;
- provide ample opportunities for students to talk about grade-level topics and to write about them in a variety of ways;
- model for students how to verbalize understandings and questions about readings and then have students practice and reflect on these strategies; and
- converse with individual students about their writing and have students assess each other using agreed-upon criteria.

Adapted from www.brown/edu/academics/education-alliance/teaching-diverse-learners/strategy.

The Nature of Reading

Reading is a complex, multifaceted process. Reading comprehension is an agreed-upon goal of the educational community, but the pathway to its achievement has been debated over the years. For ELLs, comprehension processes must take into account the relationship between English and a student's home language in regards to (a) individual differences, (b) linguistic differences, and (c) sociocultural differences (Farrell, 2009). All the while, ELLs are simultaneously developing conversational, pragmatic, and strategic competencies alongside their literacy development. With the pressures that come with schooling in the United States, ELLs must quickly begin to have oral and written discourses that encompass academic language required to succeed in content-area classrooms (Francis et.al, 2006).

Undeniably, research confirms that literacy in a student's home language influences his or her literacy development in other languages. ELLs who have a strong literacy foundation in their home language acquire English literacy at a faster pace and reach parity with their English-proficient peers sooner than those without the prerequisite skills (Christian & Genesee, 2001; Cummins, 1981, among others). In other words, a student's literacy level in the home language is a stable predictor of literacy attainment in English or other languages.

Ideas for Reading Strategies for ELLs

In a review of the ELL research, Francis and colleagues (2006) highlight important areas of attention for promoting literacy that are tied to students' oral language development. These same areas can serve as strategies for instructional assessment. For reading, such strategies center on how the language of text is organized, or its discourses, and include students

- visualizing a story in their minds while listening or reading;
- identifying how stories or informational text are constructed around one or more key uses of academic language;
- becoming familiar with and analyzing informational and narrative text; and
- understanding the language of comparison, persuasion, cause and effect.

REFLECTION

Analyzing Text for Key Uses of Academic Language

With a co-teacher or in a professional learning team, choose a grade-level text, whether literature or informational in nature. See how many key uses of academic language are present and cite your evidence. It is interesting to discover that most texts are not pure in their presentation of the key uses. How might this mixture of key uses of academic language challenge students' reading comprehension? What are the implications for assessment?

Digital literacy is a relatively new cousin on the literacy block. Let's see how it has impacted the lives of students and teachers.

Expansion of Reading to Digital Literacy

Digital literacy encompasses a variety of complex cognitive, motor, sociological, and emotional skills that are required in effectively traversing digital environments.

Digital literacy involves the processing of text and visual features that are often presented in nontraditional formats in software and in operating digital devices.

To be considered digitally literate in a school environment, students (and teachers) must be able to effectively and critically navigate, evaluate, create, and share information presented in a variety of forms in a range of digital technologies. Tasks associated with digital literacy include requiring the reader to

- interpret instructions from graphical displays in user interfaces;
- utilize digital reproduction to create new materials from existing ones;
- construct knowledge from a nonlinear, hypertextual context;
- process, manipulate, and analyze information on computer screens;
- evaluate the quality and validity of information; and
- understand the rules of cyberspace. (Eshet, 2004)

Digital literacy has expanded the scope and depth of what it means to make meaning from a combination of symbols, graphics, and text. New genres have emerged from the different forms of digital literacy, and students have to process and produce information from many different sources. Digital literacies include dealing with

- text messaging (with or without emoticons);
- receiving and sending e-mails (with or without photo attachments);
- gaming using hand-held devices;
- participating in online social networks;
- exploring the Internet for a particular purpose; and
- interacting with software programs.

REFLECTION

Assessing Language Proficiency Using Digital Devices

Students have varying degrees of comfort and familiarity with using digital devices. Assessment of digital literacy is more difficult for ELLs, who perhaps have not had experience working in digital environments and who may also be challenged by text in English. What can you do as a teacher to reassure and support ELLs in their acquisition of digital literacy?

Computers are becoming ubiquitous in schools, and in this age of technology, teachers and students alike have to deal with digital devices as tools and resources. In fact, technology in school serves various purposes. It can be (a) an interactive support for conceptual and language development, (b) a medium of delivery of information in one or more languages, (c) a venue to gain accessibility to accumulated knowledge from multiple perspectives, and (d) a generator of new genres.

Interestingly, although computers can be geared to simulate authentic learning experiences, when it comes time for assessment, the performance often reverts back to multiple-choice testing. Take, for example, the sample test for digital literacy obtained from Microsoft. How clear are the instructions for ELLs? How might they be improved? What exactly is being measured—content (skills involved in keyboarding) or language (knowing differences in the functions of the buttons or the names of each finger)? How do you think ELLs would fare on this test?

Here is the set of directions, which was retrieved from http://www.microsoft
.com/about/corporatecitizenship/citizenship/giving/programs/up/digitalliteracy/
ASMT/Instructions.aspx?lang=eng&aid=as111a:

Helpful instructions for taking the assessment
To navigate through the assessment use the **Previous** and **Next** buttons.
An option button (O) enables you to select only a single answer per question.
A checkbox (□) enables you to select multiple answers per question.
The **Question List** button displays a list of answered and unanswered questions.
The **Go** button enables you to go directly to a specific question. Enter the question number and then click the **Go** button.
The **Score Assessment** button scores your assessment and provides you with a personalized learning plan. Once you have clicked this button, you cannot change your answers or respond to unanswered questions.
The **Time Remaining** clock displays the remaining time you have to complete the assessment. When time expires, the assessment will automatically display your score report and personalized learning plan.

Here are the first couple of questions:

1. You want to view a photograph on your computer's screen.

   Which of the following actions should you perform?
   - ○ Double click the left mouse button.
   - ○ Double click the right mouse button.
   - ○ Click the left mouse button.
   - ○ Click the right mouse button.

2. The J key has a dot or a dash that you can feel with your finger.

   What does the dot or dash indicate?
   - ○ The right little finger should be placed on this key.
   - ○ The right ring finger should be placed on this key.
   - ○ The right middle finger should be placed on this key.
   - ○ The right index finger should be placed on this key.

Multiliteracies

Digital literacy is integral to technology use, and computer literacy, in turn, can be viewed as a contributor to multiliteracies—the expansion of the notion of literacy beyond text (Selber, 2004). Let's explore what other forms of literacy are wrapped into this conception of multiliteracies, which are sometimes referred to as twenty-first-century literacies. The spread of technologies has broadened the concept of literacy to open up a new world for students and educators alike. In fact, the International Society for Technology in Education (ISTE) Standards address the skills and knowledge of the many stakeholders who make use of technology as part of teaching and learning.

The concept of literacy has expanded beyond the language on a printed page to include multiple communication channels and media for meaning making.

Multiliteracies capture these increasingly multimodal representations—where print or text interfaces with oral, visual, audio, gestural, tactile, and spatial patterns of meaning. A variety of forms associated with information and media technologies now constitutes a whole new set of discourses of integrated communicative modes. These shifting forms of communication have legitimatized the interconnections that students make among textual, visual, audio, and spatial information.

Multiliteracies, so labeled by the New London group in the mid 1990s, have grown from the necessity to infuse linguistic and cultural diversity into language teaching and learning in order to increase every student's educational opportunities to interact in our interconnected world (Cope & Kalantzis, 2000). Language learners' exploration of multiliteracies has expanded their means of relating their academic understanding in nontraditional ways, such as through visual and performing arts, rather than privileging the written word. Students, by being able to see themselves in their personalized expressions of multiliteracies, have had their confidence boosted. A multiliteracy pedagogical stance enables students' voices to be heard and their languages and cultures—in essence, their identities—to be accepted (Gottlieb & Ernst-Slavit, 2014a).

The notion of literacy has been enhanced as today's youth is increasingly relying on technologies that draw on multiple semiotic modes. Students must develop abilities to interpret and understand diverse forms of text and negotiate these new discourses. That is, they must be able to manipulate the written word in combination with visual, audio, and spatial input, all within a global, multicultural context.

Multiliteracies also apply to students with disabilities who have the potential of meaning making and communication through, for example, tactile means, such as Braille, or gestural means, such as American Sign Language. Other students with disabilities, whether ELLs or not, can better express themselves through animation than print. Figure 4.10 outlines some of the many ways students can meaningfully communicate through multimodalities.

Figure 4.10   Examples of Forms of Literacies to Create Multiliteracies

Print-Based Literacy	Digital Literacy	Visual Literacy	Oral Literacy
• Books • Manuals • Magazines • Newspapers • Brochures • Outlines	• Computer games • Podcasts • Video streaming (e.g., webinars) • Blogs • Twitter	• PowerPoints and Prezis • Photographs • Videos • YouTube clips • Murals • Wordles • Graphics • Sketch noting or visual note taking	• Readers theatre • Choral reading • Book reads • Process drama • Read-alouds • Storytelling • Lyrics/songs/raps • Oral histories
Multiliteracies: A combination of two or more forms of meaningful expression			
• Movies with captions • Software with interactive figures • Social media with visual attachments • Animated cartoons with print • Semantic webs with pictures or text • Apps for digital devices • Home pages of Web sites			

Source: Adapted from Gottlieb & Ernst-Slavit, 2014a, p. 21.

Assessment of Multiliteracies: A Confluence of Modalities

Assessment of multiliteracies has its advantages, especially for ELLs, and its challenges. A multimodal approach to literacy development encompasses more than the traditional ways of tapping student mastery of a set of cognitive skills. Rather it is centered on students' ways of knowing and being in our information-based world, which are more closely tied to twenty-first-century skills (Jacobs, 2013). For assessment to reflect the principles of multiliteracies, it must take into account

- the many ways a diverse student population learns;
- the sociocultural, global, and technological contexts of life; and
- the multiple pathways to learning and language development, along with the expression of that understanding and learning.

In order to adhere to the principles of multiliteracies, assessment has to become more creative, comprehensive, and sensitive to the characteristics of its users. Project-based learning products now have the potential of combining text, graphics, sound, and video in a digital format, a powerful outcome that allows for demonstration of a variety of strengths and perspectives (Hartnell-Young & Morriss, 2007). As a result, students have choices in design and execution, teachers can observe students working collaboratively, and school leaders can maintain digital portfolios as a management tool, all in the service of a more well-rounded local assessment system.

Instructional Assessment of Reading

In a classroom setting, ongoing assessment of reading often is coupled with one of the productive domains—speaking or writing. However, for purposes of measuring comprehension, there are certain times when teachers should minimize the influence of other language domains to obtain a more accurate picture of a student's understanding of text in isolation. Varying approaches may be infused into instructional routines that revolve around the processing of literacy material. As you read the passage below on cells, make note of the interaction between language and content as either a facilitator or inhibitor of reading comprehension.

A Linguistic Analysis of a Reading Passage: The History of Cells

Cells have often been called the building blocks of life, and are indeed found to the basis of everything we generally classify as life (viruses are their own special category). Cells were discovered by a British scientist named Robert Hooke in 1665. The name was originally applied to cells found in a cork! These "cells" looked like little compartments, similar to the living quarters of monks which were called cells. Much later on, two German scientists discovered the connection between life and cells. Matthias Schleiden discovered plants are made of cells, while Theodor Schwann realized animals are composed of cells. We have since learned that bacteria are composed of single cells (unicellular), while more complex forms of life are multicellular.

Source: Creative Commons (CC BY-SA 3.0).

REFLECTION

Analyzing a Passage With a Language Lens

As you review this informational text, apply a linguistic lens while you think about your ELLs. To begin, there are numerous words with multiple meanings, a prime example of which is *cell*. Also, consider the challenges of idiomatic expressions, such as "made up" versus "made up of." In terms of sentences, there are many examples of passive voice in this passage, such as "were discovered by." What instructional strategies might you use to help your ELLs tackle these challenges as they appear in this descriptive discourse?

There are several instructional approaches, such as teacher modeled, shared, shared-to-guided, and guided reading, that, if employed systematically, result in younger students gradually gaining independence as they acquire confidence and comprehension in reading. During shared reading, whole-group activities involve enlarged print materials, such as big books, charts, or word/phrase walls; beginning readers may respond by pointing, highlighting, or underlining, or by classifying or categorizing words, expressions, or word families. Teachers frequently pause to check for comprehension or engage students in group discussions to brainstorm ideas.

Shared-to-guided reading is an instructional assessment technique developed for small groups of ELLs that bridges shared reading and guided reading, providing teacher support as beginning readers describe illustrations, make predictions, and then track print and echo read. In guided reading, students read scaffolded text independently, often in small, flexible groups under the teacher's direction, while reading strategies are introduced. Teachers build on their students' strengths and stretch language learners to new understandings through probing questions, such as, "What does the Table of Contents tell you?" "What clues tell you that this book is narrative or informational?" or, "What surprises did you find reading this true story?"

Documenting Instructional Assessment of the Language of Reading

Structured observation, in which teachers systematically maintain written anecdotal records of their students based on preselected language objectives, language targets, or language proficiency/development standards, is a powerful classroom assessment tool (Mariotti & Homan, 1994). Coupled with commercial or teacher-made checklists (Rhodes & Shanklin, 1993), teachers can focus on specific aspects of their students' use of academic language as part of their literacy development and systematically document their performance over time. This strategy is equally effective for readers of all levels, beginning to advanced, whether in English or another language.

REFLECTION

Documenting Standards-Referenced Literacy Development of ELLs

Look at the model performance indicators in the listening and speaking sections of this chapter and the corresponding ones found in your state's college and career readiness standards. How might you convert either one of those to reading? How might the language progressions in language proficiency/development standards help monitor ELLs' literacy development until the students reach grade-level reading? Share with another teacher your ideas for documenting language development during reading of ELLs at different levels of language proficiency.

As ELLs advance in comprehending text, their language and academic expectations increase as they engage in literacy-related activities, such as participating in literature circles or in book clubs. Examples of how to assess reading comprehension of ELLs include having the students engage in

- categorizing, classifying, or sorting icons, words, or phrases into groups (using illustrations or graphic organizers);
- illustrating summaries of written text or discourse;
- underlining sentences that relate to the main ideas and circling supporting details;
- completing cloze exercises using word/phrase banks (see example in Chapter 3);
- ordering pictures, sentences, or paragraphs based on sequential language;
- responding to oral comprehension questions, such as in running records;
- matching opinions and reasons or claims and evidence in text;
- identifying comparative language to distinguish between two characters, positions, or events; and
- highlighting hypotheses or research questions and the findings in different colors.

At times, such as at the end of a quarter, teachers may wish to rely on a holistic rubric to describe where ELLs fall on a reading comprehension scale. Based on evidence accrued over time, as shown in Figure 4.11 on page 114, teachers can use students' level of English language proficiency as a means of communicating ELLs' overall reading development in English and their home language, if applicable, using a 5-point scale.

As with oral language, attempting to divorce writing from reading often creates an artificial division between two naturally interrelated language domains. Be that as it may, let's investigate writing by honing in on specific genres.

The Nature of Writing

Like reading, writing is a literacy process by which students use their prior experiences and knowledge of the world to apply a variety of strategies to, ultimately, make meaning (Peregoy & Boyle, 1993). Again like reading, writing is an interactive process; in this case, it involves the writer, other writers, and written or oral text (Richard-Amato & Snow, 2005).

Figure 4.11 A Holistic Rubric of the Stages of Early Reading Development

Home Language	English	Levels of Reading Proficiency
Level 5: Competent Readers		
		Comprehend narrative, informational, and multimedia text. Draw inferences from text with teacher guidance. Consistently use multiple strategies to construct meaning from print and digital sources.
Level 4: Expanding Readers		
		Comprehend most illustrated or animated narrative and informational text. Make predictions and connections of familiar content to real-life situations with teacher guidance. Use a growing number of strategies to gain meaning from print and digital sources.
Level 3: Developing Readers		
		Comprehend familiar narrative and informational text that is visually or graphically supported. Have developed a sight vocabulary of words and phrases in context. Begin to use strategies to gain meaning from print and multimedia.
Level 2: Emerging Readers		
		Comprehend some familiar text with guidance and visual or graphic support. At times memorize and repeat language patterns in predictable narrative and informational text. Make the connection between sounds and letters, words and word families, and cognates, if applicable, with meaning. Identify some illustrated grade-level words, phrases, and short sentences.
Level 1: Beginning Readers		
		Attend to pictures, figures, illustrations, and diagrams in text and begin to connect with familiar words to ideas. Display some concepts about print. Identify some environmental print.

Sources: Adapted from Gottlieb, 2006, p. 54 and Gottlieb, M. (1999), *The Language Proficiency Handbook: A Practitioner's Guide to Instructional Assessment.* Springfield: Illinois State Board of Education.

The Difference Between Genres and Text Types

Genres and text types generally apply to written text, although they can certainly represent oral language as well. To make a distinction, we arbitrarily view writing development for ELLs from the perspective of genres. The term *genre* applies to written texts that are categorized on the basis of similar linguistic criteria—mysteries, blogs, poems, recipes, and editorials, to name a few, are different genres. Each genre serves a distinct communicative purpose. Derewianka (1991) refers to recounts, narratives, information, reports, explanations, and arguments as her genre categories. *Text types*, on the other hand, represent groupings of texts that have similar linguistic forms, regardless of their genre (Biber, 1988; Swales, 1990, Martin, 1992).

The line is blurred when it comes to the definitions of these two terms. College and career readiness standards for English language arts, for example, generally use *text types* for reading. In grades K-5, the text types under literature often include stories (children's adventure stories, folktales, legends, fables, fantasy, realistic fiction, and myths); drama (staged dialogue and brief familiar scenes); and poetry (nursery rhymes and poetry subgenres, such as narrative poems, limericks, and free-verse poems). Similarly, informational text has a broad range of text types, such as biographies and autobiographies, subject-area books, technical texts, and information displayed in graphs, charts, maps, and digital sources.

As the educational community does not make a clear distinction between *genres* and *text types*, we shall impose one. In this book we use *text types* when referring to content-based learning, generally in the discipline of language arts. As *genres* are generally more communication based and responsive to social intent, we use that term in reference to language learning across all disciplines.

REFLECTION

Contemplating the Use of Genres and Text Types

Every content area tends to have its own genres. For example, mathematics has theorems, science has research reports, social studies has treaties, and music has arias. Select a favorite genre of yours, find an example of it, and then analyze your selection using its unique linguistic features. If you are working in a team, compare your genre and analysis with others to create a compendium of genres for your subject or grade.

Documenting Instructional Assessment of the Language of Genre Writing

As in speaking, the other productive language domain, assessment of writing must tap students' direct performance. Given the variability of ELLs' writing in their home language and English, writing should be a mainstay of the curriculum, with students being offered a range of writing genres for their language proficiency level. Pauline Gibbons (2009) offers a four-stage process for introducing and scaffolding genres so that ELLs can be successful writers. This approach involves a gradual release of responsibility from teacher to learner and includes the following steps:

1. *Developing knowledge of the content topic*

   Students need information in order to be productive writers, therefore, this initial stage centers on acquiring the requisite content. Building this background knowledge, whether in the home language or in English, enables the students to have the concepts and skills of the topic or theme to produce rich writing products.

2. *Modeling the genre*

   In this stage, attention is focused on language. Students have opportunities to experiment with the forms and functions of the particular genre for their writing. Ultimately, it is expected that the budding writers will become familiar with the genre's purpose, organization, and language features.

3. *Engaging in teacher-learner co-construction*

   Joint construction entails teachers and students working together to fashion a piece of writing for the selected genre. In doing so, the student-teacher partnership delves into both content (the relevance of the information) and language (the expressed words, expressions, and forms of the genre).

4. *Forging into independent writing*

   Students are invited to apply what they have learned throughout the process and produce their own text for their chosen genre.

Each genre, which entails the key uses of academic language, is associated with certain features. Figure 4.12 lists various types of writing products eventually expected from language learners.

Figure 4.12 Sample Products Associated With Instructional Assessment of Writing, Along With a Key Use of Academic Language

Ideas for Genre Writing	Key Use of Academic Language
Autobiographies and biographies	Recount
Blogs	Discuss, explain, argue, or recount
Brochures on content-related topics or classroom newsletters	Discuss, explain
Content-based learning logs	Recount
Descriptions of places, people, objects, events	Discuss
Dialogues, poetry, prose	Explain, argue, or recount
Editorials/critiques in response to reading, such as from newspapers or videos	Argue
Expository paragraphs and essays	Discuss, explain, or recount
Interactive journal entries	Discuss, explain, argue, or recount
Letters or e-mails for social or business purposes	Explain, argue
Lists within authentic contexts, such as equipment for scientific inquiry	Recount
Multimedia presentations, including videos and movies	Discuss, explain, argue, or recount
Narrations (fictional or nonfiction)	Recount
Note-taking of lectures/outlining of text	Recount
Position papers	Argue
Structured reports, such as from science lab	Recount, explain
Summaries of oral presentations, stories, or articles	Recount, discuss

Source: Adapted from Gottlieb, 2006, p. 56.

REFLECTION

Examining Writing Assessment Using Key Uses of Academic Language

Key uses of academic language should be apparent in writing—in fact, they might serve as the organizing frame for genre development. Categorize the ideas for writing according to ELLs' language proficiency levels. Then select a key use and a task from Figure 4.12 and see to what extent it is evident in student writing.

When approaching writing from a genre-based perspective, there is a natural fit with the dimensions of academic language as each genre is organized and presents information in a distinct way. Figure 4.13 is a questioning framework built around the dimensions of academic language use that can readily be converted into a checklist to monitor students' writing, genre by genre, for each content area.

Figure 4.13 A Questioning Framework for Assessing Genres of Writing According to the Dimensions of Academic Language Use

Genre:	Dimension of Academic Language Use		
	Discourse	Sentence Forms	Vocabulary
• Which genre serves as the organizing frame for writing? • Does the genre match the writer's purpose? • Does the genre match the intended audience?	• Is the organization of the piece reflective of the genre? • Are there related ideas that are logically connected? • Are the features of the genre represented?	• Are the sentence structures indicative of the genre? • To what extent is there consistent use of forms?	• Do the words and expressions relate to the content? • Is there a variety of general, specific, and technical words indicative of the genre (e.g., *claims* and *evidence* or *opinions* and *reasons* for arguments?)

Source: Adapted from Gibbons, 2009, p. 122. © Heinemann.

Instructional Assessment of Writing

Teachers' awareness of their students' level of language proficiency is essential for selecting appropriate writing projects. Students at the beginning stages of language development may express their thoughts through drawing, labeling objects, generating lists, or perhaps providing brief responses to e-mail messages, other social media, or questions. As they move through the writing acquisition continuum, students may venture into various genres, such as narrating personal stories, describing natural occurrences, stating opinions or producing opinion blogs, or taking a stance and defending their positions. At this point, language learners start to engage in process writing. The most sophisticated writers begin to produce extended pieces, such as critiques, reports, and research papers. Writing portfolios, whether hand written or in digital form, are useful tools for maintaining and managing original student samples as well as for documenting student progress.

ELLs should have opportunities to produce social as well as academic writing. Since social writing reflects students' personal experiences, it often includes references to their home language and culture, providing insight for teachers who may not be familiar with the students' backgrounds or traditions. The following sample is a description of a special day in Poland from a fifth grader's interactive writing journal entry.

In Poland 1st June is Children's Day. On this day all children are very happy because they got a lot of presents. On this day schools are close. On Children's Day places like Grade America are free for all children. Yesterday was 1st June and I get from my parents a nice game.

For assessment of long-term assignments or projects, students' written work should be interpreted with a rubric or scoring guide. Teachers and administrators should bear in mind that the writing rubric for ELLs must clearly represent the characteristics of the student population and be descriptive of the language development process. Figure 4.14 is a 5-point holistic rubric that offers broad indicators of the developmental nature of writing for ELLs. Since holistic rubrics are general in nature, they may be used repeatedly throughout a school year; in that way, the same scale is able to document student progress over time. A cautionary note: In no way should these rubrics serve as sources for grading ELLs; rather, they should serve as a guide to viewing language development in relation to achievement.

Figure 4.14   A Holistic Rubric of Stages of Writing Development for English Language Learners

Level	Writing Proficiency for English Language Learners
Level 5: Competent Writers	Communicate in extended discourse that contains multiple related paragraphs. Message is clear, organized, and cohesive, with precise choice of words and expressions. Mechanics and conventions are consistently present in appropriate contexts.
Level 4: Expanding Writers	Communicate in discourse that contains a variety of sentence types and lengths within well-formed paragraphs. Message is clear, although it may be occasionally blurred by imprecise words, phrases, or grammatical patterns. Mechanics and conventions are generally present. Often show residual influence of home language, such as in the use of prepositions.
Level 3: Developing Writers	Communicate in sentences, often repeating a syntactic pattern. Message is present but sketchy. Mechanics and conventions are inconsistent. Often shows some influence of home language, such as in the syntactic ordering of sentences.
Level 2: Emerging Writers	Communicate in phrases and short sentences, often repetitive. A faint message is discernible. May rely on structure and phonology of home language to express ideas.
Level 1: Beginning Writers	Create pictures and isolated or strings of letters in young children. May reproduce or produce some recognizable words. Strong influence of home language is apparent in older students, especially those who are literate.

Source: Adapted from Gottlieb, 2006, p. 57.

Crosslinguistic transfer refers to the influence of one language on an individual's learning or use of another language. This influence can involve various aspects of language, from phonology (the sound system) to lexicon (words or vocabulary), syntax (word order and forms) and even discourse (the organization of language). Cognates are one form of linguistic transfer. The acceptance and promotion of crosslinguistic transfer in schools is often referred to as translanguaging. Athough translanguaging occurs across language domains, let's see how it relates specifically to writing.

Crosslinguistic Transfer

Translanguaging strategies maximize the communicative potential of ELLs' or emergent bilinguals' use of two linguistic systems. Student interaction between emergent bilinguals in two or more languages should be nurtured in naturally occurring situations, such as in classroom discussions (Garcia & Wei, 2013).

Crosslinguistic transfer or translanguaging is also facilitated when components of literacy development in one language are related to similar components in another language. Consideration of crosslinguistic transfer in literacy processes includes phonological and syntactic awareness, knowledge of genres, and strategies of meaning making. Monitoring students' use of their two languages has been helpful in distinguishing between ELLs with and without learning difficulties (Durgunoglu, 2002).

The use of crosslinguistic transfer as an instructional strategy builds ELLs' metalinguistic awareness—that is, the students start to consciously expand their linguistic repertoire by using two languages as resources. Assessment of writing, especially of emergent bilinguals in dual language settings, provides a more permanent record of how two languages contribute to biliteracy development, and rubrics must be designed that capture the totality of a student's language development (Escamilla & Hopewell, 2013).

When it comes to assessment, especially on a large-scale basis, however, the monolingual paradigm still prevails—that is, policies and practices do not acknowledge students' multilingual competencies when emergent bilinguals communicate in more than one language and culture (Shohamy, 2011; Soltero-Gonzalez, Escamilla, & Hopewell, 2012). The only way that these students can relay information from one language to another is through instructional assessment. Educators who advocate for the use of translanguaging in classrooms oppose the notion that each language is a separate linguistic system with prescribed norms. These educators also reject the idea that a bilingual person is two monolinguals in one where parallel monolingualism exists (Heller, 1999). Teachers have to be sensitive to students' strategic use of multiple languages and their metalinguistic sensitivity of knowing how to effectively negotiate in two languages simultaneously. In that way, languages serve complementary roles and enrich learning. With equal status and treatment of languages, ELLs can indeed attain linguistic equity.

THE CONVERGENCE OF CONTENT AND LANGUAGE

In his seminal book *Language and Content* (1986), Bernard Mohan introduces the educational community to the notion that content and language are inextricably intertwined and need to be integrated for students to develop conceptually and linguistically. Since that introduction to content-based instruction, teachers have slowly been moving toward a unified vision of sound educational practices inclusive

Figure 4.15 The Evolution of the Relationship Between Language and Content in the Instruction and Assessment of Language Learners from the 1980s to the Present

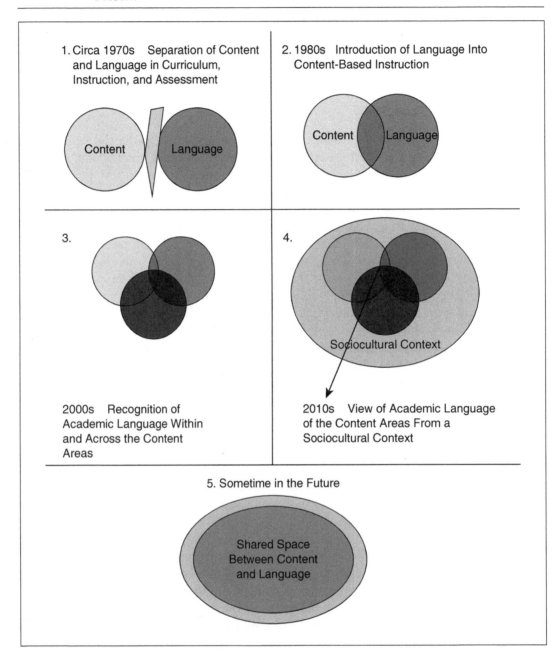

of content and language. Figure 4.15 illustrates the ever-changing relationship between content and language education as enacted by teachers. Whereas in the 1980s language and content teachers worked independently of each other for the most part, this decade is marked by a common vision and goals for students. This coming together and movement toward the integration of content and language teaching and learning has stimulated teachers to collaborate and coordinate instruction and assessment for language learners.

> ### REFLECTION
>
> **Describing the Evolution of the Relationship Between Content and Language**
>
> Ideally pairs of content teachers and language teachers should examine the set of circles above. As a content teacher, how would you describe the role of language in content instruction over time? As a language teacher, how would you describe the role of content in language instruction? What are the implications of these roles for assessment and instruction?

REACTION AND REFLECTION

Oral language and literacy are the heart of schooling. When working with language learners, teachers and school leaders must come to realize the full linguistic potential of every student, whether monolingual, bilingual, or multilingual, gifted and talented, with or without a learning disability. Each language domain contributes to students' overall language development; the integration of domains, however, is more powerful in conveying academic language use in authentic ways that have real-world relevance. With the addition of multiliteracies that are inclusive of multiple modalities for constructing meaning and translanguaging that takes multiple languages into account for sense making, it is easy to see the repertoire of language-focused instructional assessment strategies is growing. Key uses of academic language help teachers focus on organizing curriculum, instruction, and assessment.

Current theory and practice emphasize the integration of content with language for instruction and assessment. Therefore, language teachers need to convey the language of the content areas, while general education teachers express content through language. Together the pair forms a dynamite team that is sensitive to the unique and valued assets of every student.

Traditional curriculum tend to separate the arts and literacy as different meaning-making systems. Multiliteracies, on the other hand, encompass a broader view of literacy and learning in which students engage in order to excel in the twenty-first century (Crafton, Brennan, & Silvers, 2009). As educators of language learners, it is our responsibility to ensure that students use their talents and creativity to be able to communicate effectively in multiple venues. With this expanded vision of communication comes linguistic equity.

Here are some questions to contemplate how assessment might be able to facilitate and provide feedback on students' language development:

- How might you explain to other teachers or school leaders that the assessment of each domain and the language of each content area is of value? What information would it yield and how could that benefit teaching and learning?
- What are some examples of instructional assessment activities that integrate language domains? Given a grade-level, content-area topic, what are some combinations of language domains that would yield reliable information about your students (for example, oracy—listening and speaking; literacy—reading

and writing; receptive language—listening and reading; productive language—speaking and writing; multiliteracies—all language domains plus visual, tactile, or multimedia representation)?

- Of all the Reflections in this chapter, which ones resonated the most with you? Why? How might you share your responses with other teachers beyond your grade or department?
- Which key uses are emphasized in your grade or department? How do key uses of academic language help both content and language teachers plan for assessment and instruction?
- Where would you place your school, district, or state on the bridge to linguistic equity for its students?

PART II

Assessment From a Different Perspective

The Bridge to Schoolwide Equity

As we move into the second half of the book, we focus our attention on how students, teachers, and administrators—the school as a vibrant community—can all have a say in assessment and the use of data for making decisions. We offer an assessment model that encompasses these multiple perspectives (see Figure II.1). It is our vision that the implementation of this model will help bring about schoolwide equity and a sense of ownership and belonging among stakeholders.

Here is how the middle school, introduced in the first scenario in Chapter 1, grapples with multiple forms of assessment to create a fluid compendium of measures throughout the school year. Notice how each form has a unique purpose and a use specific to students, teachers, or administrators.

A School-Based Scenario

School leadership and teachers from South Side Middle School realize that the use of data from a variety of assessment tools assures a balanced and full complement among the forms and purposes of the measures. Presently, teacher teams are gathered to generate ideas for the final space exploration project and to design a common assessment for the thematic unit. Representatives from each grade-level team will create criteria for multidisciplinary projects, keeping in mind the survey results collected from the students on their preferences. The culmination of the project will be celebrated with a Schoolwide fair at which family members, business people, school board members, and school leaders will judge students' final products using a uniform rubric.

Each grade-level team is also taking inventory of its individual practices and formative processes already in place. Team members prioritize the top selections and then independently fold some of the strategies into their lesson cycles. Some teachers plan to observe students engage in academic conversations, honing in on grammatical structures highlighted in differentiated language objectives for their ELLs. Others will have students match certain expressions related to points of view to corresponding genres and text types using colored post-it notes.

Additionally, teachers are collecting data from the students on their preferred methods of self- and peer assessment. It seems that some students prefer to show their knowledge of concepts visually through doodles, whereas others are more comfortable communicating in their home language. During their weekly joint professional learning time, the grade-level teams evaluate their students' assessment strategies and note how the students are starting to take responsibility for their own learning. It seems that some students like to collaborate with a partner and use criteria of success as grounding for their oral exchanges. Others like to jot down their ideas and insights in a journal. Teachers honor both oral and written modalities since they know students enjoy charting their own progress and being held personally accountable for learning.

The educators are aware of the upcoming state achievement testing and language proficiency testing that will provide an external global index of students' annual performance. Therefore, time will be devoted to preparation for these tests, including practicing keyboarding and using technology. The school and district realize that each form of assessment contributes to a comprehensive system and together educators strive to secure the most useful data to help improve teaching and learning on an ongoing basis.

REFLECTION

Redefining Approaches to Assessment

Dissect the scenario that introduces Part II. Identify different approaches to assessment and the involvement of each stakeholder. Think about how these approaches can complement each other and how they can be or are used in your school.

Research points to three factors that are critical for successfully educating linguistically and culturally diverse students: (a) promoting their sociocultural integration into the school milieu, (b) cultivating their language development, and (c) advancing their academic achievement. In schools with a student-centered climate, there is an emphasis on high levels of achievement that are backed by equally high levels of support (Scanlan & López, 2015). These premises for linguistically and culturally responsive schools underlie student success and are the arbiters of assessment *as* learning, the centerpiece of Chapter 5.

OVERVIEW OF ASSESSMENT *AS, FOR,* AND *OF* LEARNING

The notion of assessment is expanding! The next chapters introduce an assessment model *as, for,* and *of* learning that revolves around the involvement of students, teachers, and administrators as the primary decision makers. In this model, seen in Figure II.1, five forms of assessment create a continuum across these three approaches. Keep in mind, however, that assessment *as, for,* and *of* learning all could be occurring simultaneously at the classroom, grade, and district levels. No matter whether there is co-occurrence or independence of forms, content and language standards always serve as the reference point and anchor for interpreting student performance.

Figure II.1 A Model Reflecting Assessment *as*, *for*, and *of* Learning

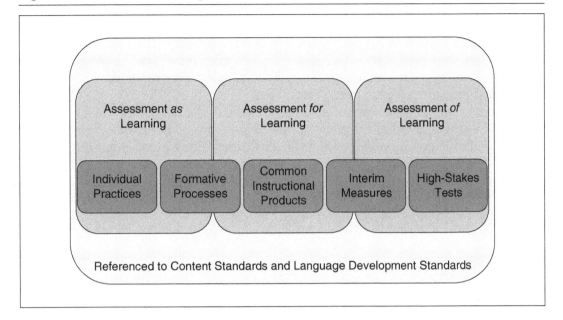

Assessment *as* learning focuses on students' self-awareness and involvement in their development and their progress in knowing, thinking, and communicating within the context of school. Within assessment *as* learning, *individual teacher practices* highlight how students take on responsibility and are agents for their own learning within a linguistic and culturally rich classroom environment. Individual practices also acknowledge and honor teachers by enabling them to assess in their own idiosyncratic ways in order to reinforce learning and push students forward academically and linguistically. As we move into *formative processes*, students and teachers collaborate in crafting and using criteria for success as learning markers. Additionally, students act on the descriptive feedback from teachers as a component of instructional assessment and engage in self- and peer assessment.

Assessment *for* learning revolves around the interaction between teachers and students. It views teachers as guides, facilitators, coaches, and designers within the process of teaching and learning. Teachers are focused on the ongoing needs of their students and how they can best match instruction and assessment to ensure ongoing improvement of their practices. Rather than a test, teachers enact a multistep *formative process* for assessment as part of their lesson design that involves collecting ongoing instructionally embedded evidence for decision making (Heritage, 2010; Brookhart, 2010; Popham, 2008; Black & Wiliam, 1999).

Assessment *for* learning also includes the design and implementation of *common instructional products* by teacher teams with support from school or district leadership. These common assessments consist of a range of performances or projects whose tasks are integrated into instruction and that culminate at the end of a unit of learning. Assessment *for* learning involves teachers and instructional leaders taking responsibility for crafting and scoring assessment, along with management of the data used for local accountability.

Assessment *of* learning implies that there are external measures produced commercially or developed under contract that have been selected for use by school districts or states. Some districts purchase *interim measures*, administered two or three times during the school year, that generally serve as a prelude to the state annual assessment. All states are required to administer *high-stakes tests* on an annual basis. The results of these tests often carry serious consequences for students and teachers, and they contribute to, or in same cases even constitute, state accountability. These tests are criterion referenced to college and career readiness standards or language development/proficiency standards.

As can be seen by the explanations above, the division between assessment *as, for,* and *of* learning is rather arbitrary, depending on the use of the data. For example, in some settings common assessment is considered assessment *of* learning and in some instances assessment *of* learning can yield feedback teachers can use to make instructional adjustment, which is a characteristic of assessment *for* learning. Within the confines of these pages, however, Figure II.2 serves as the overarching model for the consideration of assessment that occurs in schools.

REFLECTION

Responding to the Assessment Model

Figure II.1 presents a relatively new model for assessment within the United States. What are your initial impressions? Do you feel that all three assessment approaches (assessment *as, for,* and *of* learning) are useful for schools and districts? Do you think that the forms of assessment within and across the approaches portray what is happening or should happen in schools?

These three approaches to assessment were first introduced in Chapter 1, and Figure 1.2 outlines some of their distinguishing features. Figure II.2 helps further define these approaches by illustrating different aspects of comparison. After reading this figure, you might wish to refer to Resource II.1 to generate a list of examples of assessment *as, for,* and *of* learning in your school.

Figure II.2   Comparisons Among Aspects of Assessment *as, for,* and *of* Learning

Aspect of Comparison	Assessment as Learning	Assessment for Learning	Assessment of Learning
Primary stakeholders	Students, family members	Students, teachers, school leaders	District administrators, boards of education, superintendents, teachers
Purpose and use of results	Setting educational goals, documenting and reflecting on personal growth	Informing instruction, contributing to local accountability (e.g., for schools)	Contributing to district and state accountability
Time frame/window	Minute by minute, day by day	Week by week, month by month	Quarterly, semi-annual, annual
Stakes in state and district accountability	Low	Medium	High

The approaches to assessment have distinct features, as do the forms of assessment. Figure II.3 defines the characteristics of the different forms of assessment. By examining the criteria associated with each form and its corresponding approach to assessment, the fit between the two becomes apparent.

Figure II.3 Characteristics of the Different Forms of Assessment

Form of Assessment	Characteristics
Individual practices	• Revolve around students' affective, language, and academic development • Reflect the idiosyncrasies of each teacher's routine • Represent spontaneity of decisions based on individual student characteristics
Formative processes	• Revolve around teacher and student growth • Reflect an iterative routine within classrooms • Represent decisions based on the instructional cycle for a series of lessons
Common instructional products	• Revolve around teams of teachers or communities of practice with support from leadership • Reflect end-of-unit projects or performances across classrooms • Represent decisions based on standard procedures for collecting evidence and interpreting student performance for units of learning
Interim measures	• Revolve around documenting student progress on a regular basis (e.g., quarterly) • Reflect commercially produced tests or those contracted typically by districts or states • Represent decisions based on results that are generally used to predict performance on high-stakes tests for students
High-stakes tests	• Revolve around state compliance for accountability • Reflect measures that are standardized in administration, scoring, and reporting • Represent decisions that often carry consequences for students and teachers

REFLECTION

Examining the Forms of Assessment in Relation to Their Approaches

Go back to Figure II.1 of the assessment model and see how the five forms of assessment work in conjunction with the three approaches to assessment. How might you explain this model to colleagues? Which components are most relevant and useful to your setting? How might you adjust the model for use in your school or district?

We now turn our attention to the most critical stakeholder in the educational system—the students—and their contribution to assessment *as* learning. As highlighted in Figure II.4, students take center stage in the model where assessment *as* and assessment *for* learning are foundational for and a balance to assessment *of* learning.

Figure II.4   Placing Students in the Center of the World of Assessment

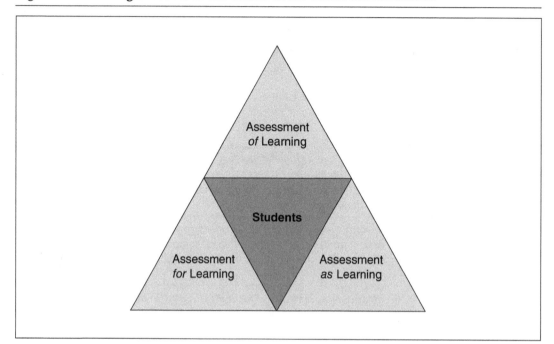

REFLECTION

Balancing the Different Approaches to Assessment

Does Figure II.4 resonate with you or your professional learning team? To what extent and in what ways does it fit your school's philosophy? How might you reconfigure it to better represent assessment practices in your school or district? What might you suggest or do to make your current approaches to assessment more balanced or student centered?

To have schoolwide equity, educators must ensure that their linguistically and culturally responsive instructional practices carry over to assessment. In your grade-level or department teams, turn to Resource II.2 and spend some time contemplating whether the rubrics you use indeed are representative of your student population. If not, make a pledge to convert them to more equitable ones as you consider their use in assessment *as, for,* and *of* learning.

THE ROLE OF RUBRICS IN ASSESSMENT *AS, FOR,* AND *OF* LEARNING

Rubrics are a stronghold for performance assessment as they provide the criteria for interpreting student work. In the first half of the book, we have sprinkled in some rubrics to illustrate how to document student performance for different language domains. Here we go a bit more in depth so that teachers and school leaders gain a sense of the importance and use of rubrics in assessment *as, for,* and *of* learning.

The use of rubrics differentiates instruction from performance assessment. While the term *instructional assessment*, used liberally throughout these pages, assumes that instruction and assessment are interwoven, it is rubrics that serve as a means of interpreting and recording student learning. Since assessment is embedded in instruction rather than being its by-product, a clear allegiance is created between the two that allows for a seamless transition from one to the other. By delineating clear-cut criteria, rubrics describe the goals for learning and identify the extent to which students have met those goals.

Of utmost importance is that rubrics are tied to the purpose for assessment. The purpose for assessment often relates to a time span; it might be short term in nature, such as when determining whether students have met a lesson's objectives; mid-range, such as when the assessment corresponds to a unit of study that spans several weeks; or long term, such as when assessment occurs every semester or on an annual basis. Rubrics serve as documentation that enable teachers to

- determine the extent to which standards have been met;
- monitor students' language development (in English and the home language);
- monitor students' achievement within and across the content areas;
- create a portrait of student performance; and
- measure student growth in language development or academic achievement over time.

No matter what the purpose for assessment, all rubrics contain criteria that describe a set of expectations, whether for content, for language, or for both. These criteria should be

- clearly delineated and scaffold from one level to the next;
- observable/confirmable;
- readily assessable in multiple ways;
- stated positively; and
- informative for students and teachers.

REFLECTION

Analyzing Different Rubrics

With your colleagues, make a list of the rubrics used for your grade, whether developed by teachers, developed by teachers and students, or found in instructional or assessment materials. Then add three columns. In the first column, decide whether the rubric matches the purpose for assessment; if so, put a check. In the second column, determine whether the criteria are meaningful and crystal clear; if so, put a check. In the last column, decide whether the criteria, even at the lowest levels, represent students in a positive light; if so, put a check. Compare your findings from grade to grade or department to department and design a plan to make adjustments to the rubrics. Use Resource II.2 if you would like to further analyze the rubrics for their sensitivity to linguistic and cultural responsiveness.

Standards-referenced rubrics, as expressions of performance assessment, are a source of evidence to use when documenting teaching and learning. Rubrics, whether adopted, adapted, or created, should

- offer a uniform set of criteria or descriptors for anchoring student, teacher, or scorer judgment of student work;
- identify learning targets to be reached by students and the requisite stepping-stones to accomplish them;
- demystify assessment for students and parents through a shared set of expectations that are student friendly and in languages understandable to family members;
- establish a uniform process for teachers to analyze and interpret student samples;
- serve as a means for translating standards into practice;
- offer a focus for instruction and assessment;
- become a basis for collaboration and coordination among teachers;
- promote articulation and continuity for teachers from one unit to the next;
- spur opportunities for consensus building among teachers; and
- provide an organizing frame for recording and reporting results.

Although there are many benefits of rubric use, there is also potential for their overuse or abuse. If rubrics become a de facto expression of standards and curriculum, teachers may make erroneous assumptions about what their students can or cannot actually do. Also, if rubrics identify the criteria by which student work is to be interpreted, then in essence they can impose limitations on the range of acceptable responses. Figure II.5 gives a balanced representation as to the pros and cons of rubric use.

When using rubrics to interpret performance, teachers must be careful not to let ELLs' language proficiency mask their academic performance. As a reminder, it might be helpful to note ELLs' language proficiency level on content rubrics so that the students' knowledge and skills can be distinguished from the language required to communicate those concepts. Better yet, perhaps language and content criteria can be presented side by side in rubrics to reinforce their close relationship.

Performance assessment can be readily captured with a variety of rubrics. Think about a project, a product, or a performance at the culmination of a unit of learning that you have used with your grade-level team or department. Which type of rubric is most appropriate for the project? Let's investigate the different types to see the one that best expresses your expectations.

Figure II.5 The Benefits and Constraints of Rubric Use

Benefits of Rubrics	*Constraints of Rubric Use*
<ul><li>Represent classroom application of standards</li><li>Describe what an assigned numeral means</li><li>Serve as a basis for consensus building</li><li>Focus on instruction and assessment</li><li>Facilitate uniform analysis and interpretation of student work</li></ul>	<ul><li>Are often restricted in their interpretation of standards</li><li>Function as an arbiter of quality of work</li><li>Constrict the range of accepted variability, such as in a 5-point scale</li><li>Prescribe instruction and assessment</li><li>Can serve as an agent of control</li></ul>

Source: Adapted from Gottlieb, 2006, p. 116.

REFLECTION

Modifying Rubrics for English Language Learners

Look for rubrics that have been designed for English-proficient students. Think of ways you might modify them to better meet the needs of ELLs or ELLs with disabilities. Perhaps you might add descriptors or language-proficiency levels. Perhaps you might incorporate visual, graphic, or interactive supports. Perhaps you might weigh the criteria differently or add another component descriptive of ELLs. Perhaps you might make provision for the students' home language. Share your ideas with other teachers at the same grade level or with your professional learning team.

Holistic, Analytic, and Task-Specific Rubrics

Analytic and holistic rubrics or scales are developmental in nature and are defined by a set of criteria that scaffold, or build on each other, from one performance level to the next to form a logical progression or sequence. Holistic scales of language proficiency or academic achievement provide an overall description of student competencies by level of performance. Several criteria or descriptors are presented along a continuum from least to most proficient. Holistic scales provide a summary and generally assign a numeral that is easily communicated to stakeholders. For a look at some holistic rubrics, refer back to Figures 4.4, 4.11, and 4.14.

Analytic rubrics generally take on the form of a matrix and define the dimensions or traits of a construct. The criteria or descriptors in analytic scales should represent what students can do at each of the designated levels of language proficiency or academic performance. For a look at some analytic rubrics, check out Figures 4.8 and 5.12.

As holistic and analytic rubrics have broad applicability, they can serve as templates for designing task-specific rubrics. A task-specific rubric specifies the criteria for a particular project or product and usually has limited applicability beyond its current use. For example, while Figure 5.12 is an analytic scale, it can also be considered task specific as its scope is limited to the genre of argumentative writing.

There are pros and cons with each type of rubric, a summary of which can be found in Figure II.6.

Now that we have a sense of the roles of rubrics, let's look at their application to assessment *as, for*, and *of* learning. By matching the rubrics to the different approaches to assessment from one grade-level to the next, schools can better articulate the developmental or vertical progression of content learning. Through collaboration, professional learning, and a commitment to a unified vision, teachers can claim equity for their school.

Using Rubrics With Assessment *as, for*, and *of* Learning

There are those who believe that rubrics are antithetical to the principles of assessment *as* and *for* learning because feedback to students is paramount and should be proximal to teaching. Others feel that rubrics indeed help clarify the

Figure II.6   The Pros and Cons of Different Types of Rubrics

Type of Rubric	Pros	Cons
Holistic	• Overall, global indicator of student performance • Easy to score against student exemplars • Results readily communicated to general education teachers and parents • Applicable across many tasks, contexts, and settings	• A one-dimensional scale with little diagnostic information • Summary scores can be mistakenly confused with grades • Broad intervals between levels; lack of precision of measurement • Need to use in combination with other types of assessment information
Analytic	• Criteria or descriptors match specified dimensions or components • Differential growth patterns emerge according to dimensions • A student portrait helps inform instruction • Diagnostic information becomes available from the multiple dimensions of the scale	• Decisions regarding which dimensions to measure are challenging • They are rather time consuming to score • Reaching consensus on scoring is difficult • It is assumed that each dimension of the rubric is of equal weight
Task specific	• Concrete feedback to students and parents • Direct link to instruction • Map of specified components of tasks or projects • Ease of scoring against specified criteria	• Not generalizable due to their discrete nature • Narrow in application • Limited usefulness outside of identified tasks or projects • Too often equated with grading practices

Source: Adapted from Gottlieb, 2006, pp. 119, 121, 123.

expectations for learning and provide guidance in terms of the specific criteria that are to be measured. Rubrics can represent coverage of standards over time and serve as a means of maintaining a record of student performance.

Rubrics have always been a component of assessment *of* learning with large-scale performance items present on district, state, and national tests. Language-proficiency assessment uses speaking and writing rubrics to interpret the productive domains to determine where ELLs fall on the continuum of language development. Mathematics assessment often requires students to explain their answers in writing, and language arts assessment generally contains a writing section, both of which are scored by rubrics.

Research shows that linguistically and culturally diverse students thrive in schools where there is a culture of collaboration and shared accountability for learning. When student data are used as a cornerstone for school reform, all students tend to have greater opportunities for academic success (Horwitz et.al, 2009). Given these optimistic findings, let's see how assessment *as, for,* and *of* learning can spearhead change in determining which data are most meaningful in contributing to teaching and learning.

RESOURCE II.1

Assessment *as*, *for*, and *of* Learning in My School

Individually, in grade-level teams or departments, or as members of professional learning communities, generate a list of all the ways in which assessment *as, for,* and *of* learning occur in your school in the first set of boxes. Then, after you read each of the upcoming chapters, use the second set of boxes to add new ideas or strategies to your current ways of assessment.

Assessment as Learning	Assessment for Learning	Assessment of Learning
Additional ideas in Chapter 5	Additional ideas in Chapter 6	Additional ideas in Chapter 7

RESOURCE II.2

A Checklist Descriptive of
Linguistically and Culturally Responsive Rubrics

Linguistically and culturally responsive rubrics take into account the full range of student variability, including the multitude of languages, cultures, educational experiences, and individual characteristics of students. Analyze the criteria in the rubrics you use and see if the features listed below are present or absent in those criteria.

Feature of the Rubric	Present	Absent
The content criteria are directly connected to college and career readiness standards.		
The language criteria are directly connected to language proficiency/development standards.		
The criteria are grade-level/developmentally appropriate.		
The criteria are linguistically appropriate, representing language variation.		
The criteria are culturally appropriate, representing multiple perspectives.		
The criteria maintain the same level of specificity across performance levels.		
The criteria scaffold at equal intervals across performance levels.		
The criteria are practical and have wide generalizability across performance tasks.		
The criteria are meaningful to students and are offered in a positive light at every performance level.		

5

Assessment *as* Learning

The Bridge to Student Equity

Everyone is a genius. But if you judge a fish on its ability to climb a tree, it will live its whole life believing it is stupid.

—Albert Einstein

S tudents are our most important asset and our promise of tomorrow. In a country built on democratic principles, we cannot exclude the thoughts and reasoning of our students during learning and only focus on elusive scores and numbers. This chapter introduces students as stakeholders and contributors to educational practice and school reform. If in fact we are preparing language learners to be college and career ready, they have to have a say in their future and we, as professionals, have to ensure there is a bridge to student equity.

Student voice should be heard, from our youngest learners to our graduating seniors. For example, efforts to gather students' insights on a host of school-related topics, such as cafeteria food, safety issues, and schoolwide policies, can be a powerful strategy and should be an integral part of school life. Most importantly, valuing students' views sends a positive message to this most important stakeholder and gives students ownership in their school community.

Students assume many identities in the context of school—mathematicians, scientists, artists, poets—but their most important role is that of learners. And for linguistically and culturally diverse students, their identity is also tied to their allegiance to multiple languages and cultures. Ultimately, content learning goes hand in hand with language learning to help form the individuality of each student.

Student agency—when students act and advocate on behalf of themselves—is the hallmark of this approach to assessment. Assessment *as* learning occurs when students have opportunities to reflect on what they have done academically and linguistically on a regular basis and to plan for their future as learners. Additionally, in assessment *as* learning, students have input in the design and use of tools to monitor their personal growth and progress in relation to their individual learning goals and targets.

Assessment *as* learning helps move students to gradually take responsibility for their own learning and become independent, capable thinkers. Grounded in the concept of the *zone of proximal development* (Vygotsky, 1978), gradual release of responsibility is a multiphase process embedded in instruction that moves responsibility in the classroom from teaching to learning. As originally described by Pearson & Gallagher (1983), gradual release minimally involves (a) teacher modeling, (b) guided practice by teacher and student, (c) independent practice by students, and (d) application of the skills to students' new learning (Fisher & Frey, 2008). Students as young as kindergarteners can become aware of how to gear their learning toward specific ends and show evidence of what they can do (Cardenas, Jones, & Lozano, 2014).

For ELLs, not only is there a gradual release of responsibility for learning that is related to the maturity of the learners but there is also a gradual release of scaffolding or instructional support across levels of language proficiency (Gottlieb, Katz, & Ernst-Slavit, 2009). As ELLs move up the scale of language proficiency and are able to tackle higher degrees of linguistic complexity in oral and written discourse, there is a relational decrease in their reliance on visual, graphic, and interactional supports for meaning making. All language learners can deal with cognitively demanding tasks when teachers provide the necessary instructional supports to make them accessible and comprehensible.

Assessment *as* learning should empower students to become self-regulated learners. Self- regulation involves the extent to which students can control aspects of their thinking, motivation, and perseverance during learning (Pintrich & Zusho, 2002). In practice, self-regulation may apply to setting individual learning goals, determining the strategies and management required to achieve the goals, reacting to descriptive feedback from teachers and peers along the way, and carrying through with the process and products of learning.

Ultimately, learners can become instructional resources for one another and can be activated to be owners of their own learning (William & Leahy, 2015; William, 2011). These strategies are particularly relevant to multilingual and multicultural students who may choose to communicate in one or more languages and who share cultural bonds. Students need to have opportunities to share learning goals that promote collaboration through face-to-face interaction, develop interpersonal skills, and engage in reflection, all strategies that are integral to assessment *as* learning.

Assessment *as* learning is personalized for students and is viewed from a perspective of their strengths as learners. Additionally, when students engage in peer assessment, there is reciprocity in learning where students also take responsibility for each other's progress. Thus, assessment *as* learning affords students the opportunity to develop metacognitive (understanding and expression of one's way of thinking), metalinguistic (understanding and expression of how to use language), and metacultural (understanding and expression of one's sociocultural identity) awareness that ultimately leads to their self-awareness and that of others.

As Lorna Earl (2013) states, "Self-assessment, self-monitoring, and self-regulation are at the heart of learning and are the focus of assessment *as* learning" (p. 109). In school, this self-regulation involves the students' affect (their attitudes and motivation) and their focus on learning. Student learning centers on thinking and reasoning, understanding the standards and related criteria for success, setting and monitoring goals, developing strategies for working towards achieving their goals, and acting on feedback.

REFLECTION

Thinking About Assessment *as* Learning

To what extent have you involved students in decision making, no matter what their age, learning disability, language proficiency, or achievement? Can you think of ways of expanding their engagement in instructional assessment? How might you begin easing students into becoming independent thinkers and doers? How might you guide students in setting personal goals and in creating an individualized plan?

It is self-assessment, with students acting as critical thinkers and using what they already know as a springboard to new learning, that allows assessment *as* learning to become a reality. By emphasizing the important role of students in the process, we consider assessment *as* learning to be an approach unto itself, rather that being a subset of assessment *for* learning. Furthermore, in this era of accountability, not enough attention has been paid to students, who are the future of our nation and our world.

CONNECTING STUDENTS AND CLASSROOMS

When students engage in assessment *as* learning, they see themselves as learners and contributors to a classroom and school culture that values student choice and voice. Teachers play a vital role as guides and facilitators, encouraging behavior that honors student interaction and student input in decision making. Through technology student relations are no longer confined to a single classroom; students now have the world at their fingertips. Here are some ideas on creating connected classrooms within and across schools:

- Amplify student presence through publishing and broadcasting.
- Establish partnerships in the community and beyond.
- Provide opportunities for service learning so that students can connect to their community.
- Design curriculum around real, authentic problems that impact students.
- Accept the ideas of students and consider them to be assets, not liabilities. (Dillon, 2015)

THE ROLE OF TEACHERS IN ASSESSMENT *AS* LEARNING

Teachers are key players in this approach to assessment, guiding and encouraging students by gently nudging each one forward until he or she reaches a comfortable level of independent learning. Referring back to the assessment model in Part II, we can see that teachers' individual practices, coupled with formative processes, form the basis for assessment *as* learning. By *individual practices* we mean the powers that teachers possess to shape students' thinking and doing each and every day. These practices entail the idiosyncratic ways in which each teacher is able to see the potential in students and push the students to view themselves as successful learners. For example, students do not often magically engage in self-reflection; in many cases it is initiated by thoughtful teachers. In a series of steps, teachers mentor students until they gain the confidence to be independent assessors. These steps are as follows:

1. Formulating criteria for success

2. Practicing using the criteria

3. Providing individual feedback on the criteria

4. Being able to set academic and language goals based on the criteria

Each teacher's individual practices are unique, as it is the ingenuity of teachers that enables classrooms to be transformed into safe havens and communities of practice. *Communities of practice* refers to a process of social learning in which people—in this case, students—share an interest—in this case, their classrooms—and build relationships through regular interaction with one another. Their classrooms, in turn, become places where students learn through apprenticeship and have opportunities to share information, perspectives, and experiences, thus learning from one another as practitioners (Lave & Wenger, 1991).

REFLECTION

Engaging in Teacher Self-Reflection

How do you see yourself as a facilitator in assessment *as* learning? Is this approach compatible with your teaching style? How might you involve students in classroom decision making? How might you assist students in forging their own course of action under your guidance?

Teachers' formative processes are woven into communities of practice or classrooms where students directly benefit from having shared expectations and interests. By *formative processes within assessment as learning*, we mean ongoing classroom procedures or strategies embedded in instruction that involve both teachers and students. Related to individual practices, teachers model for students how to (a) determine learning objectives from the criteria for success, (b) elicit evidence of learning, (c) interpret the evidence in relation to the success criteria, and (d) provide descriptive feedback that references student performance against the criteria (Heritage, 2010). Ultimately, the goal of these formative processes is for teachers to guide students in extending and deepening their learning (National Research Council, 2012). The partnership forged between teachers and students during formative processes generates powerful learning outcomes that are internal to instruction (Moss & Brookhart, 2009; William, 2011).

In defining collaborative partnerships for learning between teachers and students, Mary Jane O'Connell and Kara Vandas (2015) offer a research-based model to move learner-centered practices forward. In it, they suggest building TRUST between these most important stakeholders, an acrostic that entails the following:

Talent: Discovering every students' assets for learning

Rapport + Responsiveness: Forging relationships based on trust and mutual respect

"Us" Factor: Believing that everyone can learn and can contribute to the learning process

Structures: Setting up mechanisms that enable students to become owners of their learning

Time: Offering opportunities to nurture the relationship between teachers and students

When working with students from linguistically and culturally diverse backgrounds, it is always important for teachers to extend that trust to the students' languages and cultures as well as to their families and the community. An example of this kind of trust can be found in this kindergarten teacher of first-generation students from Mexico and Central America:

> Consuelo was able to meet her students' learning needs because she had successfully forged a partnership with her students, making them feel responsible for their own learning in a context that was characterized by a strong sense of community with caring relationships. (Cardenas et al., 2014, p. 74)

REFLECTION

TRUSTing Students

What are some effective strategies for building TRUST in your students? What are the challenges and how might you overcome them when you are not familiar with the students' languages and cultures?

THE BENEFITS OF ASSESSMENT *AS* LEARNING

The advantages of incorporating assessment *as* learning into teaching routines are enormous as they directly revolve around developing student self-efficacy. Teachers have to come to understand the power of language and culture as they honor and nurture the gifts that students possess. Acknowledging this richness and capitalizing on it in linguistically and culturally responsive ways allows students to retain their linguistic and cultural identity and become the best that they can be. When teachers put their students first and foremost, assessment becomes a vehicle, not a deterrent, for helping students develop as unique individuals and independent thinkers.

Assessment *as* learning is an approach that takes time for teachers to nurture and for students to gain their independence. As the climate in an assessment *as* learning classroom is student centered, teachers should take small steps to seamlessly embed student voice into their daily routines. As a result, students are afforded more and more opportunities to collaborate with one another and directly engage in promoting their own learning. Listed below are some of the positive results of actively engaging students in assessment *as* learning.

- *Developing of habits of mind in inquiry.* In acquiring the knowledge, skills, and attitudes necessary to tackle complex problems when solutions are not readily apparent, students become critical thinkers and problem solvers. Being able to confront and think through challenges is a critical attribute of the twenty-first century (Costa & Kallick, 2013).
- *Increasing learner autonomy.* Giving students strategies to engage in self-reflection and incorporating student self-assessment into instructional tasks help create self-starting learners. Being aware of the criteria for success, or even having a hand in creating rubrics, gives students a sense of the expectations for learning so they can plan, execute, and judge their own work.
- *Advancing intrinsic motivation.* When students are offered choices and feel that they indeed have some decision-making power in shaping what and how they learn, they become internally motivated to push themselves forward. The greater the motivation, the more students develop the curiosity and enthusiasm to investigate topics, issues, or problems.
- *Honoring the intellectual and life experiences of students.* When teachers utilize the students' background knowledge as a starting point and springboard for further and deeper learning, students become respected and sought-out members of their classroom community. There is respect for the students' linguistic and cultural integrity and it holds a privileged place in the classroom. Teachers welcome multicultural perspectives, and multilingualism contributes to the linguistic repertoires of the classrooms.

ASSESSMENT *AS* LEARNING PRACTICES

Students of all ages and proficiency levels may engage in assessment *as* learning. There are a variety of ways in which students can actively participate throughout the instructional cycle, such as contributing to the planning of lessons or units, helping to monitor their implementation, and evaluating their effectiveness. Here are some suggested practices for involving students in planning, implementing, and evaluating instructional assessment. By partaking in these practices, students can become experts at collecting evidence of learning in relation to standards, analyzing the evidence, and presenting the evidence to peers and others (Davies, 2011).

1. Student Involvement in Planning Assessment *as* Learning

Teaching and learning should be a reciprocal process between teachers and students. Students should have many opportunities to participate in planning for learning.

- *Setting academic and language goals with teacher guidance.* At the beginning of each semester, or, if preferred, each quarter, students should have dedicated time to think about where they are in terms of their achievement, language development, and social-emotional development; where they want to go; and how to plan their journey. Teachers, acting as facilitators, may model for students or share a format to help students organize their thoughts and record their goals on paper, digitally, or orally.
- *Providing personal preferences.* Before starting a unit of learning, teachers should investigate students' interest in the topic, how their linguistic and cultural experiences allow them to relate to the topic, and which aspects of the topic they may wish to pursue. If students have opportunities to then rank order their preferences for a STEAM (Science, Technology, Engineering, Art, and Math) project, for example, and teachers take their voices into account, students will more likely be more proactive in learning. If students have personal choice, such as first graders who are able to select an animal to research, then motivation is built into learning.
- *Expressing previous learning.* One way to prepare for new learning is to reflect on what is already known. Graphic organizers, such as concept or semantic maps, offer opportunities for students to show their understanding and experience with content and language. Teachers can use that information to lure students into exciting new areas of learning.
- *Co-constructing criteria for success with teachers.* Both students and teachers need to become familiar with college and career readiness standards and, for ELLs, how content standards work in conjunction with language development/proficiency standards. With students and teachers working together, the standards can be deconstructed into meaningful segments to be subsequently converted into attainable and relevant criteria for instruction and assessment. The match between the standards and the criteria for success that define the expectations for learning provide a concrete plan for later sharing the interpretation of student work.

2. Student Involvement in Implementing Assessment *as* Learning

Instruction, along with embedded assessment *as* learning, form the heart of what happens in classrooms every day. Students may be part of the process by

- *Selecting from a choice of options to express learning.* Classrooms geared toward the development of students' multiliteracies should extend learning to multimodal projects. As each student's strength rests in distinct areas (such as digital, graphic, visual, or textual literacies), students should have a say in how they wish to engage in learning and express what they learn. To capitalize on students' strengths, projects should be designed with multiple pathways to the end product.

- *Monitoring their progress and growth in content and language learning.* One way to keep tabs on growth in language development and academic progress is through student checklists. After students gain familiarity with criteria for success based on standards, progress can readily be converted into a dichotomous scale; younger students may use happy/sad faces, while older students may respond to yes/no questions that relate to student-friendly versions of the standards. All students should participate in documenting and monitoring their accomplishments over time.

- *Reflecting on learning.* Learning is personal; individual students interpret whole-group, small-group, or partnered activities in different ways. Interactive journals or learning logs are nonjudgmental communication tools shared between students and teachers that provide some insight into students' feelings, thoughts, and learning strategies. Having students produce entries in their home language, in English, or through illustrations offers opportunities for self-expression.

REFLECTION

Using Assessment Data in Classroom Practice

Interactive journals and learning logs are student self-assessment tools that are built into the classroom routine. They provide students, in particular ELLs, opportunities to practice language in a safe environment and offer teachers insight into what students can do (Cloud, Genesee, & Hamayan, 2009). What kind of data might you secure from these assessment tools? How might you use the data from these tools to provide students with feedback and inform instruction?

---

3. Student Involvement in Evaluating Assessment *as* Learning

Students can and should participate in evaluating their own work. Starting at a young age, students are able to judge their performance against a set of familiar criteria, or are able to take descriptive feedback from peers and teachers and convert it into a plan to reach content or language target. Below are some assessment *as* learning practices that revolve around students working with teachers, with peers, and independently.

Assessment *as* learning practices facilitated by teachers:

- *Devising ways of expanding student learning.* Having students brainstorm ideas using graphic organizers like concept or semantic maps is one way to help students see the interrelationships of concepts they have learned from content-related topics. Working in partners or small groups, students can recreate and rearrange ideas and information presented in boxes or circles connected with arrows, such as the one on different modes of transportation featured in Figure 5.1. Taking it one step farther, students may explain to each other the relationships among their ideas.

Figure 5.1 Example of Generating Categorical Relationships Among Words Using a Semantic Map

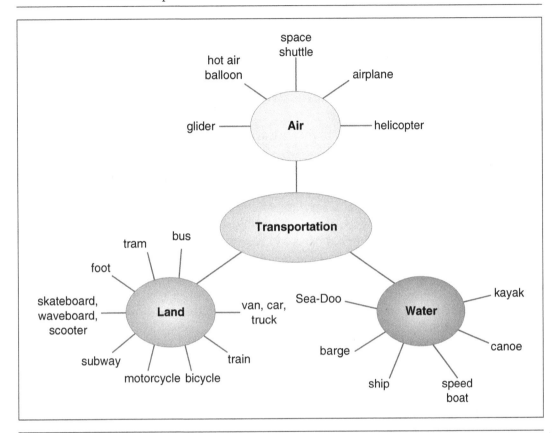

Source: Gottlieb & Ernst Slavit, 2014a, p. 47.

- *Planning student-led conferences.* Fostering student accountability for learning and sharing learning with others are the primary goals of having students take the lead in preparing and leading conferences either with teachers or family members. In essence, students take on leadership roles and are responsible for organizing and evaluating their work as well as conveying the information to others. Preparatory time before the conferences is invaluable; during this time, teachers can role play, pretending to be the student, while the student can act as the teacher or family member. In that way, the conferences become an authentic way for students to practice interacting in one or more languages, and students feel empowered and ownership in the process.
- *Discussing student work.* When students have contributed to and are aware of learning targets for units of learning and objectives for individual lessons, they have a keener sense of what to produce and how their work is to be measured. When this is coupled with criteria for success and exemplars of work, students then have the necessary tools to engage in productive discussions with their peers. Academic conversations, when intentionally geared to grade-level content tasks, provide ideal opportunities for students to work with each other in using language in meaningful ways—for example, to negotiate, clarify, and paraphrase.

- *Maintaining student portfolios.* Portfolios contain representations of students' original work products, often with an introductory letter, and are a reflection of their key learning and their immediate goals. Teachers guide students to develop the management skills to organize their work, to select representative pieces for their portfolios, and to maintain their portfolio organization throughout the year. The portfolios, amassed in a folder or stored digitally, are to be reviewed on a regular basis using guiding questions to build students' metalinguistic and metacognitive awareness.

Assessment *as* learning practices revolving around feedback from peers or mentors:

- *Engaging in peer assessment.* Once students become familiar with criteria of success and can identify examples in their own work, they then can apply the same criteria to the work of their peers. Teachers often convert the criteria into checklists and model for students how to offer evidence or justification for interpretation of their peers' performance. Students need to become familiar with a set of norms, such as always wording feedback positively, as they work through the process.
- *Acting on peer feedback partners.* Performance tasks and academic conversations are ideal for inviting students to respond to each other. However, teachers should be sensitive to the fact that older students' views towards peer feedback may not be positive due to differences in learning styles and cultural orientation. Therefore, teachers should gradually introduce the notion of having peers evaluate each other based on specified, standards-referenced criteria.
- *Collaborating with partners or in small groups.* Collaboration among students is built into college and career readiness standards and is recognized as a valuable twenty-first-century skill. Students are encouraged to engage in academic discussions where they freely offer their ideas and feedback to others on grade-level topics. Ultimately, students learn to work through unresolved issues that lead to consensus in decision making.

Assessment *as* learning practices for working independently:

- *Self-reflecting orally or in writing.* Opportunities for self-reflection provide insight into students' interests, feelings, strengths, preferences, accomplishments, and needs; it is a self-advocacy tool that pushes students to think critically about themselves in relation to what and how they learn. Journal writing and personal blogs are two genres that, maintained over time, allow students to see their personal growth and development. Students can also record their impressions orally on personal devices.
- *Recounting learning experiences.* Classrooms, as communities of learners, should acknowledge and value the uniqueness of each person's way of learning. Students should feel safe in their ability to express themselves, whether in their home language, in English, or in both through translanguaging. Giving students time to think deeply about their learning within a class or throughout the day enables them to judge the worth of the experience during self-evaluation.

> ### REFLECTION
>
> **Evaluating Assessment *as* Learning Practices**
>
> Which assessment *as* learning practices are most valuable to you as a teacher or teacher leader? Which practices do you believe are most advantageous to your students? As a grade-level or department team, you might even think about creating a survey to glean information on the students' personal interests and learning styles.

Exemplifying Assessment *as* Learning: Students as Self- and Peer Assessors

Researchers and practitioners alike endorse student self-assessment as an exemplary twenty-first-century skill for college and career readiness. ELLs in particular should have opportunities to reflect, in their home language and in English, on the processes and products of learning content within language and language within content.

Student self-assessment is a natural outgrowth of classroom assessment where students are the creators of original work. By being student centered, it facilitates self-regulated learning and promotes direct involvement in the task at hand. Student self-assessment, as an extension of performance activities, tasks, or projects, also responds to today's standards.

Self-assessment has numerous benefits. It

- provides a venue for students to convey their depth of understanding;
- invites students to take responsibility for their own learning;
- values student input in the assessment process;
- recognizes the student perspective as a valid data source;
- fosters the creation of a shared set of expectations between teachers and students;
- encourages students to do their best work;
- helps students set realistic goals based on their accomplishments;
- promotes metacognitive, metalinguistic, and sociocultural awareness;
- motivates students to analyze the quality of their work;
- offers personalized feedback to teachers; and
- stimulates students to become lifelong learners.

The concept of student self-assessment may be unfamiliar to some ELLs, especially older students who have been schooled outside the United States. Teachers should gradually introduce this idea, perhaps initially as a whole-group language experience. Later, individual students can express their thoughts on learning through interactive journal writing—during which teachers provide feedback—prior to engaging in self-assessment independently. The rest of the chapter provides different ways that students might engage in self- and peer assessment.

Questions and Prompts for Self-Assessment

How do teachers begin to engage students in self- and peer assessment? Reflective questions or statements might be placed on a sentence wall, a poster, or a digital file, or even be given orally to students. Until students become familiar with how to respond, reflective prompts, or sentence starters, might be helpful supports as well.

Sample Reflective Questions

Here is a set of questions you may wish to ask students about a topic, a procedure, a process, or a learning strategy. As you will see, the earlier questions are more general in nature, but the later ones probe a bit into specifics. Do not use all the questions in one sitting; rather, introduce them one or two at a time. You may even let students select the ones they prefer to answer. Over time, students should also be able to provide some reasoning behind their responses.

What did you know about this topic?

What did you learn about _____?

What did you find most interesting about _____?

What did you find challenging about _____?

How would you change this topic _____?

Some Personal Prompts

Student self-assessment can occur before, during, or after lessons. Here are some sentence starters for students to think about before answering them orally or in writing. Teachers should vary which ones to use in introducing a unit of learning and at the unit's conclusion.

My Preferences for Learning

The most interesting ideas for me are _____.

I prefer to work by myself when _____.

I like working with others when _____.

My Learning Style and Strategies

A strategy that helps me remember is _____.

I find it easy to understand when _____.

When I don't understand something, I _____.

My Strengths

I'm getting better at _____. Here is evidence of my improvement: _____.

I do well when _____.

In school, I enjoy working hard at _____.

Areas for Me to Improve

I'm still not sure how to _____ .

I would like some help with _____ .

My next steps for improving are _____ .

Types of Student Self-Assessment

An array of formats exists that students can use for self-assessment and that can be readily integrated into instruction. This section explores how students of all ages, including ELLs and ELLs with disabilities, can participate in assessment as they learn.

Criterion-Referenced Exemplars

One type of student self-assessment focuses on the standards-referenced criteria that shape or define the work products and the steps students take to produce evidence of learning. In this case, teachers formulate a series of questions or statements that guide students to produce a response or work sample that conforms to the criteria or specifications of the task. For young students, methods for self-assessment may consist of answering yes/no questions, using happy/sad faces, or giving answers in their home language. For older students or those with more developed language proficiency, rating scales, once they are familiar to students, may be an appropriate format for self-assessment.

By second grade, students are able to reflect on their academic language use and produce written responses. In one international school in Taiwan, students engage in self-assessment across the curriculum, including the content areas of mathematics, language arts, and social studies. They do so by first reading the criteria of a child-friendly rubric and discussing them with a partner. By using the same format, process, and rubric for every content area, the students, especially the ELLs, are able to focus on their use of language rather than on a correct answer to a problem (personal communication with V. Blais).

The following is an example of a self-assessment of the language of science from an ELL second grader at the completion of a unit on life cycles. First the students draw, label, and explain the life cycle of an insect of their choice using a word bank. Then, the students state what they did well in using academic language and what they need to work on.

> I used lots of life cycle vocabulary and I used a lot of transicein words. The transicein words help the reader know another part is coming up. Science vocabulary helps by making sence.
>
> I need to re-reading my stories to add more punctuations and comas. The punctuation helps by letting the reader know where to stop if there is no periods or comas it will just keep on going.

Another second-grade example is found in Figure 5.2. It is a checklist that mirrors a primary-grade task reflective of both college and career readiness standards and language development standards; in it students identify and describe the elements of story grammar through multicultural storytelling. Following a structured interview with family members consisting of questions that parallel the criteria in

Figure 5.2 A Story Recount Self-Assessment Checklist, Grade 2

College and Career Readiness Standard: CCSS ELA-LITERACY.RL.2.2, SL 2.4

Recount stories, including fables and folktales from diverse cultures, and determine their central message, lesson, or moral.

Tell a story or recount an experience with appropriate facts and relevant, descriptive details, speaking audibly in coherent sentences.

Language Development Standard: WIDA ELD Standard 2, The Language of Language Arts, Example Topic: Storytelling/ Experiential recounting, Language Domain: Speaking (2012, p. 59)

My Folk Tale: _____

Country: _____

I can describe **where** the story takes place (its **setting**).	YES	NO
I can tell **when** the story takes place (the **time of day or season**).	YES	NO
I can describe **who** the **characters** are in the story.	YES	NO
I can tell **what** the **characters** did.	YES	NO
I can tell (**describe**) what happens (the **events**) in the story.	YES	NO
I can tell (**describe**) what happens in the end (**conclusion**) of the story.	YES	NO

Source: Adapted from Gottlieb, 2006, p. 143.

the checklist, students are asked to share an oral folk tale from their home culture with classmates. For self-assessment, students write the name of their folk tale and the country or region from which it came; the teacher or more proficient students read the questions on the checklist as individual students respond.

The next self-assessment 4-point rating scale is based on a multidisciplinary unit of science and language arts. These third graders explored ecosystems through informational and narrative texts. They used the rating scale in Figure 5.3 to communicate the language of science when discussing environmental change with their classmates.

Similarly, Figure 5.4 on page 150 is a student self-assessment tool designed for middle school students to use as a guide as they produce a gothic tale reminiscent of the one they are studying, *The Cask of Amontillado* by Edgar Allen Poe. As the majority of students in the class are learning English as an additional language, the checklist is referenced to both English language arts standards and English language development standards. Thus, the skills of language arts are fortified by the academic language expectations of language development. Students provide evidence for each criterion on the checklist, which is integral to this self-assessment.

Student self-assessment can also center on how students react or feel as a result of participating in a task or project. Teachers create a set of open-ended questions or statements that prompt higher-order thinking. Students then summarize or recount what they have done by drawing, speaking, or writing; describe their favorite or most challenging activity; or explain some aspect of learning.

Figure 5.3 An Example Rating Scale for Student Self-Assessment on Ecosystems, Grade 3

College and Career Readiness Standard: NGSS 3-LS2.C Ecosystems: Dynamics, Functioning, and Resilience, LS4.C: Adaptation, and LS4.D, Biodiversity and Humans

Language Development Standard: WIDA ELD Standard 1, Social and Instructional Language, Example Topic: Research interests (p. 64)

When Speaking to My Class/Group or Partner,	Not Quite Yet	Some of the Time	Most of the Time	All of the Time
I use environmental change terms and expressions from the word wall.				
I compare/contrast good (positive) and bad (negative) environmental changes.				
I discuss causes/ effects of environmental change using the graphic organizer.				
I talk to my family about ways to reduce, reuse, and recycle.				
I share my reduce, reuse, and recycle data with my group.				

Source: Adapted from Young & Hadaway, 2014, p. 81.

Depending on the authenticity or real-life application of the task or project, students may assume the role of mathematicians, scientists, historians, or researchers as they reflect on their learning. Figure 5.5 is an example of student self-assessment at the upper elementary grades built into science class where students, including ELLs, reflect on their experiences as inventors. Students are invited to respond to the questions independently or in small groups, either by writing a narrative or responding orally, in their home language or in English, depending on how instruction has been delivered.

Student self-assessment can be incorporated into any content area or language domain. This next example of reflective self-assessment is taken from a unit of instruction for high school English language arts. In Figure 5.6 on page 151, students

Figure 5.4   A Student Checklist for Evaluating Narrative Writing, Grade 8

College and Career Readiness Standard: CCSS ELA-LITERACY.RL.8.2, W.8.3, W.8.5, SL 8.4, L.8.3

Language Development Standard: WIDA ELD Standard 2, The Language of Language Arts, Example Topic: Literature analysis, Language Domain: Listening (p. 95)

My Discourse, Sentence, and Word/ Phrase Writing Checklist.	*Absolutely!*	*Evidence From My Narrative*
My gothic story has an introduction, a body, and a conclusion.		
My story has a main character, plus other characters and devices for unity of effect (setting, tone, foreshadowing, and symbols).		
My story has multiple sequential paragraphs with several complex sentences, linked with connectives, and also quotations and dialogues to make my ideas clear.		
My sentences have subject-verb agreement, multiple verb tenses, and varied word order.		
My story uses words with shades of meaning, along with idioms and expressions of gothic genre.		

Source: Adapted from Minaya-Rowe, 2014, p. 177.

Figure 5.5   Inventor Self-Assessment Questions

Would you like to continue your exploration as an inventor? Why or why not?
How do you feel being an inventor?
What was the research question or hypothesis you wanted to address? What did you find?
Did you like inventing something to test your hypothesis? Why or why not?
Did your hypothesis lead to an interesting invention? Why or why not?

Source: Adapted from Gottlieb, 2006, p. 143.

think about the usefulness and application of having compiled a personal résumé as they respond to the questions.

The next example of self-assessment focuses on a unit on social justice based on Civil War biographies and how students can take social action to make a difference in their lives and those of others. Figure 5.7 is a descriptive checklist of the major steps students are to take in thinking through their project.

Figure 5.6 Résumé Reflective Questions, High School

What did you discover about yourself in making your résumé?

How do you plan to use your résumé? When might you use it?

How does making a résumé prepare you for life after high school?

Was making a résumé important to you? Why or why not?

Source: Adapted from Gottlieb, 2006, p. 144.

Figure 5.7 An Expanded Self-Assessment Checklist for a Project, Grade 4

My Project: —————————————————————————————

☐ **Content**—Did I describe my topic, include my prior knowledge, and ask inquiry questions? Give an example.

☐ **Intent**—Did I state my purpose? What is it?

☐ **Audience**—Did I identify my audience? Who did you include?

☐ **Collaboration**—Did I work well with others? Did I select an effective way to communicate my learning to others (such as a report, a slideshow, or a video)?

☐ **Social Action**—Did I use my learning to make a difference for others and myself? How?

☐ **Reflection**—Did my thinking change as a result of the project? How?

Source: Adapted from Silvers & Shorey, 2012, p. 104. © Stenhouse.

Self-assessment can help build students' metacognitive awareness—that is, knowing how one thinks. During self-assessment, students are checking their own learning and developing a repertoire of strategies to apply to that learning for different tasks. This internal monitoring is essential for self-regulation (Heritage, 2010). Figure 5.8 lists those metacognitive strategies that students might engage in when attempting to solve math problems.

Figure 5.9 is another variation of student self-assessment. It is a rating scale specifically crafted for ELLs that gives them the opportunity to think about how well they process language in various contexts.

REFLECTION

Evaluating Self-Assessment Exemplars

Which of the exemplars of assessment *as* learning in this chapter do you think your students will find most appealing? How might you modify a student self-assessment rubric or checklist to better fit your class or projects? How might your students contribute to it?

Figure 5.8   A Self-Assessment Checklist of Math Strategies for Language Learners

What do you do to solve math problems? Put an X in each box to answer YES or NO.

Math Strategy	YES	NO
Sometimes I use my home language to help me understand what to do.		
I draw pictures to help me figure out the answer.		
I use different things in my classroom (objects) to help me.		
I ask my friends to help me.		
I look for examples in the book.		
I read the problems aloud.		
I ask the teacher questions to help me understand.		
I try to see the problem when I do mental math.		
I use oral and written directions to understand what to do.		
I check what I have done.		

Source: Adapted from Gottlieb, 2006, p. 117.

Figure 5.9   Listening Self-Assessment Rating Scale for English Language Learners

Think about all the times you listen to English or another language. Put an X in the box that says how well you understand what is said, from *Not Well Yet* to *Great!*

When Listening to _____, I Understand	Not Well Yet	OK	Quite Well	Great!
Questions that ask who, what, where, or when				
The lyrics (the words) of songs or raps				
Programs and news on TV or the Internet				
Information on the radio or podcasts				
Announcements at school				
What people say on the phone				
What teachers say in class				
Oral reports my classmates give				
The main idea when someone reads aloud				
Jokes my friends tell				

Source: Adapted from Gottlieb, 2006, p. 118.

Combined Process and Product Exemplars of Self-Assessment

Product and process self-assessment can be combined into one. In this type of assessment, students respond, using a checklist or other tool, as to whether they complete each activity or task descriptor and then reflect on the most gratifying or challenging aspects of the activity. An example of this type of self-assessment is one in which students follow a step-by-step process to compose a biographical summary. In Figure 5.10, part 1 is a project-based descriptor to guide students in completing the task, and part 2 consists of an open-ended reflective question.

Figure 5.10   An Example of a Recount Self-Assessment on Biographies

Biography of _____

Part 1: Here are the steps for creating the summary of a biography. As you complete each step, put an X in the box.

☐ 1. I wrote a list of persons who I admire and respect. Then I chose a person to study and put their name on the Learning Wall along with mine.

☐ 2. I collected information on the person from two sources (books, the Internet, newspapers, magazines).

☐ 3. I made a chart or Venn diagram of the similarities and differences about the person from the two sources.

☐ 4. I summarized the information from the two sources.

☐ 5. I found photographs about to the life of the person.

☐ 6. I used the information to write a two-page biographical summary or multimedia presentation with photographs.

☐ 7. I included the references of my two sources of information.

Part 2: Think about the person you selected for your biography.

Why is the person you chose important to you? What did this person do to change the way you think or act? Write a paragraph of four or five descriptive sentences.

Source: Adapted from Gottlieb, 2006, p. 145.

STUDENT SELF-ASSESSMENT AS INFORMATION GATHERING AND FEEDBACK

There are times when teachers would have a better sense of what their students were able to do if only they would ask, and there is no reason why ELLs cannot be a part of this information-gathering process. The objective is to collect accurate, relevant, even insightful data about students; therefore, teachers of ELLs should consider modifying questions or formats, reading surveys aloud, or allowing students to respond in their home language.

Narrative forms of self-assessment are another venue for gaining student perspective. Less proficient ELLs may begin to delve into student self-assessment through graphic organizers, such as a KLWH (what I **K**now, what I **L**earned, what more I **W**ish to learn, and **H**ow I plan to learn it) chart. Teachers gain a sense of students' depth of understanding as well as their use of metacognitive strategies. Figure 5.11 illustrates how an advance organizer can serve as a self-assessment tool throughout a unit of study, such as this one on ocean ecosystems.

Figure 5.11   An Example of a Self-Assessment Advance Organizer of Content, Grade 5

What I Know, What the Text Says, and What I Learned About Ocean Life			
Column A: Read the statement.			
Column B: Answer TRUE (T) or FALSE (F) before you read the text.			
Column C: Answer TRUE (T) or FALSE (F) after you read the text. Put the page and line where you find the answer.			
Column D: Tell what you learned from the reading.			
A. Statement	B. My answer before I read the text (T/F)	C. What the text said (include page/line)	D. What I learned after I read the text
Corals are plants.			
Corals live in the tropics.			
In the tropics, the water is very cold.			
Reefs are underwater walls and platforms.			
Reefs are made only of living coral.			
About 2,000 kinds of fish live in coral reefs.			
The largest organism in the coral reefs, the giant blue-lipped clam, can eat people.			

Source: Adapted from McCloskey & New Levine, 2014, p. 166.

Assessment *as* learning also extends to peers as they can offer a unique perspective. If this type of assessment is incorporated regularly into the classroom routine as part of a collaborative partnership, peers can become rich resources to provide feedback to their fellow students.

Peer Assessment

All too often teachers dominate and control speech in class, leaving few opportunities for ELLs or other students to interact among themselves in meaningful discussion. Peer assessment is an effective means for having students practice academic language with each other that is grounded in standards and tied to a lesson's or unit's activities and tasks.

Most rubrics, checklists, or rating scales can be used with multiple stakeholders. Figure 5.12 shows how to collect feedback from both students and their peers. In this analytic scale on argumentative reports, students, along with their teacher, mutually decided to use the students' home language, Samoan, to create an analogy in which

CHAPTER 5: ASSESSMENT AS LEARNING **155**

Figure 5.12 An Example Self- and Peer-Assessment Rubric for Argumentative Writing for Middle School

Dimension	O'o (Maturing)	Popo (Reaching)	Niu (Approaching)	Tama'i Niu (Beginning)
Research evidence	I use important evidence (e.g., facts instead of opinion) from texts to develop my argument or claim.	I use evidence from texts that is relevant to the topic to develop my argument or claim.	I use evidence from texts that is relevant to the topic, but the evidence is not complete.	I try to use evidence from texts to develop my argument or claim, but the evidence is not about the topic
Connections between claims and evidence	My writing shows clear connections between the arguments and claims and helps readers understand the issue.	My writing shows rather clear connections between the argument and claims.	My writing shows an unclear connection between the argument and claims.	My writing does not make connections or the connections do not match the argument or claims.
Language of argumentation	I use strong signal words and sentence structures to show relationships between ideas.	I use signal words and sentence structures to show relationships between ideas.	I use some signal words and sentence structures to show relationships between ideas.	I use few to no signal words and sentence structures to show relationships between ideas.
Organization of the argument	My writing presents my claims and enhances the logical development of my argument.	My writing addresses its purpose and my argument has a logical development.	My writing addresses its purpose, with incoherence in some parts.	I try to organize my ideas, but my writing does not follow a pattern that matches its purpose.
Use of conventions	I consistently use a variety of words and sentence structures with few errors. My word choice and sentences match the audience and purpose. I consistently cite the sources I use in my writing.	I use a variety of words and sentence structures with few errors. My word choice and sentences are written for the audience and purpose. I cite sources with minor errors in format.	At times I use a variety of words and sentence structures with some errors. Some of my word choice and sentences do not match the audience and purpose. Sometimes I cite sources.	I try to use a variety of words and sentence structures, but with errors. My word choice and sentences do not match the audience and purpose. I use sources but do not cite them.

Source: Adapted from Lam, Low, & Tauiliili-Mahuk, 2014a, p. 91.

the stages of a coconut's development, from fully ripe to a seedling, represent the progression of five aspects of the students' writing.

The final example of a peer-assessment comes from a first-grade classroom in which young learners are just beginning to think about themselves as writers. In this unit on animal habitats, each student selected a favorite or interesting animal to explore, researched it, and then produced a report. In Figure 5.13, students assess themselves and then their peers on the content of their writing project.

Figure 5.13   An Example of a Self- and Peer Assessment Guide, Grade 1

Self-Assessment: Preparing for Sharing Content

☐ My animal: _____

☐ Its habitat: Where it lives _____

☐ Food sources: What it eats _____

☐ Its behavior: What it does _____

☐ I want to know more about: _____

Peer Assessment Guide for Content

My friend has:

☐ The name of the animal _____

☐ The habitat: Where it lives _____

☐ Food sources: What it eats _____

☐ Its behavior: What it does _____

Source: Adapted from Mora-Flores, 2014, p. 109.

Self- and peer assessment are powerful tools that help students gain maturity and move toward independence in their thinking and doing. The recognition of students' important roles within the classroom community makes assessment *as* learning an invaluable approach and a perspective that educators should incorporate into their instructional repertoire. If we want our students to grow into young adults who are poised for success, there are three key factors to promote in teaching: (a) agency, or students' positions and interaction with the world; (b) integrated identity, or the ability of students to make decisions consistent with their own values, beliefs, and goals; and (c) competencies, or the effectiveness of students in approaching different tasks (Nagaoka, Farrington, Ehrlick, & Heath, 2015). Languages and cultures are also integral to the competency base of students when they leave the K-12 cocoon.

REACTION AND REFLECTION

Assessment *as, for,* and *of* learning represents a paradigm shift in how most educators envision educational assessment. By expanding the scope of assessment to embrace multiple stakeholders and acknowledging that each represents an important perspective, we open our eyes to the use of each data source for a specific purpose. Ultimately, the implementation of these approaches will enable schools to cross the bridge to student equity.

Assessment *as* learning revolves around students. The goal of promoting student agency becomes a reality when students gradually take responsibility for their own learning and become integral to it through self- and peer assessment. Students become familiar with the role of content standards and language proficiency/development standards in shaping their academic expectations. They have input in formulating and communicating their long-term language and achievement goals and the accompanying criteria for success that they use in evaluating their performance. Here are some questions related to assessment *as* learning to prompt more attention to student involvement in the assessment process.

- There is a Hawaiian expression, *"E lauhoe kākou,"* which means "let us all paddle together." How does this expression apply to the assessment model presented in Figure II.1? How do you envision multiple stakeholders, including students, working together for the greater good of the educational community?
- How can student voice in assessment *as* learning have more of a presence in your classroom? How can planning and enacting ways to engage students up front in their own learning be reinforced with descriptive feedback?
- Based on the information in this chapter, how can you as an individual educator or as a member of a professional learning team provide a rationale for having greater involvement of students in decision making within classrooms? How can you promote more student advocacy throughout the school?
- How do you see ELLs, ELLs with disabilities, or other students with disabilities participating in assessment *as* learning? Which of the practices do you consider most appropriate for each of these subgroups of students? How can assessment *as* learning help promote student equity?
- How might you introduce assessment *as* learning through a gradual release of responsibility? How do you see assessment *as* learning as a motivator and a confidence builder for students? Share some strategies you might use to instill assessment *as* learning.

6

Assessment
for Learning

The Bridge to Teacher Equity

Pedagogy is a teaching and learning relationship that creates the potential for building learning conditions that lead to full and equitable social participation.

—The New London Group

As educators, we are constantly assessing our students. But what exactly does assessment within a classroom context entail? Assessment is a process that relies on planning, collecting data from multiple measures or sources over time, analyzing and interpreting that information in light of its specified purpose, and using the accumulated information or evidence to improve teaching and learning. Continuous feedback ensures that data are constantly being updated to provide the most relevant and accurate information for decision making.

In examining assessment from a stakeholder's perspective, this chapter focuses on teachers, rather than students, as the central figures and decision makers. It explores the choices that teachers make in designing and implementing sound assessment practices that help guide instruction. Valuing teachers' input in assessment and honoring teachers as assessment leaders facilitate building a bridge to teacher equity.

In today's elementary and secondary schools, all students are expected to reach grade-level college and career readiness standards, while ELLs have the additional charge of meeting language proficiency/development standards. Assessment must support this integrated learning by providing meaningful data to make informed decisions. In Chapter 5 we witnessed how students can exert their voice in assessment *as* learning. Now we attend to how teachers make instructional choices based on assessment *for* learning (Stiggins, 2006). Throughout the prior chapters we have referred to assessment *for* learning as either classroom assessment or instructional assessment; from now on we will use assessment *for* learning exclusively.

FORMATIVE PROCESSES

Looking back to the assessment model illustrated in Figure II.1, formative processes straddle two approaches: assessment *as* learning and assessment *for* learning. That's because in assessment *as* learning, the students are the benefactors; under the guidance and mentoring of teachers, students are developing into independent, productive learners. As we move into assessment *for* learning, it is the teachers who become more reflective and gear feedback from assessment data toward improving their own instructional practices that, of course, ultimately impact student performance.

The notion of formative assessment is prominent in the literature for the general student population (Wiliam, 2011; Moss & Brookhart, 2009, Popham, 2008; Bailey & Heritage, 2008, to name a few); for ELLs (MacDonald, et.al, 2015; Abedi, 2010); and for students with disabilities (Elliott, Kettler, Beddow, & Kurz, 2010). However, assessment *for* formative purposes represents a wide range of thinking in terms of its use; it may be viewed as a set of continuous instructional practices (Stiggins, 2005); a comprehensive system grounded in the classroom (Frey & Fisher, 2014; Marzano, 2010); or a set of tools (Kahl, 2010).

The Council of Chief State School Officers' (CCSSO) Formative Assessment for Students and Teachers (FAST) State Collaborative on Assessment and Student Standards (SCASS) uses a definition for formative assessment that forms the basis of assessment *for* learning: "Formative assessment is a process used by teachers and students during instruction that provides feedback to adjust ongoing teaching and learning to improve students' achievement of intended instructional outcomes" (2012, p. 4). Many researchers as well as states have adopted and contributed to this definition and have suggested how to operationalize it within classrooms (Popham, 2010; Heritage, 2010; Wiliam, 2011, to name a few).

The notion of assessment as applied to formative processes, practices, or purposes has gained wide acceptance by teachers and school leaders alike. What makes assessment *formative* is not *what* it is, per se, but *how* the data are used—that is, the information or evidence collected in an instructional setting is converted within a very short time span into adjusting instruction. What is undeniable about these formative processes is their value for improving teaching and learning, especially for students challenged by school (Black & Wiliam, 1999). Given this strong research base, these student-level data are tremendously worthwhile for everyday decision making in classrooms.

Figure 6.1 (a subset of the model in Figure II.1) encompasses two pathways to decision making: *formative processes,* which are multistep processes that are internal to classrooms, and *common instructional products,* which are formed by a consensus among groups of teachers across classrooms. These two formats, anchored in content and language development standards, are central to assessment *for* learning.

Figure 6.1 Forms of Assessment That Contribute to Assessment *for* Learning

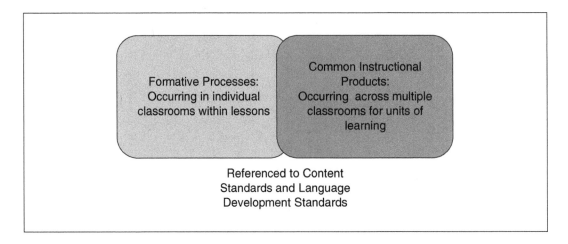

REFLECTION

Contemplating Formative Processes

Before we get into the heart of this chapter, jot down what you consider to be the steps of formative processes and the uses of the data. Share your impressions with your grade-level colleagues or department team, or as a schoolwide discussion. Make sure you revisit your initial impressions and finely tune them as you dive deeper into the discussion in the upcoming pages.

What the Literature Says

A classroom environment that supports assessment *for* learning is one that has established mutually agreed-upon ways for how students are to cooperate in working and learning together (Davies, 2011). In the safe space of classrooms, students and teachers realize that making mistakes is part of learning and that success takes on many different faces. By creating shared learning experiences around a theme of interest, students not only establish a bond through a common frame of reference but they are more willing to take risks (Silvers, Shorey, Eliopoulis, & Akiyoshi, 2014).

Research shows that assessment for formative purposes within instruction is a powerful contributor to the enhancement of student achievement (Hattie & Timperley, 2007; Black & Wiliam, 1999). Formative assessment data help teachers identify the current state of learners' knowledge, skills, and language development and propose next steps. That information enables teachers to modify their instruction and provide feedback throughout the process so that all students have opportunities to meet the criteria that have been set for success (Fisher & Frey, 2014).

Formative assessment data enable teachers to modify their strategies and differentiate instruction based on students' conceptual understanding and language proficiency in the moment. Additionally, information gained from formative assessment processes helps teachers determine (re)grouping of students, selection of materials and resources, and the allocation of time (and languages) to learning activities. In essence, assessment functions formatively when it improves instructional decisions made by teachers independently or in conjunction with learners and peers (Wiliam, 2011).

There are a variety of conceptual schemes that are descriptive of the formative assessment process. Margaret Heritage (2010) defines the process as an ongoing cycle with a continuous feedback loop that occurs within the flow of instruction. It begins with teachers identifying the goals (or objectives) for a lesson or a series of lessons, along with the criteria for success. Teachers elicit evidence of student learning using a variety of strategies; this information is then interpreted in order to identify the "gap" between the students' current performance and the intended learning objective(s). Based on the findings, teachers or peers give descriptive feedback regarding the status of the students' learning in relation to the success criteria. Subsequently, teachers plan or make adjustments to instruction so that it is synchronized with the students' needs.

For many, formative processes are interchangeable with assessment *for* learning. As conceptualized within the assessment model proposed here, we believe that formative processes center on teacher actions to ultimately advance student learning, as opposed to their presence in assessment *as* learning, where students have a greater role in the process. So what might this teacher-directed process look like?

Assessment *for* Learning: A Teacher-Directed Process

When planning curriculum, instruction, and assessment, the starting point is for teachers to think about their students. In order to be inclusive and equitable, we must consider all students, from those new arrivals who perhaps have limited or interrupted formal education to those who have had the luxury of continuous educational experiences since their early years. We have to contemplate how students' multilingual and multicultural backgrounds may influence the classroom dynamic, consider how to tap those who have or are developing multiliteracies, and how to advantage those who may have learning disabilities, whether ELLs or not.

Thus, when looking at the assessment *for* learning process in Figure 6.2, the students' life experiences and expertise are at its core and are the lens through which all data pass. The same five-phase or five-step cycle applies to the two forms of assessment *for* learning; it encompasses both the formative processes and the common instructional products depicted in Figure 6.1.

REFLECTION

Considering the Steps of the Assessment Process

Are any of the steps in the assessment process outlined in Figure 6.2 already in place in your classroom? Are they used for both content and language learning? What exactly do you do in each step? Have you shared your assessment process with your grade-level team or professional learning community? What have you discussed?

Figure 6.2 Teacher-Directed Steps in the Assessment *for* Learning Cycle

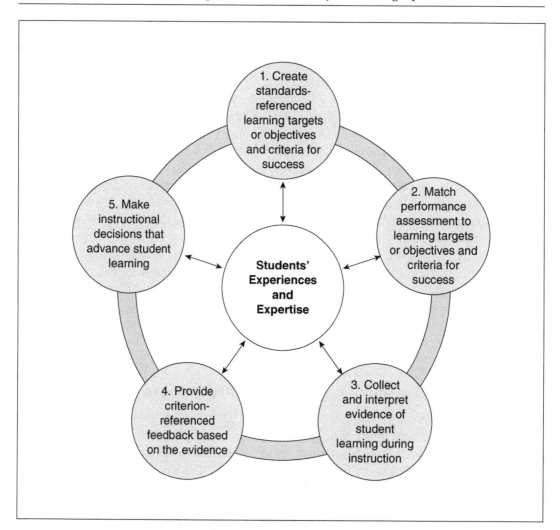

Assessment *for* learning acknowledges backwards planning, first proposed by Grant Wiggins and Jay McTighe as a central tenet of Understanding by Design or UbD (1998). The framework begins with outcomes posed as essential questions and big ideas as the basis for crafting curriculum units, performance assessments, and classroom instruction. Teacher preparation for student learning is flipped in that instruction, is contingent on assessment rather than having textbooks and other resources dictate the direction of teaching. In UbD, educators identify the desired results of student learning for a unit by using content standards or college and career readiness standards, collecting evidence of student understanding through performance assessment, and describing learning activities or tasks that will lead students back to the desired results.

The assessment *for* learning process, designed and implemented by teachers either independently or with students, applies to content and language teaching and learning. As envisioned in our assessment model outlined in Figure 6.2, it consists of five steps described and illustrated in the upcoming pages. The process or cycle begins with matching the students' experiences and expertise to a set of student expectations that is measured within instruction. It is renewed when students' evidence for learning indicates that those expectations are met or when instructional adjustments provide additional opportunities for students to succeed.

Step 1. Create Standards-Referenced Learning Targets or Objectives and Criteria for Success

There are three coordinated components to this first step of the assessment process: (a) standards, (b) learning targets or objectives, and (c) criteria for success. Together they represent a unified vision of how to begin to tackle assessment *for* learning orchestrated by teachers. The strength of the cohesion among these components helps determine the usefulness of the results.

Standards. Content that is expressed in college and career readiness standards and the academic language that is associated with language proficiency/development standards are both the primary sources for identifying clear and measureable learning targets and corresponding criteria for success. The standards, translated in student-friendly language, can readily be converted to learning targets (in the case of units of study) or learning objectives (for a single or a related series of lessons).

Learning Targets. There should be a clear content target and a language target for the unit as a whole that originate from their respective standards. Learning targets serve as the umbrella for subsequent lessons for all students. Content targets center on one of the levels of Bloom's revised taxonomy—remembering, understanding, applying, analyzing, evaluating, and creating—and provide a guide for the expected level of cognitive engagement. Language targets can be represented by one of the key uses of academic language: recount, explain, argue, or discuss. For students with disabilities, learning targets might be wrapped into learning goals in their individualized education plans (IEPs) and then matched to appropriate learning strategies.

Differentiated Learning Objectives. While language targets are all inclusive, to be equitable for ELLs, language objectives for individual lessons or related sets of lessons should be differentiated according to a student's levels of language proficiency. In that way, ELLs can demonstrate what they can do linguistically while engaged in the same mental process or level of higher-order thinking when working with grade-level content. In a heterogeneous classroom with a mix of proficient English speakers and ELLs, it is best to have no more than three groups of language learners: beginners, intermediate and advanced.

Model performance indicators in language development standards can serve as the basis for formulating differentiated language objectives. The following strand of model performance indicators represents language used for peer assessment. The language functions are bolded to illustrate how ELLs are able to evaluate their classmates' presentations when given instructional supports. Resource 6.1 at the close of the chapter offers another differentiated language pathway for ELLs.

**ENGLISH LANGUAGE DEVELOPMENT STANDARD 1:
SOCIAL AND INSTRUCTIONAL LANGUAGE, A STRAND OF
MODEL PERFORMANCE INDICATORS FOR GRADE 5, SPEAKING**

Language Proficiency Level 5: **Justify** ratings of peers' presentations with evidence and suggest improvements using rubrics.

Language Proficiency Level 4: **Explain** ratings of peers' presentations with evidence and suggest improvements using sentence frames.

Language Proficiency Level 3: **Discuss** ratings of peers' presentations and suggest improvements using sentence frames.

Language Proficiency Level 2: **Describe** ratings of peers' presentations using illustrated sentence frames.

Language Proficiency Level 1: **State** ratings of peers' presentations using simple illustrated sentence frames and word banks.

Source: WIDA, 2012, p. 76.

REFLECTION

Grouping English Language Learners

How might you take this strand of model performance indicators and convert it into differentiated language objectives? Think what you might do for three groups of students—beginning, intermediate, and advanced ELLs.

Educators have to maintain high expectations for all students and have a repertoire of supports to scaffold instruction (Dove & Honigsfeld, 2013). The progressive levels of language proficiency within language proficiency/development standards that are referenced to grade-level content provide a natural venue for generating ideas on how to differentiate instruction and assessment for ELLs. This macro-scaffolding, where teachers attend to the purposeful integration of content and language during planning, must also be coupled to micro-scaffolding or the minute-to-minute work of teaching (Bunch, Kibler, & Pimentel, 2012). Teachers' awareness of the performance definitions of standards and the performance indicators helps with lesson and unit planning.

To illustrate how scaffolding might be linked to language proficiency, let's look at the Next Generation of Science Standards (NGSS) in combination with the language of science expressed in language development standards. How might teachers capture the practices of inquiry or engineering design and their related discourses for ELLs? Figure 6.3 identifies some middle school language that invites students to pursue different kinds of scientific investigation. If matched to content expectations, it might be used as a checklist for specified objectives to show what ELLs can do at a given level of language proficiency, or, if preferred, it can be converted to "I can" statements for students.

Figure 6.3 An Assessment Checklist for ELLs Based on Key Uses of Academic Language in Scientific Inquiry

Language Proficiency Level	Language Expectations for Scientific Inquiry for English Language Learners
Level 5	• Explain in detail how the results of scientific inquiry relate to the hypotheses or research questions • Recount by connecting cause and effect based on results of scientific inquiry • Argue results of scientific inquiry using claims matched to evidence
Level 4	• Explain with details how the scientific questions or hypotheses relate to the conclusions • Recount the inquiry process in short scientific reports • Argue the extent of impact of scientific questions under varying conditions (e.g., if, then) on the results
Level 3	• Explain how scientific questions lead to conclusions • Recount steps in conducting scientific inquiry using sequential language • Argue pros and cons of possible results
Level 2	• Explain by stating how scientific questions are different from conclusions • Recount research questions or hypotheses • Argue by making statements to be verified or negated
Level 1	• Explain by showing how the language of claims is different from the language of evidence • Recount using labeled illustrations that are descriptive of scientific questions and conclusions. • Ask wh- research questions or state hypotheses (in home language)

REFLECTION

Differentiating Instructional Assessment for ELLs

Although your state's language proficiency/development standards may have five levels of language proficiency, don't think that you have to differentiate for five distinct groups of ELLs! How might you consolidate the levels to reflect the linguistic proficiencies of your students? Brainstorm with your grade-level team on ways in which the same instructional activities, tasks, and projects can have different pathways to success for your ELLs.

Criteria for Success. The criteria for success should mirror the major features of a performance task that exemplify both challenging content standards and language proficiency/development standards. The content-related criteria refer to the big ideas and grade-level concepts of a topic or theme, while the language-related criteria pinpoint the academic language necessary to access and achieve those concepts. Success criteria, generally teacher generated with or without student input, are a touchstone of the classroom culture. It is critical that there is a shared understanding with students as to what each criterion looks like since the criteria ultimately serve as the barometer of student progress in meeting learning expectations. Therefore, teachers either have to model each criterion or have exemplars of student work. Figure 6.4 illustrates the relationship among the three components of the first step of the assessment *for* learning process as teachers prepare for content and language teaching, using college and career readiness standards as the anchor for the process.

Figure 6.4   Standards-Referenced Learning Targets or Differentiated Objectives and Criteria for Success

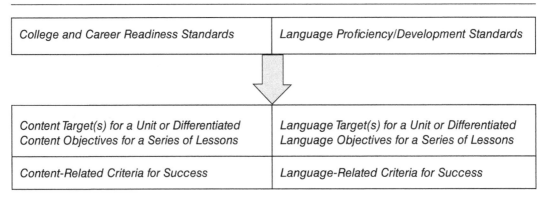

College and Career Readiness Standards	Language Proficiency/Development Standards
Content Target(s) for a Unit or Differentiated Content Objectives for a Series of Lessons	Language Target(s) for a Unit or Differentiated Language Objectives for a Series of Lessons
Content-Related Criteria for Success	Language-Related Criteria for Success

Success criteria can take on various formats. At the lesson level, criteria may be reminders to students that are either written on poster paper with bullets as a whole-class activity or digitized, perhaps as a class wiki, in a format that is easily accessible to students. Feedback could also serve as oral reinforcement of the lesson's objectives to students. Such examples might include the following:

- A series of commands, such as for a persuasive paragraph:
  - State your point of view or opinion.
  - Support your opinion with reasons or evidence.
  - Make a convincing conclusion.

- "I can" descriptors, such as to explain how to do something:
  - I can demonstrate how to _____.
  - I can use transition words or expressions to show each step.
  - I can give directions to other students.

- "I/we" statements, such as to recount an experience:
  - I/we have an introduction that tells who, what, where, and when.
  - I/we support my/our main ideas with descriptive details,
  - I/we summarize the experience and share my/our feelings.

REFLECTION

Formulating Criteria for Success

How do you compose criteria for success—independently, with other teachers, or with students? Why is it effective this way? Do you use any of the example formats illustrated above? If not, what do your criteria look like and how might you share them with others? If you have not yet shared criteria for success with your students, which model might you choose?

Within the formative process, it is easy to convert differentiated learning objectives into criteria for success that are shared with students, such as in Figure 6.5. Here you see how the content objectives for a cluster of lessons can be differentiated for beginning ELLs, including SLIFE. The project deals with weather patterns and is described more fully toward the close of the chapter. As students display evidence for meeting an objective, it is checked off with the date by their name.

Figure 6.5   Formative Assessment Processes: Converting Differentiated Content Objectives Into a Checklist of Success Criteria for a Group of Beginning English Language Learners

Level 1 ELLs	Juan	Sara	Ina	Raj	Kai
Identify different kinds of weather from illustrations					
Label words and expressions related to descriptive statistics (e.g., mean temperature)					
Classify weather patterns by location					
Level 2 ELLs	Lina	Habib	Jorge	Sofia	Ivan
Identify weather patterns from TV or newspapers					
Match words and expressions of descriptive statistics to weather examples					
Compare elements of weather patterns in two different locations					

Source: Adapted from Gottlieb, 2006, p. 95.

Step 2. Match Performance Assessment to the Learning Targets or Differentiated Objectives and the Criteria for Success

This particular step introduces performance assessment as an expression of learning targets or differentiated objectives and their criteria for success. Performance assessment refers to students' original work produced individually or in groups for curriculum-related tasks and projects, along with a form of documentation. This work may be written or presented orally or via multimedia. Students are actively involved in ongoing discussions; constructing models, figures, and maps; conducting science experiments; delving into technology; self-assessing their accomplishments and applying strategies; or articulating key uses of academic language through process writing. Performance assessment requires a set of well-articulated criteria for success grounded in standards that are shared with or co-constructed with students.

Performance assessment, in which students express their learning in direct, hands-on ways that reflect real-life situations, is integral to the classroom routine. Because performance assessment connects students' experiences with the curriculum through active engagement, the assessment itself is part of the learning process. Participation of ELLs in performance assessment, regardless of their levels of language proficiency in their home language and English, is advantageous. Hands-on assessment allows language learners to

- use multiple modalities or multiliteracies to express themselves, such as using actions, technology, or oral expression combined with other media rather than being confined to paper-and-pencil tasks;
- access support materials, such as visuals, graphics, and manipulatives, used for scaffolding instruction;
- work and interact with partners or in small groups; and
- reinforce learning through building on previous educational and personal experiences.

The collection and interpretation of evidence of learning is based on student performance that serves as the source of assessment *as*, *for*, and *of* learning. Performance assessment includes the following features:

- Topics or themes of high interest to students that are reflective of their identities (languages and cultures), are thought provoking, and encourage exploration
- Key principles, concepts, and "big ideas" of content
- Discourse, sentence structures, and vocabulary (the academic language use) associated with a theme or topic
- High-order thinking and processing
- Multiple avenues as options, which often rely on multiple resources, and acceptance of multiliteracies to reach conclusions or solutions
- Questions that lead to related issues or new ideas.

REFLECTION

Identifying Features of Performance Assessment

Think about an assessment that is currently in place for your students. What percentage of it would you say requires students to collaborate in producing a product, creating an original piece of work, or demonstrating their expertise? How might you convert more traditional means of assessment (e.g., fill in the blank, multiple choice) into ones in which students take ownership of their learning?

Figure 6.6, on the next page, gives examples of the components for steps 1 and 2 of the formative assessment process for a fourth-grade unit on fractions. In this activity the students are following a recipe to make brownies for their class. Notice how the content and language standards, the learning targets, and the differentiated learning objectives and the criteria for success complement and reinforce each other.

REFLECTION

Integrating Content and Language in Formative Processes

To what extent do you integrate content and language in planning instruction and assessment? What do you see as the benefits of combining the two for ELLs? Do you see any challenges in addressing both content and language throughout a unit of learning?

Figure 6.6   Example Standards-Referenced Learning Targets, Differentiated Objectives, and Criteria for Success for an Integrated Fourth-Grade Unit in Mathematics

College and Career Readiness Standards, Grade 4:	Language Proficiency/Development Standards, Grade 4:
CCSS for Mathematics 4. NF.1, 4. NF.2, 4. NF.3, 4. NF.4a Explain, compare, and understand fractions CCSS for English language arts, Grade 4 SL.4.1 Engaging in a range of collaborative discussions	WIDA ELD Standard 3, the language of mathematics Language domain: writing, explain problem-solving
Content Target for the Unit: Students will apply real-world solutions in solving mathematical problems involving fractional parts.	*Language Target for the Unit:* Students will explain how to convert recipes involving fractions by describing and comparing their uses in a variety of ways.

Differentiated Content Objectives for a Set of Lessons:
 	
a. For students with conceptual understanding:
 	
   ○ Represent fractions with creative examples
   ○ Determine equivalency of fractions using recipes or other analogies
 	
b. For students challenged by the concepts:
 	
   ○ Represent fractions relying on physical models
   ○ Determine equivalency of fractions using a baking analogy
	Differentiated Language Objectives for a Set of Lessons:
	
	a. Intermediate ELLs:
	
	   ○ Use comparative phrases such as "is more than" or "is equal to" in identifying fractions
	   ○ Use sequential terms such as *first second*, or *finally* to describe steps involving fractions in recipes
	
	b. Beginning ELLs:
	
	   ○ Distinguish between "is more than" and "is less than" using visually supported fractions
	   ○ Follow illustrated steps of recipes involving fractions

Criteria for Success for Content: ✓ Name fractions using numerators and denominators ✓ Multiply fractions to double or triple amounts ✓ Convert fractions to mixed number equivalents	*Criteria for Success for Language:* ✓ Compare size of fractions ✓ Explain how to use fractions in following recipes ✓ Describe steps in converting fractions using sequential language

Source: Adapted from Ernst-Slavit, Gottlieb, & Slavit, 2013, pp. 92, 98–99, & 115–116.

Step 3. Collect and Interpret Evidence of Student Learning During Instruction

Once the standards, targets for units, differentiated objectives, and criteria for success are in place, we have established the pathway for collecting and interpreting evidence. Formative assessment processes embedded in the ongoing learning environment revolve around instructional activities, tasks, and projects. The evidence for learning that is generated based on student performance is used for the primary purposes of monitoring student progress and improving instruction.

Figure 6.7 Collecting Evidence of Student Learning: The Relationship Among Performance Projects, Tasks, Activities, and Questions

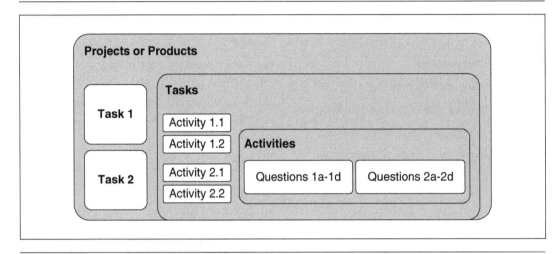

Source: Adapted from Gottlieb, 2012, *Common language assessment*, Bloomington, IN: Solution Tree. ©Solution Tree.

Figure 6.7 shows the relationship among questions, activities, tasks, and projects as the means for collecting evidence for student learning. In this nested diagram, we see how the many questions asked within the context of teaching and learning help shape classroom activities. Multiple activities combine to create tasks. Questions, activities, and tasks form the heart of lessons or a related series of lessons. Tasks, in turn, are aggregated into projects or products for a unit of learning. Resource 6.3 offers a graphic of the figure with a completed example.

Activities form the core of daily instruction. They are often composed of a set of interrelated questions or a single in-depth question that integrates content and language, such as showing the steps to solving a problem. Other examples of activities include comparing points of view in excerpts of two texts and asking and answering wh- questions (who, what, where, when, and why) for a content-related topic.

Tasks are broader in both scope and depth than activities. As one activity builds on the next one, generally higher levels of cognitive engagement are possible with tasks than with activities. Examples of tasks include researching a topic (which consists of examining several sources and summarizing their contents) and conducting an interview (which consists of formulating and asking questions then recording or reproducing the responses).

Projects involve several tasks and are the broadest in range, giving students the opportunity to explore an issue or topic in depth across a unit of learning. Theme-based or interdisciplinary instruction across the content areas lends itself to student creation of different products. In project-based learning, students may be invited to design models, debate research-based issues, act in a mock trial, or create multimedia presentations.

REFLECTION

Identifying Questions, Activities, Tasks, and Projects

Instructional tasks are composed of activities, and projects consist of tasks. Now that you have a sense of the relationship among these different components of assessment *for* learning turn to Resource 6.2, which gives you more examples of each.

As shown in Figure 6.8, there are obvious differences among activities, tasks, and projects. When collecting and interpreting data within the formative assessment process, however, remember that activities and tasks correspond to a series of lessons, while projects or products more aptly go with units of learning.

Now that we have a clear sense of the roles of activities, tasks, and projects in formative assessment processes, we can add the key use of academic language to better delineate the purpose for communicating. Figure 6.9 illustrates the applicability of the key uses to performance assessment that has been folded into instructional activities and tasks.

Figure 6.8 Distinctions Among Activities, Tasks, and Projects

Activities	Tasks	Projects or Products
• Are short term (in minutes up to the length of a class period) • Consist of a single in-depth question or a set of related questions • Correspond to a single learning objective • Provide spontaneous feedback based on the learning objective	• Involve multiple class periods (perhaps up to a week) • Consist of a series of scaffolded activities • Correspond to multiple learning objectives • Provide feedback based on criteria for success	• Are long term (in weeks or months) • Consist of two or more tasks • Correspond to learning targets • Provide feedback based on criteria for success expressed in rubrics

Figure 6.9 Examples of Oral Language and Literacy Performance Activities, Tasks, and Projects for Key Uses of Academic Language

Key Use of Academic Language	Discuss	Explain	Argue	Recount
Oral language (listening and speaking)	• Describing and comparing language-learning strategies with their peers • Presenting options for solving problems	• Stating how to do a process or procedure • Telling why something happened	• Giving personal opinions with reasons • Defending points of view in debates	• (Re)telling stories from experiences or text • Summarizing academic conversations
Literacy (reading and writing)	• Confirming use of feedback in revising informational or narrative text to peers or teacher • Classifying sentences by genre and checking with a peer	• Comparing how texts on the same topic are similar and different • Relating cause and effect in a series of events	• Providing evidence for claims in text • Producing critiques of controversial issues	• Paraphrasing text • Creating autobiographies or reproducing biographies

Deciding on Student Performance

Depending on the purpose and context for language use, student performance might be centered on activities, tasks, or projects. How might you convert the key uses of academic language in Figure 6.9 into these different types of student performance? How might you take an activity and combine it with another to form a task? Which examples could be composed of multiple tasks?

Evidence Based on Differentiated Instruction and Assessment

Differentiation of instruction and assessment maximizes students' opportunities to succeed in school. Instruction is differentiated when it is organized into multiple, simultaneous, diversified activities and tasks around a central topic that allow students to work toward the same standards and learning targets. Assessment is differentiated when teachers gather data before, during, and after instruction from multiple sources to address an individual learner's strengths and challenges (Chapman & King, 2005).

Students, with their differing levels of conceptual understanding, and ELLs, with their differing levels of language proficiency, can benefit from this strategy for lessons and units of learning. The use of differentiation strategies encourages teachers to share responsibility and collaborate in planning instruction and assessment (Fairbairn & Jones-Vo, 2010). Although challenging for teachers to implement, differentiation can prove effective in instilling confidence and drive in students, especially in ELLs. Referring back to Figure 6.4, we can see how differentiation of content and language objectives does not diminish the rigor of instruction and assessment but makes learning more developmentally appropriate and equitable for ELLs.

Teacher observation is a powerful tool for collecting evidence of student learning. When planned within formative processes, anecdotal information can be gathered traditionally, by taking notes when students are interacting with each other or when they are approached individually by the teacher. Teachers using note cards, perhaps placed in alphabetical order on a clipboard, to jot down standards-related information can observe a few students at a time. More and more teachers are relying on hand-held technology to record a student's oral responses or maintain notes on individual students over time.

Step 4. Provide Criterion-Referenced Feedback Based on the Evidence

The formative assessment process, although initiated by teachers, is of equal value for students. Data collected within instruction allow teachers to

- respond in real time to individual student interests, needs, and preferences;
- analyze student performance in light of the criteria for success;
- provide students criterion-referenced feedback rather than strictly relying on grades;
- plan differentiated instruction for students' achievement and language development;

- document individual student performance over time;
- examine personal instructional practices and make spontaneous adjustments; and
- facilitate educational decision making that impacts individual students and classrooms. (Gottlieb, 2015)

In the world of assessment *as* and *for* learning, feedback is criterion-referenced information about student performance in relation to the instructional objective or learning target. The performance may be reflective of students' language development, content learning, or both. Feedback may be self-directed or given by teachers or peers; instructional feedback is not praise, advice, value judgments, or a grade.

Research undeniably shows that feedback positively impacts learning and improves student achievement (Hattie, 2008; Black & Wiliam, 1999). Wiggins (2012) offers seven essential features of effective feedback. According to him, feedback is

- referenced to a learning goal (target or objective);
- tangible and transparent, with performance results related to the goal;
- actionable, providing concrete, specific, and useful information;
- user friendly so that it is comprehensible to students;
- timely (that is, the sooner it is given, the sooner it can be used);
- ongoing, with multiple opportunities to apply the information; and
- consistent, with the same message tied to high-quality work.

Feedback may be oral or written, depending on the strengths of the students. Based on mutually agreed-upon criteria for success, the response is as important to students as it is to their teachers. In formative assessment processes, descriptive, constructive feedback is based on the preset criteria for success derived from learning objectives, learning targets, and standards rather than being evaluative in nature. For example, a teacher might say, "I see in this paragraph that you support your opinion with two reasons," or, "Your feelings about the experience come through in your conclusion." Student feedback and reflection can aid in decision making by alerting teachers of the need to modify or expand their instructional approaches to allow for multiple pathways for students to reach expected learning targets or objectives.

Step 5. Make Instructional Decisions That Advance Student Learning

A fundamental idea behind the formative process is that teachers should not collect evidence of student performance unless they have a plan to deal with it. Knowing what kinds of decisions need to be made should inform the kinds of evidence to be gathered (Wiliam & Leahy, 2015; Wiliam, 2011). The formative process must yield information in a timely fashion about learning targets or objectives that are expressed as criteria for success and understood by all students. In that way students will be aware of subsequent instructional expectations and what they have to do to meet them.

Formative processes are one form of a comprehensive assessment system in which teachers have control over crafting instruction, measuring student performance, and making minute-by-minute and day-to-day decisions. Formative processes are closely tied to common instructional products as together they comprise assessment *for* learning.

COMMON INSTRUCTIONAL PRODUCTS

Imagine teachers collaborating in grade-level teams, in professional learning communities, or even in district committees in the creation of end-of-unit projects as part of curriculum design. These products, along with their accompanying rubrics, represent assessment *for* learning that can contribute to local accountability. Common assessment abounds for content courses in middle and high schools and for the content side of thematic units at elementary schools, but it often does not embed the intentional use of academic language.

Assessment *for* learning is inclusive of both content and language learning for all students. As we have seen, in formative processes attention centers on teachers enacting a related series of lessons individualized for students. In common instructional products, teachers must agree on the product and the rubric to interpret student work for a unit. Although students may be encouraged to pursue different pathways to success, inevitably, student performance leads to measuring the identical learning targets and standards. Figure 6.10 compares some of the features of these two forms of assessment for learning, formative processes and common instructional products.

Figure 6.10 Assessment *for* Learning: Comparing Formative Processes With Common Instructional Products

Formative Processes	Common Instructional Products
Implemented at a lesson level	Implemented at a unit level
Anchored in differentiated objectives that lead to learning targets	Geared toward learning targets
Centered on classroom activities and tasks	Centered on cross-classroom projects
Based on an individual teacher's decision on criteria for success	Based on teachers' group decision on criteria for success, generally expressed in rubrics

As mentioned earlier in this chapter, the teacher-directed steps in the assessment *for* learning cycle are motivated by backward design. We can visualize these steps in a more linear fashion using Figure 6.11. With content and language standards as the umbrella, learning targets and performance-based projects, along with their rubrics, are the primary components of common instructional products. The remaining components, starting with the week-by-week differentiated learning objectives, are more reflective of formative assessment processes and can also occur with students at the helm in assessment *as* learning.

Defining Common Assessment

Why is it important to distinguish between the two forms of assessment *for* learning? The role of the teacher is equally important in formative processes and in common instructional products. Rather, the question is how to accept different types of data for decision making. For local educators who, in large part, have been excluded from federal policy initiatives since the early 2000s, common assessment (based on common instructional products) has become the counternarrative to state and federal accountability. Built by consensus by groups of teachers, common assessment is more directly aligned to instruction, and the data are as valid, at least at face value, as those generated from standardized measures. Additionally, common language assessment in two languages

Figure 6.11 Looking Forward With Backward Design: From Common Assessment Products to Instructional Assessment Tasks and Activities

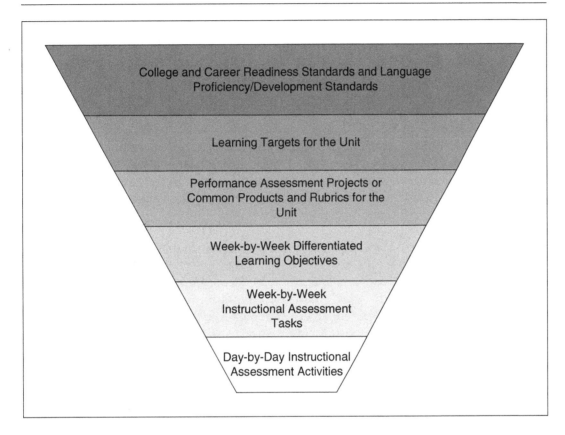

offers more authentic, relevant, and useful data for improving everyday teaching and learning for our growing numbers of dual language learners (Gottlieb, 2012a).

> **REFLECTION**
>
> **Defining Common Instructional Products**
>
> How does common assessment fit within the approach of assessment *for* learning in your setting? Brainstorm with your grade-level team or professional learning team how common instructional products might specifically be used with ELLs, gifted and talented ELLs, ELLs with disabilities, or dual language learners. If your school or district has common assessment in place, how might you modify or retrofit it so that it addresses the academic language students need in order to access grade-level content?

For the purpose of assessment *for* learning, common instructional products are a form of assessment seamlessly interwoven into instruction where tasks scaffolds within a unit to ultimately create an end product. Both the product and its rubric or documentation form have been mutually agreed upon or crafted by a group of teachers within the district, not by outside groups, who have the support of school or administrative leaders. There is intentionality built into common instructional products, which are implemented with fidelity across classrooms.

Defined from the vantage point of teachers, common assessment sets a collective vision and attainable learning targets for students. It represents what teachers value, what has been taught, and what data are meaningful in making decisions (Gottlieb & Nguyen, 2007). One of the tenets of common assessment is that teachers reach consensus on its parameters and there is sustainability over time. The *common* in common assessment or common instructional products involves participating teachers coming to agreement on

- setting a timetable for collecting data on the products;
- formulating a uniform set of directions or a series of assignments for the students;
- using the same scoring guides or rubrics to interpret the products;
- checking for reliability of scoring of student work among the teachers;
- ensuring that feedback based on the results is given in the same way; and
- reaching the same instructional decisions based on the information. (Adapted from Gottlieb, 2012a, p. 7)

Common assessment is an expression of the curriculum that is created and implemented by local teachers who know the students and the community, thus enhancing opportunities for student learning. Due to the burgeoning population of ELLs, teachers and school leaders must be aware of the integration of academic language and content in product design. Figure 6.12 is a checklist to help in the collaborative planning of common instructional products. Resources 6.4 and 6.5 at the close of the chapter are two other checklists that may be useful to educators in planning and implementing common instructional products.

Figure 6.12   A Checklist for Planning Common Instructional Products for Teacher Teams and School Leaders of ELLs

Steps in Planning Common Instructional Products	*Done!*
1. We select grade-level teams or professional learning communities of language and content teachers for the year.	
2. We choose content standards and pair them with language standards for our units of learning.	
3. We create learning targets for content and language for each unit.	
4. We ensure that there is common performance assessment for each unit with multiple pathways to reach it.	
5. We determine the academic language demands of the standards and instructional materials for each unit.	
6. We craft or revisit end-of-unit products, projects, or performances.	
7. We formulate differentiated language and content objectives for lessons in the unit.	
8. We extend differentiation of instruction into assessment.	
9. We score each common assessment together with a linguistically and culturally responsive rubric and enter the data into our local system.	
10. We use the results to improve our teaching, to monitor student progress, and to contribute to local accountability.	

Source: Gottlieb, 2015, adapted from Corwin Connect blog, http://corwin-connect.com/2015/05/its-the-end-of-the-year-what-can-we-do-to-measure-ells-progress/.

> **REFLECTION**
>
> **Using Checklists for Common Instructional Products**
>
> Often it is quite complex to plan and implement a project for a unit of learning across classrooms, especially one that is inclusive of ELLs. Review Figure 6.12 and Resources 6.4 and 6.5 to create a checklist of your own, for your grade level, or for your department for common instructional products.

Academic Language Use Within Common Assessment

Of late there has been renewed interest in project-based learning because it benefits all students. However, ELLs, by definition, require language support that is built from and connected to their linguistic, cultural, and educational experiences. The academic language, along with cognitive demand of projects, must match the characteristics of the students. If you are in a middle or high school that contains large numbers of students with limited formal or interrupted education, tasks and projects would be crafted differently for these students than for those who have had continuous education in their home language or who were born and raised in the United States. Likewise, if you are in an elementary school setting that serves ELLs with disabilities, your curriculum, although representative of the same standards, would contain a different set of scaffolds or instructional supports, plus specific accommodations to advance students' language development.

Let's revisit the key uses of academic language since they provide the guiding light for formulating language targets that connect to common instructional products. Assuming that the interactive and collaborative nature implied in *discuss* will make it a candidate for all the products, Figure 6.13 gives some ideas of projects that emphasize other key uses, with a primary focus on oral language and literacy.

Figure 6.13   Examples of Oral Language and Literacy Performance Projects for Key Uses of Academic Language

Key Use of Academic Language	Explain	Argue	Recount
Oral language (listening and speaking)	• Relating the "how" or "why" of research-based processes • Creating and giving multimedia presentations on content-related procedures	• Engaging in debates on content-related issues • Conducting and giving results of opinion surveys	• Producing and participating in historical reenactments • Recreating news broadcasts or documentaries
Literacy (reading and writing)	• Producing informational reports using multiliteracies • Comparing and contrasting informational and narrative text on the same topic	• Producing persuasive essays • Creating editorials based on claims and evidence	• Reproducing biographies from multiple sources • Narrating familiar stories or giving descriptions of events

Applying Key Uses of Academic Language to Product Design

How might your grade-level or department team incorporate the key uses found in content standards, along with English language proficiency/development standards, as foundational for common end-of-unit products? Brainstorm some ideas regarding the key uses of academic language that apply to interdisciplinary products.

The Importance of Inter-Rater Agreement in Documenting Common Instructional Products

Inter-rater agreement is a form of reliability; it is the degree to which different judges or raters agree on their decisions to assign a score or give specific feedback on a performance assessment, such as an oral presentation or an opinion piece. Inter-rater reliability establishes consistency in interpreting what students do so that the meaning of the results and consequent decisions are based on the same understanding from teacher to teacher and classroom to classroom. Not only is agreeing on scoring procedures among teachers important for maintaining uniform interpretation of student performance, it also provides an excellent opportunity for teacher teams to interact with each other as part of job-embedded professional learning.

It is critical to document the inter-rater agreement on common instructional products if the data are going to be used for local accountability, such as for determining student growth in language development at quarterly intervals or monitoring student achievement from semester to semester. If this is the case, classroom teachers should not score samples of their own students, but rather other students within their grade. Below are some easy steps you may follow in establishing inter-rater reliability of performance tasks, whether those products are oral or written language samples or multimedia entries.

1. Form teacher pairs within grade-level teams; select one teacher as the arbiter in case of a dispute and one teacher as a facilitator and manager of the process.

2. Review the rubric to be used for interpreting student work (make sure it is linguistically and culturally responsive); discuss and reach consensus on the meaning of each descriptor and performance level.

3. Remove all student names from their samples and replace them with an identification number or code. Transfer the information onto an Excel spreadsheet or computer program.

4. Select anchor papers from the student samples that best represent each score point or performance level on the rubric.

5. Rank the anchor papers by scores or performance levels and make sure that each student sample represents the same interval between each score—for example, the difference between 2 and 3 in a holistic rubric should be identical to the difference between 3 and 4. Discuss any discrepancies until agreement is reached.

6. Have each teacher work independently to record single scores for a holistic rubric, or scores for each dimension for an analytic rubric, for each student.

7. Repeat the process with a second teacher scoring the student samples and placing the results alongside the first set of scores or performance levels.

8. Determine the initial reliability by calculating the percentage of exact scores between raters and adjacent (plus or minus one) scores.

9. Have teachers provide evidence and justification of their selection of scores they assign, especially if there is any disagreement. Continue until the group reaches consensus on the scores for the set of products.

10. Debrief the experience as a whole group.

The ideal inter-rater agreement among teachers is 100%; that means that each student sample receives the exact same score from the teacher pair. An acceptable range of agreement is usually between 80% and 90%, which includes the exact scores and usually their adjacent ones. The higher the percentage of agreement, the more confidence teachers can have that their decisions are based on the same interpretation of student work. Having a similar mindset helps design common instructional products as assessment *for* learning.

DESIGN AND IMPLEMENTATION OF COMMON INSTRUCTIONAL PRODUCTS

We have seen how formative assessment processes occur at the micro level for related lessons within classrooms. Common instructional products, on the other hand, function at the curricular or macro level and represent assessment across classrooms. Ideally, in crafting common instructional products, teachers have opportunities to create or modify a curricular template that can be articulated across grade levels. Often there is a template or framework in place for the content areas, but rarely has there been an integration of the necessary dimensions of academic language. Designing standards-referenced units of learning that integrate content and language should be part of teachers' sustained professional learning and supported by school and district leadership.

In this section we examine the macro components that deal with the unit "Weather Around the World," a project for K-5 classrooms that could be extended to middle school and beyond. It is intended for all students, with focus on ELLs, and represents a collaborative effort by a team of content and language teachers, including instructional coaches.

Resource 6.6, a blank template for personal or team use, is one tool for conceptualizing curricular design. Resource 6.7 is a curriculum framework that has been used to generate K-8 integrated language arts and mathematics units of learning in a series centered on academic language in diverse classrooms (see Gottlieb & Ernst-Slavit, 2013, 2014a, and 2014b); in this framework, assessment *as* and *for* learning is visible within and across classrooms.

Planning a Unit of Learning With Common Instructional Products in Mind

In mapping out common instructional products, as in formative processes, we follow the steps in the assessment *for* learning cycle (see Figure 6.2). After determining the topics of interest, we select academic content and language proficiency/development standards that illustrate the unit's theme, formulate content and language targets, match the learning targets to the product and rubric, and define the tasks that fold into the final project. In the planning phase, we begin by naming the unit's theme and identifying its burning issue or "big idea"—in this case, "Variations in weather patterns affect how people live."

Content Components

We start unit planning with grade-level content—a theme, an issue, or a problem of interest for the students that has potential for multiple pathways for students to pursue—as it is the anchor and foundation for instruction and assessment. College and career readiness standards for projects can be drawn from the areas of language arts, mathematics, science, social studies, and more, including technology and the arts. In particular, the content standards in Figure 6.14 may be used as the source for the common instructional product for the weather unit.

Figure 6.14 Coverage of Content Standards in a Unit Project

Content Area	Grades K-5 Content Standards
Language arts	CCSS.ELA/Literacy RI.4.7 Interpret information presented visually, orally, or quantitatively and explain how the information contributes to an understanding of the text.
	CCSS.ELA.W4.7 &4.8 Conduct short research projects that build knowledge through investigation of different aspects of a topic. Gather relevant information from print and digital sources.
Mathematics	CCSS.MATH.CONTENT.3.MD.B.3
	Draw a scaled picture graph and a scaled bar graph to represent a data set with several categories.
Science	NGSS Science and Engineering Practices
	4-ESS1-1 Constructing Explanations and Designing Solutions
	Identify the evidence that supports particular points in an explanation.
Social studies	D2.Geo.2.K-2 &3-5. Use maps, satellite images, and photographs to describe places and explain relationships between the locations of places and regions.
	D2.Geo.4.K-2. Explain how weather, climate, and other environmental characteristics affect people's lives in a place or region.

Content targets come next; they focus on the academic concepts or ideas expected of all students that will be displayed in the unit's product. Remember content targets are often seen as cognitive functions (think Bloom's revised taxonomy—remembering, understanding, applying, analyzing, evaluating, and creating) that mirror the selected content standards. Here is one way of conceptualizing a content target for the weather unit that crosses content areas:

Content Target: Students will

Apply mathematical operations to everyday weather scenarios, *analyze* weather patterns in two global locations, and *evaluate* the impact of weather conditions on people's lives.

You cannot have content without language. The language target, intended for all students, helps teachers highlight grade-level academic language use for the unit theme to help foster students' deeper conceptual development. Figure 6.15 distinguishes the features of content and language targets.

Figure 6.15 Learning Targets: A Comparison Between Content and Language

Content Targets	Language Targets
Represent content standards	Represent language proficiency development standards
Focus on conceptual knowledge and cognitive skills	Focus on academic language use associated with content knowledge
Capture the big idea(s) of a unit	Reflect key use(s) of academic language
Are the basis for differentiated content objectives	Are the basis for differentiated language objectives

REFLECTION

Examining Content and Language Targets

There are many different ways to organize assessment *for* learning based on common instructional products. However, the starting point is always standards, along with content targets and language targets. Read over the learning targets of the weather project and discuss with your colleagues how you might approach the content and the language of this unit or one of your own.

Language Components

For this project, students will interact with text and each other using all language domains (listening, speaking, reading, and writing), but we will concentrate on assessing the productive areas of speaking and writing. Language targets complement content targets for the unit; the integration of language and content within delivery provides comprehensible input for the students. Here is an accompanying language target:

Language Target: Students will

Recount weather reports, *explain* weather patterns in different locations, and *discuss* the impact of weather events on people.

This multidisciplinary unit of learning is broad in scope, spanning all the language domains and the language of the core content areas. As seen in Figure 6.16, while the content expectations remain constant, the language expectations are subsequently differentiated into language objectives that reflect ELLs' levels of language proficiency when it comes time for lesson planning.

Figure 6.16 Coverage of Language Development Standards in the Unit Project: Integrated Productive Strands, Kindergarten-Grade 5

Level 1 Entering	Level 2 Emerging	Level 3 Developing	Level 4 Expanding	Level 5 Bridging
Name weather conditions and their effects on people using calendars, maps, charts and graphs	Restate weather conditions and their effects on people using calendars, maps, charts, and graphs	Describe weather conditions and their effects on people using calendars, maps, charts, and graphs	Discuss weather conditions and their effects on people using calendars, maps, charts, and graphs	Explain weather conditions and their effects on people using calendars, maps, charts, and graphs

Source: WIDA, 2012, p. 19. ©Board of Regents of the University of Wisconsin System, on behalf of the WIDA Consortium. www.wida.us.

> **REFLECTION**
>
> ### Determining the Common Instructional Product
>
> Now that your team has selected content and language standards to generate content and language targets, the next step is to think of various common instructional products that reflect the multidisciplinary nature of the unit. What are some products and pathways that might appeal to your students? For example, students might produce a poster, a PowerPoint slide show, an i-movie, a video clip, or an illustrated essay. How might you ensure that you are motivating your ELLs?

Student Evidence of Learning

Planning a common instructional product for a unit goes hand in hand with planning a common rubric that defines the criteria for success. Rubrics are a good starting point because they organize the criteria for students into descriptive levels on various aspects of their work. You can determine whether students comprehend the levels of a rubric by asking them to state the levels in their own words or in their home language. Students can learn to recognize levels of performance when they see real-life exemplars. Students who can identify performance levels in sample papers (or oral samples) have more precision in self-assessment and at producing expected levels of work themselves (Moss & Brookhart, 2009).

Up to this point, we have tied assessment to the language of the content areas (see Chapter 3) and to the distinct language domains (see Chapter 4). In elaborating on assessment *as* and *for* learning here in Part II, we have purposely integrated content across disciplines and language across modalities or domains. Figure 6.17, a holistic rubric for common instructional products, can be used as a template to exemplify this combined effort.

> **REFLECTION**
>
> ### Converting Rubrics to Match Common Instructional Products
>
> How might your grade-level team convert the generic or holistic rubric in Figure 6.17 into a task-specific one—that is, how would you make it applicable to your specific project? Perhaps you would simply take each criterion and substitute one reflective of your project.

You might also consider breaking up the holistic rubric into different dimensions to create an analytic scale. Whatever you decide, consider using what you adopt or adapt for multiple common instructional products so indeed you will be able to document student growth throughout the year using the same scale.

Figure 6.17   A Sample Rubric for Common Instructional Products

Level 4: Champion

- Develops and implements a comprehensive action plan from project descriptors
- Uses extensive materials and resources to develop related ideas
- Connects ideas through visual and graphic representation
- Justifies decisions based on evidence from multiple and varied sources

Level 3: Contender

- Develops and implements an action plan based on project descriptors
- Uses a variety of materials and resources to develop ideas
- Presents logical ideas through visual and graphic representation
- Provides reasons or rationale for decisions based on evidence from multiple sources

Level 2: Competitor

- Follows a given action plan based on project descriptors
- Uses materials and resources (in the home language) to develop ideas
- Expresses ideas through visual or graphic representation
- Relates decisions based on some evidence from multiple sources

Level 1: Challenger

- Attempts to follow the project descriptors
- Uses some materials and resources in the home language to relate to the theme
- Includes some visual and graphic representation
- Makes decisions loosely related to information or evidence

Evaluation of Common Instructional Products

Peer or student self-assessment promotes students' involvement in their own learning and provides built-in monitoring of their progress. Students can be taught to maintain an illustrated learning log in which they note one or two new concepts or language patterns after each activity. They may also use a checklist to pace their content and language learning.

Teachers can provide students with a product descriptor and a timeline for each activity or task and its associated product. In the reporting summary, language is separated from content so that ELLs, in particular, can gain a sense of their accomplishments on both dimensions. The same set of criteria, if used over time, allows teachers and students to monitor and create portraits of student learning.

In this final phase of common instructional products as part of assessment *for* learning, students have opportunities to apply their new skills by viewing each other's products and offering feedback to one another, following a standard format, such as a project descriptor, a checklist, or a rubric. In addition, teacher-student conferences can be held to promote interaction and bring closure to the project. As common instructional products involve multiple classrooms, teachers should have dedicated time to come to agreement on each point or criterion in the project rubric and match evidence of the criteria with student samples. The culmination of a multiclass, multiweek project should involve a celebration of students' accomplishments by having a gallery walk, a fair, or an exhibition for the grade, department, or school.

REFLECTION AND REACTION

Assessment *for* learning is broad in scope, covering formative processes and common instructional products for units of learning that are planned within the instructional cycle. It features standards-referenced performance assessment that integrates content and language. In assessment *for* learning, teachers come together in designing and implementing activities, tasks, and projects around criteria for success. Although assessment *for* learning relates to teaching, teachers never lose sight of its power when combined with assessment *as* learning.

Embedded in assessment *for* learning, evidence is systematically gathered, organized, and analyzed. Standards-referenced results are used to inform various stakeholders, including students, other teachers, and multi-tiered teams of support, with the ultimate goal of advancing teaching and learning. This information reveals how students are performing in relation to content and language standards (that is, the extent to which they are meeting their criteria for success) and provides feedback to teachers on how to improve their instructional repertoire.

Evidence collected from assessment *for* learning is as valuable as that gained through assessment *of* learning data, which we shall inspect in the next chapter. By having a challenging standards-driven curriculum; delivering it through rich, content-based instruction with concurrent attention to academic language use; and assessing student performance comprehensively throughout and at the close of the unit, teachers can make worthwhile decisions based on evidence acquired in the moment or accrued over time. As teachers are at the heart of assessment *for* learning, formative processes and common instructional products serve as a bridge to teacher equity. Below are some questions that reference this approach to assessment.

- Explain to other teachers, school leaders, or district administrators how the formative assessment process is a form of assessment *for* learning and is not another test. Then argue for the value of the process and the benefits it yields.
- The formative assessment process represents both assessment *as* learning and assessment *for* learning. Do you believe that there should be a distinction in emphasis between students and teachers in these two approaches? Explain why or why not to your colleagues or school leaders.
- How do common instructional products exemplify assessment *for* learning? How do you or your grade-level team think that common assessment yields different kinds of information than does the formative process? Do you believe that both of these forms of assessment are necessary or are they redundant?
- How might you collaborate with your grade-level team or department in expanding a content rubric to infuse components of academic language use? Or, conversely, how might a language proficiency rubric be amended to also express content?
- As seen in the chapter, learning targets are quite different from learning objectives. How would you explain the difference and why do you think the distinction between the two is useful? How is it helpful to teachers in designing units of learning?

RESOURCE 6.1

Example Language Expectations for Language Learners at Varying Language Proficiency Levels

Language Proficiency Level 5	• Justify and defend positions through speeches, multimedia reports, or essays • Investigate language of academic topics using multiple resources • Explain relationships, consequences, or cause and effect • Debate issues and provide evidence to support claims • React and reflect on articles, short stories, or essays of multiple genres • Author a variety of genres for varied purposes and audiences
Language Proficiency Level 4	• Explain processes or procedures with extended discourse/paragraphs • Describe in detail original models, demonstrations, or exhibitions • Summarize and draw conclusions from grade-level speech and text • Discuss pros and cons of research-based issues • Reflect on use of multiple learning strategies • Compare and contrast objects, people, events • Author various narrative and informational genres
Language Proficiency Level 3	• Outline speech and text using graphic organizers • Explain phenomena using information from charts, graphs, or tables • Make predictions or hypotheses based on illustrated stories, events, or inquiry • Argue points of view with others • Produce short stories, poetry, or structured reports with interactive support • Describe with details objects, people, or events using visual support • Author informational and narrative pieces
Language Proficiency Level 2	• Describe events or problems using timelines, number lines, or schedules • Define and categorize objects, people, or events with visual or graphic support • Compare information in charts, diagrams, and illustrations • Sequence pictures per oral directions to show processes, procedures, or cycles • Produce multiliteracy projects in collaboration with peers
Language Proficiency Level 1	• Name and describe pictures or real-life objects related to grade-level themes or topics • Produce movies, videos, or multimedia presentations with grade-level content • Categorize labeled pictures, words, and phrases using graphic organizers • Take a stance and illustrate it through collages or photojournals

Source: Adapted from Gottlieb, 2006, p. 30.

RESOURCE 6.2

Activities, Tasks, or Projects?

How you would categorize the following activities, tasks, and projects as examples of performance assessment? Place an A, T, or P in front of each example. (Answers follow.)

1. _____ Asking and answering questions related to a topic or issue

2. _____ Contributing entries to a journal, learning log, or a blog

3. _____ Constructing and presenting a model and a chart of its statistics

4. _____ Producing a process-writing report

5. _____ Conducting a survey and discussing the results

6. _____ Explaining answers to math problems

7. _____ Producing an argumentative essay using information gathered from multiple sources

8. _____ Creating an illustrated brochure

9. _____ Comparing and contrasting two stories, articles, or works

10. _____ Conducting an experiment and completing a structured lab report

REFLECTION Answers for Activities, Tasks, or Projects

1. Activity; 2. Activity; 3. Project; 4. Project; 5. Project; 6. Activity; 7. Project; 8. Project; 9. Task; 10. Task

Source: Adapted from Gottlieb, 2006, p. 100.

RESOURCE 6.3

Planning for Common Instructional Products

Here is a completed graphic organizer exemplifying Figure 6.7. Think of how you or your team might use it to help organize a unit of learning. How might assessment fit into this representation?

Unit Theme: On a Mission

One day humans may have to leave the Earth and travel to another planet to settle down and live.

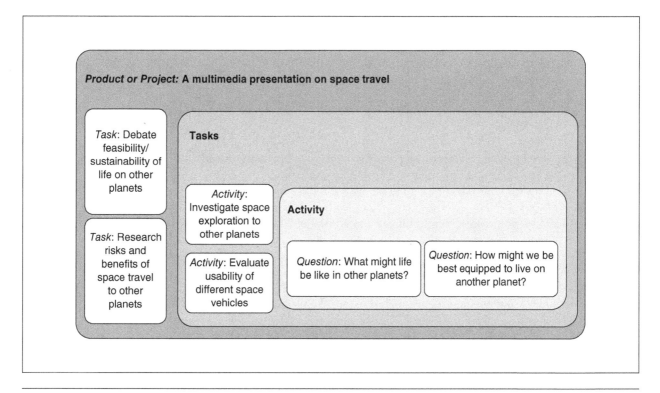

RESOURCE 6.4

Common Instructional Products: A Checklist for Use Prior to Implementing Performance-Based Projects

_____ 1. Is the project created for all students, with special attention paid to ELLs, gifted and talented ELLs, and ELLs with disabilities?

_____ 2. Does the project represent a collaborative effort by a team of teachers, including the partnering of content and language teachers?

_____ 3. Is the project realistic for the time allocation?

_____ 4. Does the project encompass multiple standards, specific learning targets, and multiple language domains, including multiliteracies?

_____ 5. Are students welcome to use their personal, family, and community resources as sources of evidence?

_____ 6. Are there provisions of supports for instruction and assessment?

_____ 7. Can students pursue multiple pathways in designing the project?

_____ 8. Have students been informed of the criteria and practiced using the rubric for the project?

_____ 9. Have teachers agreed upon the selection of anchors of student performance that represent the scoring points on the rubric?

_____ 10. Have teachers shared the anchors or model projects with students?

_____ 11. Are these teacher-crafted projects considered part of local accountability?

RESOURCE 6.5

Common Instructional Products: A Review Sheet for Projects Involving English Language Learners

Name of project: _____

Grade level(s) or departments: _____

Teachers involved: _____

The Project	YES	NO*
Covers a representative sample of grade-level college and career readiness standards and language proficiency/development standards		
Makes provision for multiple levels of language proficiency for ELLs		
Insists on demonstration of oral language in two languages and biliteracy development for students in dual language settings		
Is linguistically and culturally responsive		
Requires student work samples or products for the designated language domains and content area(s)		
Covers grade-level curriculum yet is authentic, relevant, and of interest to students		
Relies on multiple resources, including those in the students' home languages		
Follows a logical sequence of scaffolded activities and tasks		
Contains visual, graphic, and interactive supports		
Allows students to follow different pathways, such as using multiliteracies, to meeting learning targets and standards		

*For every NO response, offer a suggestion on how to enhance the project.

RESOURCE 6.6

A Template for a Unit's Common Instructional Product

Theme/Topic:

Name of the project: _____

Content area(s): _____

Burning issue or big idea: _____

Teachers and school leaders involved (ESL, bilingual, general education, special education in grade-level teams or professional learning communities): _____

Grade or grade-level cluster(s): K 1 2 3 4 5 6 7 8 9 10 11 12

Duration of project: _____

   I. Planning: The parameters for assessment

      A. Content

          1. Content area college and career readiness standards to be assessed:

              Language arts standards: _____

              Mathematics standards: _____

              Science standards: _____

              Social studies standards:_____

              Other content standards :_____

          2. Content target: _____

          3. Language(s) of instruction and assessment of content:

              English _____

              Spanish _____

              Other _____

      B. Language

          1. Language development/proficiency standards, performance indicators, and language domains to be assessed:

              Listening _____

              Speaking _____

              Reading _____

              Writing _____

          2. Language target: _____

          3. Language(s) of instruction and assessment of language development:

              English _____

              Spanish _____

              Other _____

      C. Performance assessment: _____

          1. Product(s): _____

          2. Criteria for success: _____

3. Materials and resources, including visual, graphic, and interactive supports:

    _____

4. Type(s) of documentation (rubrics) or scoring guide(s): _____

II. Implementing: The instructional assessment sequence for a product or project

Task 1 Duration _____

Grouping of students: Individuals _____ Pairs _____ Small groups _____

Description of what students do when integrating language and content:

Task 2 Duration _____

Grouping of students: Individuals _____ Pairs _____ Small groups _____

Description of what students do when integrating language and content:

Performance-based product

Combining tasks into a final project:

III. Evaluating: Results, feedback, and use of the information

A. Peer or student self-assessment: _____

B. Teacher-teacher agreement on student work based on a common rubric: _____

    _____

C. Lessons learned and decisions made: _____

Source: Adapted from Gottlieb, 2006, pp. 103–104.

RESOURCE 6.7

Curriculum Design Highlighting Academic Language Use

There are many ways of conceptualizing the design of curriculum. Here is a template that highlights academic language use as the crosswalk between content and language. It is the basis of thematic units of learning created by teachers in the academic language series (Gottlieb & Ernst-Slavit, 2013, 2014a, 2014b).

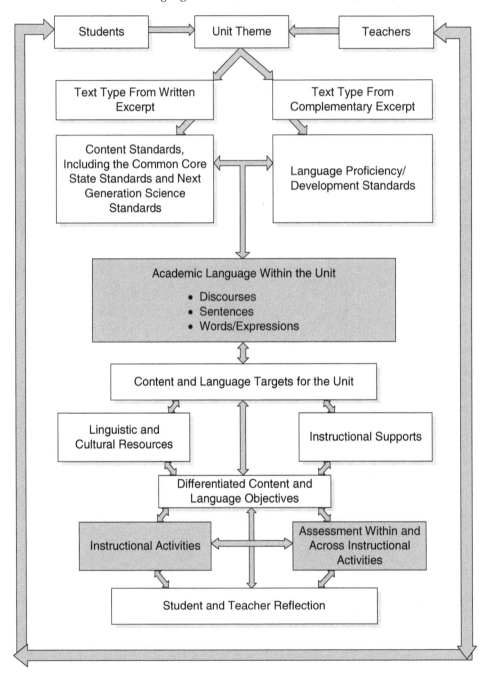

Source: Adapted from Gottlieb & Ernst-Slavit, 2014a, p. 188.

7

Assessment of Learning

The Bridge to Administrator Equity

Leadership and learning are indispensable to each other.

—John Fitzgerald Kennedy

We have come to the final approach of assessment, one that is quite distinct from the other two as it is external to the day-to-day functioning of the classroom. In fact, it is generally imposed upon teachers rather than created by them. The purpose of assessment *of* learning is also unique as most likely the results contribute either to local or state accountability. As it is tied to the academic status of schools and districts and is often public in nature, data from assessment *of* learning have become one means of defining administrator equity.

For decades, standardized achievement tests have been the mainstay of the American educational system. Standardized testing serves a specific purpose: It allows for comparisons to be made among schools, districts, and states in regards to student performance based on the same measure. Looking closer into the technical qualities of these tests, however, may lead to skepticism in the interpretation of the results and doubt in the inferences or decisions made for students outside the norming population. As we shall explore in this chapter, interim (sometimes called benchmark) measures and standardized achievement tests that comprise assessment *of* learning (see Figure 7.1) may not be appropriate for ELLs or ELLs with disabilities.

Forty years after the Supreme Court decision on the *Lau v. Nichols* civil rights case and the enactment of Congress's Equal Educational Opportunities Act, the U.S. Department of Justice, Civil Rights Division, and the U.S. Department of Education, Office for Civil Rights, issued joint guidance on the equitable treatment of ELLs in

Figure 7.1 Forms of Assessment That Measure Assessment *of* Learning

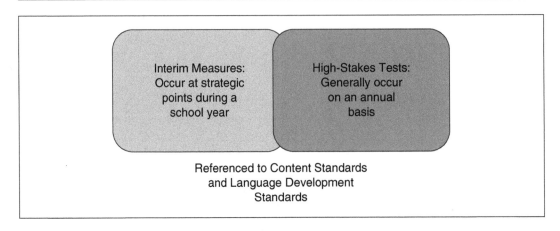

public schools under the civil rights laws (2015). The guidance, along with an accompanying toolkit for states and local education agencies (see http://www2.ed.gov/about/offices/list/oela/english-learner-toolkit/eltoolkit.pdf), stipulates that schools and school districts must have systems in place to reliably identify ELLs and provide plans to enable ELLs to reach proficiency in English. At the same time, ELLs must be offered the identical learning opportunities as all students, such as magnet schools or honor societies, to ensure meaningful and equitable participation in educational programs and services.

The guidance goes on to state that students identified as ELLs with disabilities are to receive both language support and disability-related services. The policies inherent in this legal document have implications for administrators who deal with assessment *of* learning and accountability of ELLs and ELLs with disabilities—the focus of this chapter.

REFLECTION

Examining Federal Guidance

If you are not familiar with the U.S. Department of Justice/Department of Education letter of January 7, 2015, which can be found at http://www2.ed.gov/about/offices/list/ocr/letters/colleague-el-201501.pdf, take some time to read through the guidance. Make a list of all the issues that deal with assessment of ELLs. Then determine the extent to which your school is compliant.

Accessibility features and accommodations in annual state assessments are intended to offset disparities between ELLs and their proficient English peers, but do they? In examining some sample items from the newest generation of tests, you will be able to conclude for yourselves whether these measures are valid for all students and whether their high-stakes nature is warranted. Given that assessment *of* learning is directed from the outside, and assessment *as* and *for* learning are more sensitive to the internal workings of a school, it is difficult to conclude that a bona fide assessment system, especially for ELLs, truly exists (Bailey & Carroll, 2015).

THE DISTINCTIONS AMONG TESTING, ASSESSMENT, AND EVALUATION

Let's make sure we are all on the same page. When discussing assessment *of* learning, we tend to concentrate on testing, so let's clarify some basic terms. *Testing, assessment*, and *evaluation* are often used interchangeably, but they actually represent quite different constructs. *Testing* is a systematic procedure of collecting a sample of student behavior at one point in time and is generally quite narrow in coverage. *Assessment* is a comprehensive process of planning, collecting, analyzing, interpreting, reporting, and using information over time. It typically includes data from tests as well as documentation from other sources, such as projects, anecdotal information, and student self-assessment. *Evaluation* is broadest in scope and involves a process of gathering and analyzing an array of evidence matched to a set of goals to judge the worth of services, programs, or interventions in order to make informed decisions about their effectiveness. Figure 7.2 is a set of concentric circles that illustrates the relationship among these three terms.

Figure 7.2   Viewing Assessment in Relation to Testing and Evaluation

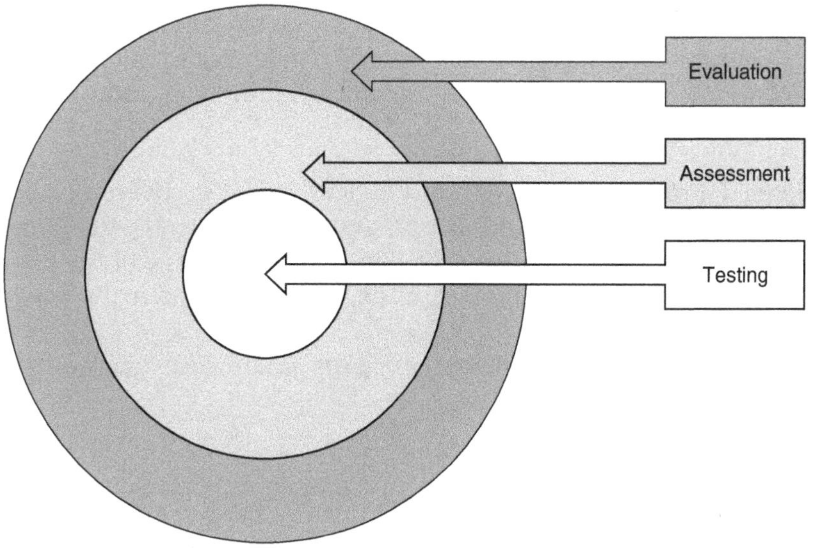

Source: Adapted from Gottlieb, 2006, p. 86.

REFLECTION

Distinguishing Terms

How have the terms *evaluation, assessment,* and *testing* been applied in your setting? Give some examples of the measures associated with these terms and the kinds of decisions that are made with each.

This book centers on assessment as the primary source for decision making in schools. *Assessment* is quite an all-encompassing term as it includes testing and it contributes to evaluation. Assessment relies on establishing a purpose, planning a course of action around multiple measures or data sources, gathering information at multiple data points (a span of time), involving multiple stakeholders, and using the results to make decisions in relation to the purpose. Continuous feedback ensures that data are constantly being updated to provide the most relevant and accurate information.

As educators, we must be attentive to how our students learn and how they demonstrate their learning; therefore, it is our responsibility to provide all language learners with the appropriate tools and techniques to enable them to thrive within a standards-based environment. Assessment *as* and *for* learning equip students and teachers with those resources. We must also be aware of how assessment operates outside our individual classrooms—at a grade level or at department, district, or state levels—and its subsequent impact on ELLs and ELLs with disabilities.

VALIDITY

Due to their high-stakes nature, measures of assessment *of* learning must be, above all else, valid. Without validity, there is no equity. This means that the interpretations or inferences that are made from the results must be accurate in representing the meaning of the construct being tested. For ELLs, one might ask, is the content of the test true to either the construct of academic achievement or of language proficiency? When testing ELLs, systematic error that impacts validity can often creep in due to

- irrelevant information in the items;
- students not having the opportunity to learn what is covered on the test;
- assumptions that students are familiar with the context of the items;
- assumptions that students are proficient in the language of the test;
- assumptions that students' cultural backgrounds match those of the items; and
- items that are not developmentally appropriate for the age group. (Chatterji, 2003)

REFLECTION

Maximizing Validity and Minimizing Bias

Which of the potential sources of test error identified above do you believe is most destructive to the integrity of a measure, especially for ELLs? Investigate a commercial measure to find some evidence of your claim by examining its technical manual. You might also consider examining sample items of the test for potential bias. Share your findings with members of your grade-level team and present your argument, if warranted, to others in your school.

All these sources of potential error lead to tests that yield invalid results. On top of these caveats, even a well-designed test can be unfair or biased towards specific test users if the results are misapplied. Case in point, an oral reading test is used to measure comprehension, not to diagnose a speech disability, a purpose other than the one defined by the test. In evidence-centered design, types of validity evidence are collected to prove the argument that a test indeed measures what it is intended to measure, but we will leave that work to psychometricians. One of the takeaways from this discussion is that all tests associated with assessment *of* learning have some degree of bias; this has to be minimized, however, so that we can maximize our confidence in the results when making decisions.

Validity also extends to assessment *for* and *as* learning. By definition, by being closer to teaching and learning, these approaches have greater real-world applicability. In assessment *for* learning, the teacher must have a notion of quality that is appropriate to the task; the judgment of students' work in relation to that quality or criteria directly relates to the feedback given. In assessment *as* learning, students must develop the capacity to monitor the quality of their own work during actual production to be able to improve (Sadler, 1989). Clear expectations of authentic tasks that are directly matched to student learning are an expression of validity.

What the Scores for Assessment *of* Learning Mean

Rather than relying on oral or written feedback within the teaching-learning cycle or the interpretation of student work using a rubric, assessment *of* learning typically generates test scores. Let's take a minute to clarify different types of scores and how they are reported. Raw scores are the total number of correct answers on items; they give us little information and cannot be compared from one test to another. Often test results are converted to percentages or averaged, often for the sake of grading, but this still does not add meaning. Think about it: While 8 out of 10 correct answers is 80%, does this really tell you anything in terms of a student's quality of work?

For large-scale tests of achievement or language proficiency, results are often reported as scale scores. Scale scores are the conversion of a test's raw scores to a common scale that allows for a numerical comparison of student performance. As every test has an associated degree of error, scale scores are often presented within a confidence band. A confidence band takes the amount of error into account in depicting the upper and lower limits of a range of data. For example, if a student's scale score on a test is 500 and the standard error of measurement (the test's variability) is 25, then the confidence band would lie between 475 and 525. This means that you can have 95% confidence that the student would score within these 50 points if the test were to be administered again within a short window of time.

REFLECTION

Interpreting Test Scores

Examine several test manuals to note the scale scores and standard error of measurement. Then look to see whether they are reported in a data table or visually, such as with a histogram. Select the way that you think students and family members can best understand the test results.

INTERIM MEASURES

According to the Glossary of Education Reform, there is no official definition for interim measures, but there is general consensus on their purposes or uses. Interim measures are a form of assessment where educators gather data to determine (a) where students are in their learning and (b) to what extent students are on track to performing well on end-of-course or annual tests. Interim measures are administered periodically during a course or school year (for example, every several months) and are separate from and not necessarily reflective of instruction. The premise behind interim measures is that these tests can inform and improve practice, thereby contributing to increased student achievement (Goertz, Oláh, & Riggan, 2010).

Going back to the assessment model in Figure II.1, we consider interim measures as assessment *of* learning. Why? They fit the parameters of common instructional products in that results are easily aggregated and analyzed across classrooms. However, there is one huge difference: Interim measures are not part of the instructional cycle and are not designed by teachers who work together as a team. Instead, interim measures are commercial products, sold by testing companies or publishers and purchased by districts or schools. Often management systems come with the package so that stakeholders can identify students' strengths and weaknesses based on the analysis and display of data.

Interim measures are administered at regular intervals, such as at the beginning, midpoint, and toward the end of a school year. These testing intervals are usually determined at the district level. As these measures are given multiple times, the breadth of content is less than that on annual tests, although each topic may be treated in more depth. The multiple test rather than single test approach can be advantageous when results inform high-stakes decisions (Bergan, Bergan, & Burnham, 2009). An example of an interim measure for the primary grades might be an informal reading inventory; for middle grades and high school, it might be a digital multiple-choice reading test.

Benchmark tests are frequently used interchangeably with interim measures. Similar in nature, standardized benchmark tests typically

- are administered on a periodic basis, from twice a year to as often as once a month;
- focus on the primary areas for state accountability (reading and mathematics for all students and language proficiency for ELLs);
- are anchored in academic standards, either content (state college and career readiness) or language proficiency/development standards;
- have standardized, often computer-generated scoring that increases reliability;
- give (almost) immediate results to teachers and other stakeholders; and
- serve to predict results on state achievement tests or measure student growth in language proficiency.

As early as 2005, in response to the accountability demands of the reauthorization of the Elementary and Secondary Education Act of 2001 (known as No Child Left Behind), an *Educational Week* article reported on the burgeoning benchmark test market. Seven in 10 superintendents surveyed admitted to using these measures in response to the elevated high-stakes environment of their districts (Olson, 2005). The appeal of these published benchmark tests is that many include extensive reporting

> **REFLECTION**
>
> **Figuring Out More Terms**
>
> Does your district administer interim or benchmark measures? If so, what are their purposes? When are they given? Which standards and content areas are addressed? Are there interim measures of language proficiency? For dual language learners, have you identified measures in the languages of instruction? How are the results used? How do the interim or benchmark measures exemplify assessment *of* learning?

systems whereby test results are categorized according to federal requirements, such as by race, socioeconomic status, disability, and English proficiency. In addition there are multiple reports that are issued at the district, school, classroom, and student levels.

Rounding out the continua of assessments presented in Figure II.1, we have now reached the measure that educators have come to equate with personal, school, and district accountability: high-stakes tests.

HIGH-STAKES TESTS

We have reached the final form of assessment, the one that epitomizes assessment *of* learning. Yes, high-stakes testing, with its primary purpose of gauging student achievement on an annual basis and its contribution to the accountability of districts and states, remains a time-honored tradition of schooling. In the last decades, national legislation has elevated the status and significance of testing academic achievement in American schools, yet many challenges remain with the use of standardized achievement measures in English for ELLs. These include

- only tacit acknowledgement of the role of language in achievement;
- the propagation of an English-only orientation rather than a recognition of the research that has solidified bilingualism and biliteracy as assets; and
- the continued use of ineffective accommodations on state and consortia tests. (Menken, 2015)

What would you say constitutes high-stakes testing, especially for ELLs or ELLs with disabilities? The primary criterion is that the data generated from the single use of one of these measures heavily weigh on decisions that carry specific consequences for the test-taker—in this case, the student. It is not the test per se that is "high stakes" but how the results are used, such as for retaining students or determining graduation. Some high-stakes tests are standardized, with the assumption that if administered under the same conditions, they are consequently equitable for all examinees. However, that's not necessarily true.

The validity issue present in high-stakes tests of academic achievement for linguistically and culturally diverse students, in particular ELLs with lower levels of English language proficiency, stems from various sources. The reasons extend across the test development process—from conceptualization of the blueprint to test construction to administration to data analysis and reporting. In other words, validity concerns are not only internal to the test but are, in fact, systemic (Weir, 2005). Overlaid onto that scenario is the notion that culture shapes our thinking and is a form of validity unto itself that must be taken into account in test construction and test-taking (Basterra, Trumbull, & Solano-Flores, 2011).

The following list of statements reflects the primary inadequacies of high-stakes tests of academic achievement for ELLs that lead us to question their validity.

- Universal design has not truly guided the test development.
- The language development process is not considered in item construction.
- Language complexity and density confound students' ability to express conceptual understanding.
- Access to meaning or understanding is dependent on text.
- Bias and content review panels have not focused on linguistic or cultural influences of the items.
- Cognitive labs, pilot testing, and field-testing phases of test development do not include ample representation of ELLs or ELLs with disabilities across various language proficiency levels.
- Modifications or accommodations for ELLs and students with disabilities have not been piloted, field tested, or empirically examined.
- ELLs being instructed in their home language do not have comparable standards-referenced tests to demonstrate their language proficiency or achievement.

REFLECTION

Experiencing High-Stakes Tests

Think about some high-stakes tests that you have experienced, such as getting your driver's license, auditioning for a role in a play, trying out for a sports team, or securing college credit from an AP test. How did you handle taking the test? What was your reaction when you received the results? Now put yourself in the shoes of students for whom English is an additional language. How do you think they would feel?

Despite the prevalence of high-stakes testing in the United States, debate continues over its appropriateness. Menken (2015) asserts that these tests pose a threat to standards-referenced reform efforts since educators are pressured to teach to the test rather than the standards. Andrea Honigsfeld and Vicky Giouroukakis (2011) take a different stance. Rather than looking at improving test characteristics, they contend that by utilizing curriculum and instructional practices that are inclusive of students' unique backgrounds, educators can create opportunities for advancing language learners' achievement on high-stakes tests.

These arguments have been supported by a host of organizations and agencies. The National Center for Fair and Open Testing (FairTest) has been a persistent opponent of standardized testing, claiming that performance assessment is a more equitable and authentic means of accountability for both teachers and students. Others specifically oppose the use of high-stakes tests and their sanctions. The U.S. Department of Education's Office for Civil Rights (2000) has been critical of the misuse of high-stakes testing from an equity standpoint, whereas the American Educational Research Association (2000) has denounced high-stakes testing on the basis of evidence gathered from scientifically based research.

Numerous teacher organizations have joined the cry for testing reform and have issued policy statements or resolutions to this effect. Many have taken the stance that overdependence on the results from a single test for educational decision making is irresponsible. The International Literacy Association, formerly the International Reading Association, insists that high-stakes decisions be based on a more comprehensive picture of students' literacy performance (2013–2014). Teachers of English to Speakers of Other Languages (TESOL) notes how high-stake achievement tests are "unfair to English language learners and cannot be relied on to provide an accurate measure of an English language learner's abilities in content areas" (2003). The National Council of Teachers of Mathematics (2012) states that large-scale tests are only one form of assessment that is to be used to make high-stakes decisions that significantly impact students and schools. The National Education Association typifies the argument posed by many organizations by stating the claim that testing is not teaching (Flannery, 2015). The National Council of Teachers of English (2015) "strongly opposes the use of high-stakes test performance in reading as the criterion for student retention," reinforcing 40 years of research on the negative consequences of grade retention as punishment for students.

Standardized tests are designed to measure a broad band of competencies, whether for academic achievement, such as in the areas of language arts, mathematics, or science, or, in the case of ELLs, in English language proficiency as well. Standardized tests are outside the direct control of teachers and removed from classroom assessment. High-stakes standardized tests are secure, and educators do not have access to them except during administration. However, all teachers need to be knowledgeable about standardized testing and understand how the data affect teaching and learning. The pros and cons for using standardized tests are outlined in Figure 7.3.

Figure 7.3 The Advantages and Disadvantages of Using Standardized Achievement Tests

Advantages of Standardized Content Measures	Disadvantages of Standardized Content Measures
Produce consistently reliable data	Often serve as a gatekeeper for students (and teachers)
Require uniform data collection and analyses on large numbers of students	Do not represent in-depth conceptual knowledge
Provide a state or national perspective	Do not allow for individual student creativity or imagination
Are not confounded by individual teacher effects	Development may not be inclusive of all students
Are readily scored	Generally adhere to time limits
Easy to train teachers on procedures for administration	Can lead to misinterpretation of data and overgeneralization of results

Source: Adapted from Gottlieb, 2006, p. 153.

Linguistic Appropriateness of Assessment Measures: Implications for ELLs and ELLs With Disabilities

Achievement tests measure content, yet they often contain complex linguistic structures that lead to inaccurate results for ELLs (Abedi, 2004). Ideally there should be a match among a student's experiential background, his or her language proficiency, and the linguistic features of a test. Besides familiarity with vocabulary, the following syntactic structures may confound ELLs' understanding of content:

- Passive voice (e.g., Florida *was discovered* by Ponce de Leon.)
- Complex noun phrases (e.g., "professional learning community")
- Prepositional phrases (e.g., *on* v. *in* the desk)
- Relative clauses (e.g., "that dangled from a clean kitchen towel")
- Use of negation (e.g., use of *none, never, neither*)
- Subordinate clauses (e.g., "until I have my first cup of tea . . .")

Linguistic complexity affects the reliability and the validity of tests. When the measures have high stakes, such as when they are being used to determine special education placement, problematic results lead to misplacement of students (Klingner, Hoover, & Baca, 2008).

Norm-Referenced and Criterion-Referenced Tests

There are generally two types of standardized tests. Norm-referenced tests rank students by measuring their relative performance against that of the group on which the test was field tested. Criterion-referenced tests, on the other hand, gather information about student progress or achievement in relation to specified criteria. In a standards-based assessment model, standards serve as the criteria or yardstick for measurement.

The primary advantage of criterion-referenced measures is that they allow us to make inferences about the amount of language proficiency, in the case of language proficiency tests, or knowledge and skills, in the case of academic achievement tests, that students initially have (their baseline) and their subsequent gains over time. Criterion-referenced tests are concerned with the extent to which students have mastered the representation of standards along a continuum rather than with ranking students' performance on a bell curve. Thus, for ELLs, with English language development standards as the criterion, we are able to see their individual language proficiency growth from year to year alongside their academic achievement measured by college and career readiness standards.

Types of Item Responses in Assessment of Learning

There are generally two types of responses associated with standardized tests. In *selected-response* tests, items list all possible answers for the students. Dichotomous scales offer students two choices, such as in true/false or yes/no questions, or perhaps involve the classification of pictures, words, phrases, or sentences for content, such as distinguishing between vertebrates and invertebrates, or, for language, using words with multiple meanings in two different contexts. A checklist is another example of a dichotomous scale.

Selected response also refers to items that involve multiple choice, categorization, or sequencing where the number of possible options for correct responses is expanded to three or four. For categorization on a mathematics achievement test, for example, students may be asked to read some problems and decide which operation to use: addition, subtraction, multiplication, or division. For achievement in social studies, language learners may be asked to sort phrases or sentences as to whether the event described occurred before, during, or after a major event; to show their language proficiency, ELLs may recount an event choosing sequential language to indicate chronology.

Obviously, scoring is easy when there is only one correct answer, and reliability is greater with selected-response items. (*Reliability* refers to the internal consistency among the test items, the consistency in the scores for the test-taker, or the consistency of scoring among the raters when dealing with constructed response questions.) Now that states are moving toward more computer-based testing, the notion of selected response has been extended to drag-and-drop items.

REFLECTION

Thinking Like an Item Writer

If you were given the opportunity to produce items for a test publisher, what kinds of selected-response items do you think would be most effective for your different groups of students? What reasons might you give for your choice? You might choose to analyze the different kinds of selected-response items with your grade-level team by examining non-secure interim or benchmark measures.

Constructed response items, in contrast, offer more latitude to students by allowing them to produce original work and to be creative in approaching complex issues. In doing so, items can be more cognitively demanding and reach higher-order thinking. With open-ended responses, there may be multiple solutions to questions or acceptance of various perspectives. Constructed-response items that take ELLs' levels of language proficiency into account may range from illustrating and labeling math problems to producing a persuasive essay that includes claims and evidence.

The 2014–2015 academic year ushered in a new wave of achievement testing for students in grades 3–12 in the United States. This was unique in that these high-stakes tests were

- grounded in college and career readiness standards;
- most likely conceptualized by a consortia of states; and
- significantly driven by technology.

Provisions for Annual Testing of English Language Learners Under the Every Student Succeeds Act

Since its inception in 1965, the ESEA has intended to bring equity to the education landscape by addressing the academic needs of "disadvantaged" youth. In December 2015 Congress reauthorized the ESEA after a 14-year hiatus; the new version of the act is known as the Every Student Succeeds Act (ESSA). The law maintains high academic standards and annual statewide assessment minimally in grades 3 through 8 and in high school for reading/language arts and mathematics, along with science in each of three grade spans (3–5, 6–9, and 10–12). With this federal legislation comes special provisions for assessment regarding annual achievement testing and accountability. These provisions include the following:

- For ELLs newly arrived to the United States, two options are available to states. The first is to have annual test scores for mathematics count immediately for ELLs, then after one year to have test results for both mathematics and reading/language arts count toward accountability. The second choice is to have ELLs take both tests in year one and publicly report the results but do not include ELLs in a state's accountability equation. By year two, there should be some measure of growth in both disciplines, and by year three there should be no distinction made between ELLs and their peers.
- Former ELLs can be factored into state accountability up to 4 years after reclassification; this change will help equalize the performance of the subgroup and the addition of time will add to the stability of the results.
- Subgroups under Title I, including ELLs, students with disabilities, racial minorities, and students in poverty, are to be disaggregated and reported by state test data as in prior years.
- For each subgroup of students, states are to design long-term goals and measurement of interim progress on academic achievement and graduation rates.

In addition, under the ESSA annual language proficiency testing will continue to mark the progress of K-12 ELLs in reaching a state's designation of English language proficiency.

REFLECTION

Improving Opportunities for ELLs?

Research has repeatedly shown that acquiring an additional language (in this case, English) within the context of American schooling is a lengthy process. It generally takes 4 to 10 years for ELLs to reach academic parity with their proficient English peers. That said, how do you respond to the amended provisions for ELLs under the ESSA? Do you believe that the ESSA brings student subpopulations closer to educational equity? Do you believe that there is fairer treatment of these students? Why or why not?

The Next Generation of Achievement Testing

With the launch of college and career readiness standards in 2010 has come a cry for assessment with corresponding content and rigor. Yet, once again, the inherent problems related to achievement testing surface for ELLs, for when "large-scale academic content assessment [is] primarily developed for and field tested on native speakers of English and those proficient in academic English, the outcomes for ELLs may not be reliable and valid" (Abedi & Linquanti, 2012). The academic language competencies inherent in these standards are indeed challenging, and when it comes time for assessment, it is important to be able to tease out extraneous language demands on the students so as not to corrupt the content that is being measured.

REFLECTION

Assessing the Impact of Language on Achievement Testing for English Language Learners

As educators, how do we begin to tackle the enormous issue of determining the effects of academic language on achievement testing, especially when the stakes are so high for ELLs and other subgroups? How do we implement reform efforts to reduce the amount of achievement testing in schools to positively impact language learners, particularly ELLs?

It is understood that a test *in* English is a test *of* English for ELLs until they reach a level of English language proficiency where language no longer masks their academic achievement. To mitigate the effects of language on their content tests, test consortia and states have developed a set of accessibility features and accommodations. The assessment consortia that measure achievement have taken slightly different stances, however, on how to approach this issue.

Accessibility and Accommodations for Achievement Tests

In 2010, the U.S. Department of Education awarded millions of dollars to groups of states that formed two consortia, the Partnership for Assessment of Readiness for College and Careers (PARCC) and the Smarter Balanced Assessment Consortium (SBAC), which were charged with the development of a comprehensive assessment system. Test development in reading/language arts and mathematics has been undertaken from a position of universal design inclusive of all students. Universal design is a set of principles that applies to the use of "products and environments (including educational testing) for all individuals to the greatest extent possible without the need for adaptation or specialized design" (Connell et al., 1997). As a result of the desire to maximize students' potential for success, accessibility features are either embedded within a test, often digitally, or are provided by test administrators. However, the advantages of including these features are negated if students do not have opportunities to practice using them prior to actual test administration.

In combination with universal design requirements, PARCC claims its "comprehensive accessibilities guidelines ensure . . . that all task/items are bias-free, sensitive to diverse cultures, stated clearly, of appropriate linguistic complexity, and consistently formatted" (2014, p. 16). For Smarter Balanced, "the overarching goal (of accessibility) is to provide every student with a positive and productive assessment experience, generating results that are a fair and accurate estimate of each student's achievement" (2014, p. 6).

So far, so good, you say? Now let's go on to part two, accommodations. As specified, accommodations are "considered to be adjustments to the testing conditions, test format, or test administration that provide equitable access during assessments for students with disabilities and who are English learners" (PARCC, 2014, p. 28). Accommodations are to be valid and not to alter the construct that is being measured. ELLs who have individualized education plans (IEPs) are dually identified, therefore, they are eligible for both sets of accommodations. Interestingly, for Smarter Balanced, accommodations are only designated for special education students with IEPs or 504 plans. All students, including ELLs and ELLs with disabilities, can be afforded universal tools and designated supports, as appropriate. Resource 7.1 at the end of the chapter is a worksheet for you to list and compare the accommodations for ELLs and ELLs with disabilities for your state annual assessments.

The vast majority of students identified as ELLs with disabilities should be working on the grade-level, standards-based curriculum in the mainstream classroom. When testing ELLs, there are several considerations that should be taken into account before deciding on the most appropriate designated supports or accommodations. These factors should include a student's (a) time in the United States, (b) level of language proficiency, (c) level of literacy, (d) instruction in the home language for a particular content area, (e) experience with technology, and (f) documented disability, if applicable.

REFLECTION

Determining Accessibility and Accommodations for Achievement Tests for English Language Learners

Whether your state is a member of either of the content assessment consortia or is independently developing achievement tests, questions of accessibility and accommodations must be addressed for students with disabilities, ELLs, and ELLs with disabilities. What is the policy of your state regarding these issues? Do you agree or disagree with it? Why or why not? What can you or your professional learning team do to maximize students' opportunities to demonstrate their true achievement?

Practice Items From the Next Generation of Testing: Language Implications

In anticipation of states administering achievement tests that are aligned with college and career readiness standards, two consortia have released sample items. To better understand the complexity of language in content assessment, below are a couple of sample reading/language arts texts and mathematics items.

English Language Arts

Let's revisit some of the tenets of the content assessment consortia in light of sample English language arts texts. To reiterate, the PARCC consortium asserts that their items are "bias-free, sensitive to diverse cultures, stated clearly, and of appropriate linguistic complexity." Read the following excerpt with fifth-grade language learners, particularly ELLs, in mind to see if you agree with these claims and, if not, note the evidence in the text to produce counterclaims. Italicized phrases (personally added) in the passage emphasize a sampling of the key concepts, contexts for understanding the passage, linguistic structures, and words/phrases students are expected to comprehend in processing this biographical text. One illustration of text complexity is the use of complex noun phrases, a compact series of nouns and adjectives that add to the linguistic density of text. For example, "professional learning community" is a structure quite unique to English. See how many instances of complex noun phases you or a group of teachers can uncover in the passage.

Life in the Limbs by Heather Kaufman-Peters

Imagine *stepping out* your front door to find yourself 40 feet above the ground overlooking *a dense forest* and *a winding stream*. Instead of *hopping* on your bike, *you grab the handles of your very own zipline* and fly 1000 yards over a pond, landing safely on the *far bank*.

Sound crazy? Not to Jonathan Fairoaks, who lives in *a four-story tree house* that he designed and built! In fact, as *a tree house architect*, Jonathan has built more than 380 *custom tree houses* across the United States.

Jonathan's love of *tree-house living* began when he was a kid. He started climbing trees when he was 10 years old, and he became an arborist *(a person who cares for trees)* in high school. He built his first tree house and lived in it while he was in college.

"It was delightful—*like being on a ship* because it moved with the wind," Jonathan says. "It was the most fun I ever had."

Designing *unique tree houses* may *sound tough*, but Jonathan says *it's no sweat*. "I let the trees decide the designs," he says. "Hardwoods such as oak, maple, or hickory make the best trees for houses—but I did once build a wonderful tree house in a crabapple tree."

"If you want a bigger tree house than the tree can support," he adds, "*you can use braces.* My tree house is in two trees—an oak and a fir—and has three posts to support the weight."

As a certified arborist, Jonathan tries to never harm the trees.

"I build a tree house so it helps the tree," he says. "*The tree's center of gravity is at the top and the ends of its branches, so I build a house down at the center of the tree, which shifts the center of gravity and makes the tree more balanced.*"

Source: Retrieved from http://oldtappanschools.org/cms/lib6/NJ01000542/Centricity/Domain/191/2Grade5Reading Passage.pdf

If you were to deconstruct the sentence structures in this narrative, you would come across a whole series of complex noun phrases. Here are the complex noun phrases found in this short story; imagine how a 10-year-old attempting to navigate this text might interpret their meaning.

- His first tree house
- A bigger tree house
- A tree house architect
- Tree-house living
- Custom tree houses
- Unique tree houses
- A wonderful tree house
- A four-story tree house

Here's another sample fourth-grade text—an historical fiction story to be specific. Again, take some time to analyze it in light of its academic language demands, especially for ELLs or ELLs with disabilities. Some of the phrases and sentences have been italicized to highlight examples of linguistic complexity.

Grandma Ruth

Last night I learned that my grandma was named after Babe Ruth, the greatest baseball player of all time. I learned this six hours *too late.*

Yesterday I wanted to work on throwing a baseball. I needed a baseball, since my brother wouldn't let me borrow his. *Unfortunately, I knew right where one was.*

I tiptoed into my grandma's bedroom. *Sunlight from the late morning sun filtered in* through the leaves of the dogwood tree outside the open window. I moved slowly through my favorite room in the house, *which belonged to my favorite person in the world, my grandma.*

I reached into the back of her closet and pulled out a shoebox full of old baseballs wrapped in tissue paper. I shoved my hand in and grabbed the first one I touched. *I threw off the paper and ran out into the yard with our dog, Bowie, who would always play a game of catch with me.*

We had a spectacular game of catch. By the end of our session I was throwing *straight as an arrow* and Bowie was bringing it back as fast as he could. It was perfect.

I went back into my grandma's room and *wrapped the ball back up* in paper, just like I'd found it. Except now it looked dirty and used, like a good baseball should.

At dinner, though, I heard the story.

"Have I ever told you that I'm named after the greatest baseball player who ever lived?" Grandma asked suddenly.

James and I shook our heads. We leaned forward to listen. It isn't often we hear new stories from her.

My grandmother stood up and walked into her bedroom. She came back with the shoebox in her hands. She sat down and started her story.

"So, your great-grandfather was the dentist for the *Detroit Tigers* back in the 1920s. His favorite player was Ty Cobb, the best player *the Tigers* have ever had. *When Ty found out that your great-grandparents were going to have a baby, he brought your great-grandfather a big package full of baseballs signed by the best-known players of the time.* He said, 'Doc, you can have these under one condition: name your daughter Tyrina. After me.' And my father, too excited to say no, agreed.

"*When my mother heard about this she told my father to go to Ty Cobb and give him back the baseballs, because she had her own ideas for names.* Ty just laughed when he heard this. He said to my father, 'Doc, I'll tell you what: keep the baseballs but name her after my good friend Babe Ruth.'

"My father smiled and said, 'I'll see what I can do. Keep these for me until then.'

"It turned out my mother loved the name Ruth. That's how I got my name and how my father got these: he let Ty Cobb name me after Babe Ruth."

I tried to swallow but couldn't. I hoped that she wasn't going to say what I thought she was going to say. Then she said it.

"In this shoebox are the ten baseballs Ty Cobb gave my father. They are signed by some of the most famous ballplayers in history, including one that has one single signature on it: Babe Ruth's."

My grandma pulled the ball out, unwrapped it, and held it out for us to see. The ball was scarred almost beyond recognition. It had dog bite marks, *dirt scuffs, and fraying seams*. Right in the middle was a big signature in black ink that I had somehow overlooked. It was smudged now and faded, but it still clearly said "Babe Ruth." I began to shake inside.

But my grandma just looked at the ball and smiled sweetly. She said softly, "Even though it doesn't look like much, this ball has brought our family a lot of joy in its time. I remember when I was your age, Naomi, *I almost rubbed the signature right off from tossing it up and down all the time*. You see, I've always felt that a baseball should be used for a lot more than looking. My dad, your great-grandfather, used to say the same thing."

She lowered her hand and gently tossed the ball toward Bowie, sleeping by the door. It rolled in a perfectly straight line and came to rest softly between the dog's paws. A perfect throw.

Source: Retrieved from http://sampleitems.smarterbalanced.org/itempreview/sbac/ELA.htm.

In analyzing any text, it might be helpful to first think about the sociocultural context in which it is situated. By having a sense of the situational context, teachers can then readily see if the text matches the students' cultural and experiential backgrounds. Let's think about the sociocultural assumptions that are implied in the "Grandma Ruth" narrative. See if you agree that sociocultural context is truly a lens for interpreting the meaning of text. Remember, the students reading this text are 9 years old.

The sociocultural context for "Grandma Ruth" includes the following assumptions:

- Baseball is a favorite American past time.
- The Detroit Tigers is a baseball team.
- Babe Ruth and Ty Cobb are famous baseball players.
- Old baseballs that are signed by famous players are valuable.
- People make collections of valuable things and their value tends to increase if they are not used.
- Some people are named after famous athletes that have passed away.

REFLECTION

Determining Accessibility of Complex Texts for English Language Learners

As teachers, how would you rate the accessibility of these two texts? What specifically (e.g., types of sentences, idiomatic expressions, words with multiple meanings, context for the story) do you think either facilitates or inhibits accessibility for ELLs? What are the implications for assessment, especially for ELLs?

Mathematics

Analysis and interpretation of grade-level mathematics embedded in word problems is often a challenge for students. In this sample item, think about the sociocultural context in which the problem is based and then compare it to the students' experiential backgrounds. Are they compatible? To what extent do you think that the number line is or is not a support for students?

Grade Band 3-5

Students are running in a relay race. Each team will run a total of 2 miles.

Each member of a team will run $\frac{1}{5}$ of a mile.

How many students will a team need to complete the race?

Choose the correct number.

You may use the number line to help find your answer.

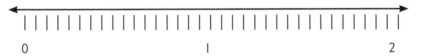

0   1   2

How many students will a team need to complete the race?

$\frac{5}{2}$ $\frac{5}{2}$ 9   10   20

Source: Retrieved from http://www.parcconline.org/sites/parcc/files/Grade4-FractionComparison.pdf

---

REFLECTION

Complicating Mathematics for Language Learners

Take some time to explore additional mathematics word problems for your grade or for the courses that you teach. Based on mathematics sample items on achievement tests, identify issues outside of mathematics that students face when solving text-based problems.

Recent research that has focused on improving the testing experience of ELLs is a cause for optimism (Kopriva & Sexton, 2011). With so much technology at educators' fingertips, new ways are opening up to explore what students are able to do to demonstrate their conceptual understanding. Let's take a look at some of these new methods.

Innovative Testlets in Mathematics and Science

The next generation of content assessment initiated in 2015 still may not adequately or accurately reflect what ELLs can do. There are other means and measures that hold promise, however. One such effort is the ongoing research on technology-driven prototypes for ELL content assessment, both on a large-scale and a classroom basis. It provides insight into text-alternative ways for students to demonstrate their conceptual understanding in the content areas of mathematics and science.

In this conceptual model, test items are multimodal, consisting of simulations, animations, image rollovers, sound, and interactive sequences. The performance tasks reflect grade-level topics, and their interpretive score reports are delivered electronically in real time. Much of this research has come from the Institute for Innovative Assessment, which is housed at the Wisconsin Center for Education Research. This innovative approach to assessing challenging grade-level content while minimizing language dependence opens up possibilities for students who may have the conceptual background but not the extensive repertoire of language— that is, an ample amount of English—to express it.

Another means to tap ELLs' conceptual development is through their home language. Spanish language arts standards and aligned assessment afford teachers of mathematics and language arts another pathway to lead students to academic success.

Spanish Language Arts Standards and Assessment

Spanish language arts standards define the knowledge, concepts, and skills for students whose language and literacy instruction is in Spanish; they are analogous to English language arts standards. Several states, organizations, and consortia have been involved in the development of Spanish language arts standards, including WIDA (2005), the state of Texas (2009), and the Mid-Atlantic Equity Center (2011) for the District of Columbia. The California *Common Core State Standards in Language Arts and Literacy in History/Social Studies, Science, and Technical Subjects: Spanish Language Version* provides a one-to-one correspondence with the CCSS. It has been linguistically augmented to guide equitable assessment and curriculum in Spanish with the vision of student attainment of high levels of biliteracy.

Language learners in dual language programs must have representation and balance of measures for the languages of instruction at the classroom and district levels. Below are some questions to consider when reviewing standards-referenced achievement tests in Spanish and other languages. They center on the equitable inclusion of ELLs and the other group of language learners (in large part, Spanish Language Learners) throughout the development process.

- In your professional judgment, do you consider content-area assessment at both the state and district levels equitable for ELLs?
- To what extent is transadaptation—that is, a translation of items that takes into account the unique linguistic and cultural characteristics of Spanish or a language other than English—used and if so, is it appropriate?
- To what extent is the test aligned to high achievement standards and classroom practices?
- Have there been a content review as well as a bias and sensitivity review of the measures?
- Have experienced and knowledgeable teachers with language expertise in Spanish (or other languages for other achievement tests) been included in the development and review processes?
- Are the test items relevant, developmentally and experientially appropriate, with universal access?

- Have there been cognitive labs, pilot testing, and field testing on each form completed on a representative sampling of students?
- Are multiple linguistic and cultural (Spanish) communities represented in the student samples and are there sizeable numbers of students in each group?
- Has there been a separate standards setting for each major language group?
- Do the data fulfill the designated purpose of the test and are decisions made in a timely fashion?
- Do you consider the test to be a valid indicator of what language learners can do?

REFLECTION

Ensuring the Validity of State or Commercial Achievement Tests

Think about converting the above questions into a checklist or a rating scale. Either individually or as a professional learning team, use a technical manual from your state or district achievement test and determine whether the measure is valid for ELLs. Make sure you create an argument with evidence so that you can defend your response.

The Next Generation of Assessment for Students With Significant Cognitive Disabilities

After the awarding of a federal grant in 2010, two assessment consortia for students with significant cognitive disabilities were formed. The alternate assessment system created by Dynamic Learning Maps (DLM) lets these students show what they know using means other than multiple-choice tests. DLM's Essential Elements represent and are aligned to college and career readiness standards. Data are collected during instruction throughout the year using embedded items and tasks.

The second consortium, the National Center and State Collaborative (NCSC), offers an end-of-year assessment for English language arts and mathematics referenced to alternate achievement standards for students with significant cognitive disabilities. Its wiki provides curricular and instructional resources based on its Core Content Connectors. The secure test, given in grades 3–8 and 11, with stage-adaptive delivery over several weeks, relies heavily on multiple-choice items. Like the other assessment consortia, spring 2015 was the time set for its first operational administration.

With initial funding secured through a federal grant, WIDA first administered Alternate ACCESS, an English language proficiency test designed specifically for ELLs with significant cognitive disabilities in grades 1–12, during the 2012–2013 school year. As stipulated in the ESEA and the IDEA (the Individuals with Disabilities Education Act), all students who are identified as ELLs, including students who receive special education services, are to be assessed annually for English language proficiency. There are tutorials on test administration, webinars on score reports, and interpretive guides that inform teachers on how to use the test results.

The Next Generation of English Language Proficiency Tests

Of the six assessment consortia, WIDA, created from the first federal Enhanced Assessment Grant in 2002, is the consortium with the longest history and the deepest resources. Its mission, "to advance academic language development and academic achievement for linguistically diverse students through high-quality standards, assessments, research, and professional learning for educators," and its principal value, "believing in the assets, contributions, and potential of linguistically diverse students" drive its expansive, standards-centered work forward. Its English language development standards, first formulated in 2004, have served as the anchor for its language proficiency test, ACCESS for ELLs, which as of 2015–2016 will be moving online as ACCESS for ELLs 2.0.

English Language Proficiency Assessment for the 21st Century (ELPA21) is the other consortium building a new language proficiency assessment based on its English language proficiency standards. Formed in 2011 from a round of federal funding, it addresses the language demands needed for ELLs to reach college and career readiness. According to ELPA21's mission statement, the consortium acknowledges the "diverse and rich languages experiences ELLs bring to school," and

> we recognize their English language proficiency is constantly growing. ELPA21 measures that growth based on its new English Language Proficiency Standards and provides valuable information that informs instruction and facilitates academic English proficiency so that all ELLs leave high school prepared for college and career success.

Four states with the largest numbers of ELLs have chosen to remain independent and to create their own English language proficiency/development standards and English language proficiency tests. Arizona, California, New York, and Texas, which contain the lion's share of the over 5 million ELLs in the United States, have each designed a unique statewide system.

Standardized English language proficiency tests, besides being a required response to a federal mandate and a major contributor to state accountability, are of substantive value for ELLs. First, an educator's knowledge of an ELL's composite language proficiency level and all the configurations of combined language domains (i.e., receptive language, productive language, literacy, oral language, and comprehension) assists in the placement of that ELL. Additionally, using the same metric or common measure from year to year allows districts and states to measure ELLs' annual progress and attainment of English language proficiency, which is used for reclassification purposes. Lastly, results from standardized language proficiency tests help inform students' academic achievement (Wolf, Guzman-Orth, & Hauck, 2014).

Practice Items From the Next Generation of English Language Proficiency Tests

ELPA21 and the WIDA Consortia have posted a smattering of sample items on their Web sites for the public to view. For ELPA21, items can be seen at http://www .elpa21.org/assessment-system/sample-items, and for WIDA's ACCESS 2.0 for ELLs, sample items for the public as well as a sample test are available at https:// www.wida.us/assessment/access20-prep.aspx. The samples for both consortia address each grade level cluster and contain some examples from the language domains of listening, speaking, reading, and writing.

The following two sample items are from WIDA's ACCESS 2.0 for ELLs. The receptive language items (listening and reading) are multiple choice. The illustrated item posted for grades 2-3 for Tier C, the most advanced ELLs, for reading in the language of mathematics is:

> Ji-hoon wants to buy a toy at the fair. Ji-hoon can buy a toy that costs more than $0.50 but less than $1.00. Look at the price list. Which items can Ji-hoon buy?
>
> (Note: Although there are four possible responses of different prices, the answer is contingent on the student processing the phrase "less than," not on a mathematical calculation.)

The productive language items (speaking and writing) are performance based. Here is an illustrated sample writing item for grades 6-8, Tier B/C (the diagram is not included below). The topic of this language of science item is "Measuring Boiling Points."

> Camila needs to use all the equipment in the materials list to heat three liquids and record their boiling points. Look at the diagram showing the assembled equipment. Write a paragraph of at least 8 sentences explaining how Camila will use the equipment to find out which of the liquids has the highest boiling point.
>
> (Note: The response to this item is to be an explanation based on the step-by-step process for determining boiling points, not what they are for each liquid.)

The vast majority of ELLs with disabilities (except for the 1% with significant cognitive disabilities) are to participate in the annual language proficiency test. How can we expect ELLs with disabilities to access and process items on state or consortium language proficiency tests?

Accessibility Features and Accommodations for English Language Proficiency Tests

The same principles of accessibility and accommodations for achievement tests apply to language proficiency tests, but the student population is exclusively ELLs. In other words, accessibility or universal features for state English language proficiency tests apply to all ELLs, and accommodations are only afforded to those ELLs with disabilities where they are stated in their IEPs or 504 plans.

There are accessibility and accommodation guidelines for ACCESS for ELLs 2.0 included with its comparable paper and computer forms. Additionally, a host of accessibility features and accommodations are described on its Web site at https://www.wida.us/assessment/access20-prep.aspx. ELPA21 also has an accessibility and accommodations manual in which it recognizes three categories of features for ELLs and ELLs with disabilities:

- Universal features that are embedded and nonembedded in the test
- Designated features that are embedded and nonembedded in the test
- Accommodations for ELLs with IEPs or 504 plans.

Figure 7.4 gives a glimpse into these features for ELLs and ELLs with disabilities for consortia annual English language proficiency tests.

Figure 7.4 A Sampling of Accessibility Features for ELLs and Accommodations for ELLs With Disabilities for Annual English Language Proficiency Testing

Accessibility-Designated Features for All ELLs	Accommodations for ELLs With Disabilities With IEPs or 504 Plans
• Accessibility/embedded designated tools, including highlighters, line guides, magnifiers, color overlays, answer masking, color contrast, magnifying glass, spell check • Test administration procedures, including using familiar school personnel to administer the assessment; administering the assessment individually or in a small group, or in a separate room; providing frequent supervised breaks; or allowing students to take the assessment in short segments.	• Responses scribed by test administrator while the student dictates responses orally or points to the responses • Responses from students using assistive technology • Responses by students using Braille writers or Braille note takers, using recording devices, or using external augmentative and alternative communication device or software • Large-print test booklets

Source: WIDA, 2015, pp. 6 & 14, p. 6. © Board of Regents of the University of Wisconsin System, on behalf of the WIDA Consortium, www.wida.us and ELPA21, 2014.

REFLECTION

Deciphering Terminology

This next generation of standards and assessment has ushered in a revised glossary of terms. What does accessibility mean for achievement testing and how does it differ from that of language proficiency testing for ELLs? How might you explain the difference between accessibility features and accommodations to family members or student advocates?

Approaching State Accountability Systems

It would be remiss in a book devoted to assessment not to mention its role in educational accountability and the contribution of assessment *of* learning to state and federal policymaking. As a nation, we are in the midst of challenging the test-based policies of the past umpteen years that have been pervasive in educator evaluation systems and in the evaluation of teacher preparation programs. It appears that the widespread negative consequences of these policies have not succeeded in driving greater learning and achievement of our students. We must strive for a more equitable solution.

These counterproductive policies have been offset, to some extent, by the use of multiple measures that embrace a broader set of learning goals. Additionally, this variety of measures recognizes important aspects of successful schools that cannot be measured with standardized tests. In essence, we are shifting our reliance on testing to assessment inclusive of data from other sources. We must be cautious that only documented, valid evidence is used for making decisions and policies. Extra steps in the process are important to ensure equity for ELLs and ELLs with disabilities based on soundness of the measures, relevance of the results, and usability of the data.

A different method has been proposed for accountability that holds some promise. It rests on school self-evaluations coupled with inspection from external accountability teams. It has the advantage of being more inclusive and less likely to distort teaching and learning. It comes, however, with concerns of cost.

No evaluation system by itself is capable of overcoming the shortcomings of a school, community, or district that lacks resources. In his 2015 policy brief William Mathis concludes with a set of recommendations for planning and implementing well-rounded accountability systems. It gives us some thinking points in that it encourages policymakers to

- offer students opportunities and resources to achieve each state's goals;
- continue development and validation of multiple measures that strive for balance and clarity;
- apply use of standardized test scores with caution and only in combination with other data;
- avoid data aggregation that results in a single score or an assigned grade;
- develop expert school visitation teams;
- refocus external reviews of schools and districts on guidance and support rather than sanctions; and
- insist on the involvement of multiple stakeholders, from families to administrators, in state level evaluation/accountability.

Assessment *as, for,* and *of* learning is a vision for enacting equitable education practices. From student voice to teacher input to legislative policy, assessment seems to be impacting all facets of schooling today. While ELLs have double the work (Short & Fitzsimmons, 2007) to demonstrate both their academic language proficiency and achievement, they also have double the assessment. And ELLs in dual language programs in the process of developing two languages must demonstrate progress and growth four times over. By balancing assessment *of* learning with assessment *as* and *for* learning, we will come to value students, teachers, and administrators as important data sources and contributors to successful schools of the 21st century.

REACTION AND REFLECTION

Assessment *of* learning plays a critical role when it comes to district and state accountability. In this chapter we have addressed interim measures as well as annual achievement and English language proficiency tests. As the stakes are higher in these forms of assessment, so must be the reliability and validity of the measures. In order to maintain the standardization of administration across schools, districts, and states, there are many guidelines and procedures to follow. What are teachers and school leaders to do? Here are some questions to think about and to help you reflect on your assessment *of* learning experiences.

- How have your students been impacted by interim measures and high-stakes achievement tests? What have you, your professional learning communities, teacher unions, or district administration done to counteract the negative effects of these measures on ELLs?

- If your school or district uses interim or benchmark measures, do you believe that they have made a difference in regard to using the data to inform your instruction? To what extent do they provide you with relevant data?
- Imposing accessibility features and accommodations on tests should not be a one-time event. Rather, whichever ones are either selected or identified in students' IEPs or 504 plans must be incorporated into instructional practices all year. Do you follow that guidance? If not, what can you do in the future to ensure that these students indeed are advantaged by those supports?
- The focus of this book is on equity—assessment equity. Now that you realize all forms of assessment hold the potential to contribute to a balanced system that serves multiple stakeholders for multiple reasons, how can you or your professional learning team be proactive in using the data from each form to create a comprehensive portrait of your students? With your team, try to develop an action plan to move your thinking forward.
- If you or your team were to design an ideal accountability system at the federal, state, or district level, what would it look like? What components would it entail and how would you make sure its impact would be positive for all stakeholders?

RESOURCE 7.1

Accommodations for English Language Learners on Annual State Tests

English language proficiency and academic achievement are different constructs, and the accommodations for assessment should be unique. What are the accommodations for ELLs for your state's annual achievement test? Likewise, what are the accommodations for your state's annual language proficiency test for ELLs with disabilities, and how are they different from those of the achievement test for ELLs with disabilities? Fill in each box and then compare your findings.

Accommodations for ELLs With Disabilities for the Annual Language Proficiency Test	
Accommodations for ELLs for the Annual Achievement Test	**Accommodations for ELLs With Disabilities for the Annual Achievement Test**

8

Assessment Results: Feedback, Standards-Referenced Grading, and Reporting

The Bridge to Sustained Educational Equity

Feedback is the breakfast of champions.

—Ken Blanchard

In the assessment model *as, for,* and *of* learning, where is the place of grading? When is grading appropriate and when is it not? Should feedback to students and by students contribute to grading? How do we report evidence that is accumulated over time in a standards-referenced system? And finally—and perhaps trickiest—how do we place a value on teaching and learning when it merges with evaluation?

Interestingly, Black and Wiliam's (1998) seminal research on formative assessment (inclusive of *as* and *for* learning) concludes that grades are not as effective as feedback and, in some cases, may even be counterproductive. Overall, comments

219

specifically tailored to students seem to have a more positive impact on their learning and thus improve their achievement. Black and Wiliam's claim, which is backed by evidence from their meta-analysis, is that good feedback is at the heart of good pedagogy.

Researchers have also found that the quality of feedback is of critical importance. Offering feedback is quite a complex process as it entails teachers (a) attending to an individual student's performance, (b) appraising the student's output against some reference, (c) identifying the student's strengths and weaknesses, and (d) responding to individual students. This process is invariably comparative and reflects teachers' judgment; it results in teachers giving students grades, marks on a rubric, or verbal or written responses (Sadler, 1998).

This chapter takes the stance that grading is inevitably part of life but its negative, punitive effects on students have to be eliminated. It highlights how standards-referenced feedback, grading, and reporting can be designed to reflect the *accomplishments* of students, not their failings. While grading tends to fall within teachers' responsibilities, reporting encompasses how grades are communicated to stakeholders—the students and their family members (Muñoz & Guskey, 2015). Reporting offers the opportunity for teachers and students to meaningfully interact with each other and decide on how to move forward together.

Moving past grading as the primary form of interpreting assessment results, we suggest how to promote more equitable teaching and learning through assessment portfolios. Ideally maintained in digitized form, assessment portfolios provide a means of accumulating and storing reliable and valid documentation of students' language development and academic achievement over time. Ultimately, educational equity can only be sustained if we as educators believe in the potential of our schools as change agents and judge students on their individual merits rather than on numbers or letters.

THE ISSUE OF GRADING

Grading as a form of individual student accountability has always gone hand in hand with schooling; it is very much ingrained in our educational system. Although the standards movement has shifted our focus and the criteria we use, grading is inevitably a mainstay of American education. As school districts and teachers are painstakingly restructuring classroom assessment, curriculum, and instruction to meet high academic standards, grading practices are following suit to become more standards referenced.

Grading, in many ways, tends to perpetuate inequity. We need to discard our antiquated methodologies and mindsets to prepare twenty-first-century students for twenty-first-century schools. Rethinking grading can be an incredibly powerful lever for strengthening equity in every facet of teaching and learning. As grading practices exert enormous influence on students' motivation to learn, especially that of students who have been historically underserved, improving the accuracy, fairness, and consistency of grading lends itself to opening the door to equity (Feldman, 2015).

For some, teachers giving grades is considered a type of normative feedback that is reflective of a student's performance in reference to others in the class (Marzano,

2010, for example). Normative feedback, although still commonplace, defeats the intent of improving learning. For others, grades are never to be thought of as formative feedback but rather feedback should be focused on the instructional task (Heritage, 2010, for one). When learners realize that feedback is partly cohort dependent and that they are being judged against their peers, it can be interpreted as personal criticism. Instead, both teachers and students need to focus on constructive feedback based on established criteria for success so that feedback pushes learning forward and becomes ingrained in the classroom and school culture.

REFLECTION

Weighing in on Grading Versus Feedback

Assessment *for* learning is often viewed as a grade-free zone where student-centered and teacher-directed feedback is geared to improving teaching and learning. Where do you or your grade-level team stand on this issue? What is your school's stance on grading versus feedback? If you and your school are at odds in regards to the role of grading, what might you suggest as a compromise?

To Grade or Not to Grade? The Compatibility of Grading With Assessment *as* and *for* Learning

There seems to be a dividing line on the issue of student grading. On one side are those who feel that grading is antithetical to the idea of assessment *for* learning (or assessment for formative purposes). The most ardent oppositionist is Alfie Kohn (2011), whose position is to eliminate grades altogether. In the opposite corner are those who believe that grading is a form of feedback for students, such as Douglas Reeves (2008).

Teachers can best resolve the ongoing controversy of grading—in fact, in some instances it might be a holdout for individual teacher discretion. Teachers bring expertise to instructional assessment and have expectations about what each student should be able to produce in response to the instructional assessment task. Many use criteria and grade-level standards to validate their personal thinking. Additionally, teachers are also beginning to consider the influence of students' academic language use on the expression of their content knowledge and to separate language proficiency and achievement from other classroom expectations, such as an attendance policy, or student behaviors, such as effort or participation. When grading is more accurate and equitable, students feel empowered with more control over their outcomes.

Teachers who believe that grading should reflect growth in language development or academic progress toward standards may include data from assessment *for* learning in their determination of grades. The value placed on classroom data varies among teachers and rightfully so. Keep in mind that counting some formative assessment data in grading helps to more fairly reflect the learning of students who are challenged by more traditional testing formats or who experience test anxiety. The bottom line is while the universe of classroom activity may be open for assessment, not all data have to be graded (Greenstein, 2010).

> **REFLECTION**
>
> ### Determining What Counts in Grading
>
> Here are some typical classroom activities that generate data from assessment *as* and *for* learning:
>
> - Learning logs
> - Anecdotal notes from teacher observations
> - Oral questioning by peers or teachers
> - Think-alouds
> - Graphic organizers, such as semantic webs or Venn diagrams
> - Interactive journals
>
> The question becomes, should any of the products from these classroom activities factor into grading? If so, which ones and why? Compare your thoughts with those of your colleagues to see the extent of your agreement.

Setting Learning Goals to Anchor Grading Practices

Just as all students should be engaged in formulating learning targets for each curricular unit, so should every student have individual learning goals. Teachers may guide students in setting learning goals for content and language based on specific criteria. Content goals should be derived from high academic standards, such as college and career readiness standards, and content targets, while goals for language learning should be based on language proficiency/development standards and language targets (Gottlieb, 2012a).

Learning goals tend to be quite global in nature and geared toward students' use of academic language over a quarter of a year or even a semester. If the school or district report card happens to have a narrative section, this might be a place to share a student's learning goals. Sample learning goals for upper elementary and middle school might resemble the following:

A Sample Content Goal: "I will research controversial topics, state my opinions or claims, and identify evidence to match my opinions or claims."
A Sample Language Goal: "I will practice forming opinions and using persuasive language in oral and written arguments."

Depending on the students' age, content and language learning goals can be determined by individual students from several models or in consultation with peers or mentors, including the teacher. This activity might be a motivator for students so that they can more readily see the relationship between standards-referenced criteria and their evidence of learning. The information from learning goals, in turn, helps determine the criteria for grading. Information regarding grading has to be communicated with students at the beginning of each marking period so that there is a common understanding of classroom expectations, procedures, and policies.

Grading is more evaluative in nature than assessment as it relies on the interpretation of data. Often other factors outside of academics are taken into account in determining a grade, such as effort, motivation, and timeliness. At times, these affective factors tend to take precedent over rigorous academic ones. Such can be the case with ELLs.

Giving Grades to English Language Learners

English Language Learners, by definition, have not reached academic parity in English with their English-proficient peers. Due to the increasing numbers of linguistically and culturally diverse students, especially ELLs, in their classrooms, teachers need to carefully reexamine how they make judgments about student performance and provide feedback to students.

So how can grades realistically convey what these students have learned when the language they are in the midst of developing more often than not masks their academic accomplishments? Is there any consideration for an ELL's level of English language proficiency in relation to his or her achievement during grading? What if a truer estimate of what an ELL knows in a content area were to be measured in that student's home language? How can we better promote educational equity for these students?

As teachers, we should think about the factors that influence our grading practices and what we would want to communicate to students about their language learning. Take the following scenario as an example of the dilemma of assigning grades to two ELLs in the same English as an Additional Language (EAL) class.

A Scenario About Grading ELLs

Ana is in an intermediate EAL class in her sprawling high school where the large numbers of ELLs are grouped according to their overall level of English language proficiency. She attends class regularly and always comes on time. However, she is reluctant to participate in classroom activities and completes very few homework assignments. She is attentive but rarely participates in group work or class discussions. Yet she manages to do fairly well on classroom tests, the midterm, and the final exam.

Carlos is another member of this early morning EAL class. Several times during the term he is absent as his job requires him to work late and he tends to oversleep. He tackles each homework assignment and tries his best to complete the assigned work. He makes an effort to engage in classroom activities and consistently contributes to group work. However, his downfall is testing; he just cannot seem to relate content using his new language, especially on the final exam.

At the end of the semester, Ana and Carlos receive a series of marks that form their final grade for this class; these marks are displayed in Figure 8.1. In this instance the teacher uses traditional letter grades from A, the highest, to F, the lowest. The school is just beginning the conversation of how to switch their traditional grading practices to standards-referenced ones to minimize subjectivity and to be able to share specific, common criteria with students.

Figure 8.1 Hypothetical Semester Grades for Two Intermediate-Level High School English Language Learners in the Same Class

	Ana	Carlos
Quizzes, midterm, and final exam	B	D
Classroom-based measures (including contributions to group work)	C	B
Classroom performance (including behavior and attitude)	D	B
Homework assignments	D	B
Attendance	A	C

Source: Adapted from Gottlieb, 2006, p. 171.

REFLECTION

Addressing the Dilemma of Grading ELLs

Based on this scenario, what final grades would you give Ana and Carlos? Discuss your answer and reasoning with other teachers. Are there other factors that influence grading not included in the chart that might influence your thinking?

Actually, it is difficult to determine the semester grade for these students because we only know the components, not the criteria, on which the final grade is based. If teachers use this system, they should relate to students the meaning of each component and how much (in terms of percentage or points) each contributes to the overall grade. As Thomas Guskey and Jane Bailey (2001) have pointed out, the primary goal of grading and reporting is communication and, in this instance, that is not clear. So let's use the next Reflection as an opportunity to convert arbitrary letter grades to more descriptive standards-based reports.

REFLECTION

Clarifying the Meaning of Grades

Let's reexamine Figure 8.1 and ask the following questions about grading in the hopes of more clearly communicating to students what their semester grade might mean.

- Which academic content standards are being assessed and what are the corresponding English language proficiency/development standards?
- Which language domains or combinations of domains or modalities are being assessed: listening, speaking, reading, and/or writing?
- Is there a weight assigned to each standard or language domain that determines its contribution to the grade?
- What are the specific academic expectations for classroom performance and homework assignments?
- Do students have input in helping determine their grades by providing evidence of learning?

The Dilemma of Grading ELLs

In the previous scenario, the two students happened to be at approximately the same level of English language proficiency in a classroom full of ELLs. Yet the stories of their school performance yielded such distinct portraits. In many elementary and middle schools, teachers usually work with groups of much more heterogeneous ELLs that are sprinkled in their classes. The same holds true for schools in rural areas or schools that have small numbers of ELLs. How are teachers expected to make sense out of grading when each student is so unique?

That's just the beginning of the grading controversy. How do teachers grade newly arrived ELLs who are in the same grade and classroom as ones who are ready to transition into general education classes? That is, should the same criteria be used for grading ELLs at language proficiency level 2, who are at the beginning stages of their English language development, as for those who are at language proficiency level 5? How can teachers evaluate students with limited or interrupted education whose circumstances have precluded them from having opportunities to learn? How can teachers distinguish between some students' academic language development and potential learning disabilities? What about ELLs who speak different varieties of English? More importantly, should language development be graded at all?

We differentiate instruction and classroom assessment according to ELLs' proficiencies in English (and their home language), yet often this principle does not extend to grading. Some provision must be made in grading ELLs so they are not punished for not having the necessary English or background knowledge to navigate grade-level text efficiently or write commensurately to their English-proficient peers. For example, students with limited formal schooling cannot be expected to move at the same pace as those ELLs with strong literacy skills and a solid educational foundation. Equally distressing would be to subject ELLs to the identical grading criteria as those who have been raised exclusively in an English-speaking environment.

English Language Learners who are in the early stages of their English language development should be graded within their band of English language proficiency for each language domain and, depending how the curriculum is designed, for each key use of academic language. That is, evaluating ELLs' performance in English should be in relation to descriptors or criteria specific to their language proficiency level. For example, if an ELL is at midrange on the scale, let's say at the Developing level for writing, then grades should reflect the student's performance in relation to the language expectations for that level. The resources for determining these expectations might include the performance definitions of language proficiency/development standards and other state or consortia resources.

Figure 8.2 illustrates how ELLs at language proficiency level 3 demonstrate their progress toward meeting expectations for writing. As you see, grading should not be letters or numbers but rather descriptors of where the students fall within a particular band or level. In this instance, performance definitions for speaking and writing are the basis for formulating the criteria for meeting expectations.

The main purpose for giving grades to ELLs at the higher end of the language proficiency scale is to ascertain the extent to which these students are meeting challenging content standards and approaching academic parity. Thus, grade-level achievement is stressed over progress towards meeting standards. At this stage in their English language development, it is justifiable to use identical criteria for subject-area grading for ELLs and their English-proficient peers.

Figure 8.2 Criteria Associated With Meeting Expectations for Writing for ELLs at Language Proficiency Level 3

Beginning to Exhibit Expectations	*Progressing Toward Expectations*	*Approaching Expectations*	*Meeting Expectations*	*Exceeding Expectations*
Students produce:				
←	←	←	• Discernible discourses • Short and some expanded or compound sentences expressing one or more related ideas • Repetitive grammatical structures across the content areas • Grade-level content-related language	⇒

Source: Adapted from WIDA, 2012, p. 9. © Board of Regents of the University of Wisconsin System, on behalf of the WIDA Consortium. www.wida.us.

REFLECTION

Writing Expectations for ELLs

Obviously you noticed that Figure 8.2 has only been filled in for ELLs who are meeting the criteria represented by the language proficiency/development standards at level 3. Think about a specific grade or grade span. How would your grade-level team or department extend these criteria across the other performance levels? When you reach consensus, you will be on your way to applying a uniform set of criteria for evaluating student work.

Using multiple data sources for grading is appropriate for all students, including ELLs. Reflective of assessment *as* and *for* learning, these sources should be confined to learning within classrooms. However, the relative weight of each form of assessment (or data source) may be adjusted by students' language proficiency levels, teacher discretion, and district policy. In a standards-referenced system, teachers should consider including the following in their grading scheme:

- Student self-assessment (the older the students, the greater responsibility they should take for their own learning) in relation to standards-referenced goals, targets, and objectives
- Performance assessment and common instructional products in which students have opportunities to demonstrate learning through tasks and projects that are interpreted with standards-referenced rubrics populated with shared criteria for success
- Teacher made tests—using both traditional paper-and-pencil and newer digital formats—that are reflective of standards that have been addressed during instruction.

REFLECTION

Contributing to Grading

What are the primary sources for grading in your classroom? Do individual teachers or grade-level or department teams determine these sources or do they reflect school or district policy? If you had your druthers, how would you grade your students, and what specific considerations would there be for ELLs?

Feedback, as we have described in Chapters 5 and 6, is based on criteria for success that have been co-constructed by students and teachers. However, when it comes to grading, other criteria are often applied.

Criteria for Grading in a Standards-Referenced World

According to Tom Guskey and Jane Bailey (2010), diverse sources of evidence are foundational for standards-based approaches to grading. This evidence centers on several types of criteria—namely, those for product, process, and progress learning. Equally important are performance criteria related to language learning.

Product criteria are used for communicating students' achievement over one or more units of learning. They focus on what students produce as an artifact of their learning, such as an authentic performance like a debate, a dramatization, or a reenactment with a twist (think of a fractured fairy tale applied to other content areas as an example). Teachers who use product criteria may also base grades on final projects, such as reports, exhibits, or presentations. Depending on school or district policy, the same standards-referenced criteria can apply either to assessment *for* learning, where students receive oral or written descriptive feedback, or be converted to points in a more traditional grading system.

Process criteria are additional indicators that are used by educators who believe that product criteria are not a sufficient portrayal of student learning. Teachers who take this stance believe that grades should not only reflect the final product of a unit but should also take into account a student's responsibility, effort, or work habits. Therefore, process indicators as part of grading may include classroom quizzes, homework, punctuality of assignment completion, class participation, or attendance.

Progress criteria are tied to measuring how much students gain from their learning experiences; these indicators help determine academic growth over time. Teachers who use progress criteria examine where students begin their journey in terms of their conceptual understanding and how their learning moves forward. Unlike other criteria, progress criteria rely on two data points in order to measure growth rather than relying on a single given moment. Progress criteria may be individualized given that each student starts at a different place—or, put another way, each student has a unique baseline. As a result, while grades might be based on the same content standards, students' expectations will vary as a function of where they are positioned on a standards-attainment continuum.

Performance criteria are also necessary for language learners, in particular ELLs, whose language proficiency may influence their achievement when English is the medium of instruction. Similar to progress criteria, performance criteria take into account an ELL's language proficiency level as a starting place for measuring growth in language development, whether in English or in another language. Teachers need to become familiar with the performance definitions of language proficiency/development standards to gain a sense of the language expectations within and across language domains for each grade or grade span.

REFLECTION

Selecting Criteria for Grading

The above discussion introduces four types of criteria that may be useful for grading purposes. Which ones, if any, do you rely on? Do you think additional factors should be taken into account for grading purposes? If so, which ones and why? How might the criteria apply to certain subgroups of students, such as ELLs with disabilities or gifted and talented ELLs?

When it comes to grading, remember that different types of criteria serve different purposes. Not all criteria are directly related to college and career readiness standards; some encompass the social and emotional well-being of students. Grading must be meaningful to students and their family members. At the same time, it must support standards-based learning. As such, grading, by providing useful information that centers on what language learners can do, becomes a communication tool that facilitates making informed decisions and taking action.

A Report Card for Dual Language Learners

All students are in the midst of learning content and academic language simultaneously. Grades for ELLs and for other language learners in dual language or immersion programs should represent both their language proficiency and academic achievement in the languages of instruction. Figure 8.3 shows one way of displaying grades for dual language learners. With the use of side-by-side columns, teachers, students, and family members are able to see a student's academic performance in relation to his or her language development in English and the other language of instruction. Specific

Figure 8.3 A Sample Standards-Based Report Card for Language Learners Whose Instruction Occurs in Two Languages

Academic Achievement	English	My Other Language	Language Development	English	My Other Language
Language arts			Language of language arts		
Math			Language of math		
Science			Language of science		
Social studies			Language of social studies		

Source: Adapted from Gottlieb, 2006, p. 176.

references to individual college and career readiness standards, other language proficiency/development standards, or additional content areas may easily be added.

> **REFLECTION**
>
> **Adapting Report Cards for English Language Learners**
>
> How might you create a standards-referenced report card based on your high academic standards and language proficiency/development standards for your ELLs or dual language learners? Would you add language domains or combination of domains? Does your professional learning team for your school or district have results from common instructional products that can be aggregated and transferred onto a report card?

There are other tools outside of traditional report cards that are useful for reporting students' growth or progress.

Can Do Descriptors

Formulated and validated by teachers, Can Do Descriptors are task-based examples of what ELLs can do linguistically at a given level of language proficiency. One set of descriptors, developed by WIDA, offers stakeholders, including students, family members, and teachers, concrete examples of the language expectations of ELLs at each level of language proficiency and language domain. While the descriptors serve as a resource that works in tandem with reporting scores on language proficiency measures, they often serve as a tool for the collaboration of content and language teachers in planning differentiated classroom assessment and language instruction.

In 2016 the Can Do Descriptors were reorganized around the key uses of academic language—discuss, explain, argue, and recount. Available in English and Spanish, the descriptors represent standards-referenced classroom activities with a specific language focus. Figure 8.4 provides a slice of the Can Dos from the language domain of speaking in situations where first-grade students are asked to explain something. Note that level 6 corresponds to the expectations of college and career readiness standards.

Portfolios are another resource for maintaining long-term records of student growth and achievement. While they capture assessment *as* and *for* learning, depending on their overall purpose, their contents also may be used for grading students at strategic points during the school year or may contribute to program evaluation.

USING STUDENT PORTFOLIOS FOR ASSESSMENT AND GRADING

Portfolios are representations of student accomplishments in school. There are many different kinds of portfolios (showcase portfolios of best work, pivotal portfolios of most important work, and collections of work samples, to name a few), and each one has a distinct purpose. We limit our discussion here to the assessment portfolio, a systematic

Figure 8.4 Example Can Do Descriptors for Grade 1, Speaking, for the Key Use of Explain

Level 1	Level 2	Level 3	Level 4	Level 5	Level 6
Explain by	**Explain by**	**Explain by**	**Explain by**	**Explain by**	**Explain by**
• Answering questions with words or phrases (e.g., "Go washroom.") • Describing pictures or classroom objects in one or more languages	• Demonstrating how to do something using gestures or real-life objects (e.g., tie a bow) • Describing what people do from action pictures or photos (e.g., jobs of community workers)	• Stating associations between two objects, people, or events • Telling why something happened to peers or adults (e.g., based on videos)	• Connecting ideas by building on guided conversations (such as in logical sequence) with peers • Describing in detail the function of objects or the roles of people (e.g., how to use a microscope)	• Elaborating content-related procedures or cycles in detail (e.g., life of butterflies) • Stating conditions for cause and effect (e.g., "*If* it rains, I play inside") to peers	• Asking and answering content-related *how* and *why* questions in small groups • Expressing connected ideas with supporting details (such as by using sequential language)

Source: WIDA, 2016. © Board of Regents of the University of Wisconsin System, on behalf of the WIDA Consortium. www.wida.us.

collection of the processes and products of original student work and their associated documentation (Gottlieb, 1995), and to how its contents help contribute to grading.

If assessment portfolios are part of a grading scheme in a classroom, school, or district, then certain procedures are necessary to ensure their care, maintenance, and reliability. If all teachers at a given grade are using the identical criteria in evaluating student work and rely on common instructional products as an anchor, then the potential usefulness of portfolios is expanded. A student's assessment portfolio chock-full of data can be helpful for teachers who have students who are

- moving from one grade to the next;
- transferring schools within a district;
- transitioning from language or academic support services;
- being considered for gifted and talented services;
- being considered for prereferral to special education; or
- graduating elementary school or high school.

Throughout this book we have emphasized the importance of assessment *as* and *for* learning and their contribution to our understanding of the whole student. Assessment portfolios offer a means by which this information can be stored and maintained. In this way, there is documentation and evidence (in addition to assessment *of* learning measures) of student progress and accomplishments.

Features of Assessment Portfolios

Educators have been advocating for the use of assessment portfolios since the 1990s as a more equitable lens for measuring ELL performance (Gottlieb, 1995; Farr & Trumbell, 1997; Gómez, 1998; and Richard-Amato & Snow, 2005, to name a few). Portfolios should be designed to simultaneously capture ELLs' language proficiency and academic achievement through performance assessment. Thus, by centering on authentic contexts for teaching and learning, assessment portfolios can showcase the following:

- Learning in a student's home language and/or in English
- Interdependence between oral language and literacy development
- Integration of language and content in student work
- Higher-level thinking through extended tasks and projects
- Mulitliteracies, including the use of technology and multimedia
- Students' personal reflections and self-assessment

Assessment portfolios should be portraits of the students—who they are, what they can do, and how they communicate what they have learned. For grading purposes (especially within a large district), there might be restrictions in terms of the types and numbers of entries required or how student work is interpreted. However, if assessment portfolios are to be valued, students need to have a voice and ownership in their contents.

Contents of Assessment Portfolios

There is tremendous variability in the contents of portfolios and how the samples of student work are selected for assessment and grading purposes. Several stakeholders may be the decision makers in regards to portfolio entries. Students may have a choice, within a set of general guidelines, as to what goes into their portfolios. In this type of assessment portfolio, students may use their portfolios to collect all their original work during a grading period and then select their best or most representative pieces to be graded. When students and teachers both have input, together they may reach a joint decision as to the portfolio's contents, perhaps through a student-led conference. In other cases, teachers or teacher teams may be very systematic and uniform in their selection of standards, student work samples, and rubrics to be used for grading. Finally, a school district may impose how to organize assessment portfolios, directing the types of work samples and rubrics, the timetable for the collection of entries, the inclusion of results from interim and annual measures, and even the determination of the inter-rater reliability among grade-level portfolios as a whole.

In designing assessment portfolios for ELLs, teachers need to consider students' ages, levels of language proficiency, and familiarity with handling the contents. For students with lower levels of English language proficiency or for those who have had limited formal schooling or who have a learning disability, a more structured portfolio is necessary. Once students gain familiarity with the routine of using portfolios as a reservoir of their learning, they can gradually have more freedom in their choices.

REFLECTION

Using a Report Card Format for Portfolios

Do you believe that assessment portfolios and grading are compatible? Why or why not? Should assessment portfolios influence grading? What if standards-related narratives were substituted for grades—would that make assessment portfolios more personalized and meaningful for students?

Example Assessment Portfolios Entries

Assessment portfolios should represent standards, curriculum, and the languages of instruction in proportion to their use. It is important that the portfolios are thoughtfully organized so that there is continuity from marking period to marking period or articulation from year to year. Assessment portfolios that are used for grading ELLs may contain the following entries:

- A dated student summary sheet with student characteristics, teacher and student goals, college and career readiness standards and language proficiency/development standards that have been addressed, and a list of the contents (including scores, if applicable)
- Introduction, including purpose and audience, by the student
- Original samples of student work (both oral and written) referenced to standards with accompanying rubrics or constructive narrative feedback
- Entries that demonstrate students' multiliteracies
- Quizzes and tests, if warranted
- Peer and student self-assessment or reflection on the collective body of work.

REFLECTION

Using Assessment Portfolios

Take this list of potential contents and provide concrete examples of how you and your students might create an assessment portfolio. Use the checklist in Resource 8.1 as your guide. Which entries do you find most relevant? Discuss your conclusions with other teachers at your grade level, in your department, or in your professional learning team.

With assessment portfolios, language learners have opportunities to present evidence of learning in varied formats according to their interests, learning styles, or language proficiency levels. The increased availability of technology affords teachers and students many more choices. Here is a sampling of potential multimedia entries for portfolios that illustrate the integration of content and language learning.

Ideas for Multimedia Entries for Assessment Portfolios

- Digital or scanned writing samples and reflections (stored on a district's server or in the cloud)
- Scanned pieces of creative work that include visual arts saved in individual student files
- PowerPoint, Prezi, or multimedia presentations
- Photographs of student-designed models or exhibits
- Photographs or panoramic videos of collages, murals, or other artistic renderings, along with an oral or written description
- Videos of reenactments, dramatizations, or student interactions
- Audiotapes of oral language samples, oral readings, or think-alouds of metalinguistic or metacognitive strategies
- Student-made videos or movie clips, or use of other technologies
- Evidence of use of computer software programs or computer-based research

---

REPORTING STUDENT PROGRESS IN PORTFOLIO CONFERENCES

Assessment portfolios are the perfect venue for students to showcase their newly acquired language and knowledge as well as to share their accomplishments with others. One-on-one conferences can be arranged at the close of a marking period to organize the contents, review the entries, and set common goals for the coming months. In that way, the grades that are ultimately assigned have personal meaning to the students and their family members.

Guidelines and policies regarding portfolios should fall within the purview of schoolwide professional learning communities. Teachers should have a management plan for portfolios that addresses quantity (how many entries), quality (which rubrics or documentation forms), timing (when entries are to be submitted), and presentation (how to organize the contents—in chronological order, by content area, or by language). Depending on their age, students may create a table of contents and design the cover to reflect their personal interests. Implementation of portfolio use should be embedded in the instructional routine.

Teacher-Student Conferences

Students' involvement in the creation of their portfolios carries over to conferencing with their teachers. For ELLs with mid to high levels of English language proficiency, student-led conferences can be conducted in English or in another language when instruction occurs in that language. For ELLs with lower levels of English language proficiency, the teacher should guide the students. Some key questions should form the basis of the conference. The following scenarios may be adapted by teachers for use with their students.

- "Show me your best work. Tell me why you chose this piece. What did you learn from doing it? Let's look at your goals this marking period. What grade do you think you should get? Why? Show me the evidence that this is the grade you deserve."
- "Show me your portfolio. Tell me what you did in each piece. Which one are you most proud of? Why? What grade do you think you should get for math (or any content area)? What was the goal you were working on? Did you reach it this marking period? What goal should we work on next?"
- "Let's look at your goals this marking period and the criteria for success. How have you improved? Show me a piece from the beginning of the year and one you just finished. Tell me how you are a better reader (listener, speaker, writer, mathematician, scientist). What grade do you think you should get? Why?"

The conference should strengthen individualized instruction and the bond between teacher and student (Farr & Tone, 1994). Afterward, teachers may complete the summary sheet (see Figures 8.5 and 8.6 as an example) to supplement the school's report card. For ELLs, standards-referenced grades or descriptive numerals are entered for the students' language development in English and other languages, as applicable, along with their academic achievement. In addition, there is space for a short narrative based on the evidence of learning. For students in dual language or immersion programs, progress in language development in their additional language should be noted. The back side of the report provides an overall summary of a student's performance based on the integration of content and language standards.

With the emerging trend of having students be more participatory and have agency in their learning, student-led conferences are gaining ground as a means for students to communicate to others and share evidence of their learning.

Student-Led Conferences

Student-led conferences that center on student portfolios occur across the United States and around the globe. For example, the Tokyo International School has students as young as those in kindergarten participate in this event. ELLs at the Taipei American School contribute to standards-based Academic Learning Notebooks, a collaborative partnership among the language teacher, content teacher, and student.

Figure 8.5 Side 1 of a Hypothetical Summary Sheet for an Assessment Portfolio Used for Reporting Grades for ELLs and Dual Language Learners

Student: _____   Grade level: _____

Quarter: _____   Year: _____   Teacher(s): _____

Overall English language proficiency level: _____

Overall (Spanish) language proficiency level: _____

	Language domain (or any combination of domains)	*ELD standard* *SLD or other language development standard*	*ELD standard* *SLD or other language development standard*	*ELD standard* *SLD or other language development standard*	*ELD standard* *SLD or other language development standard*	*Goals and evidence of language learning*
English language development (ELD)	Listening					
	Speaking					
Language development in Spanish (SLD) or another language, if applicable						
	Reading					
	Writing					
	Content area	Content standard	Content standard	Content standard	Content standard	Goals and evidence of content learning:
Academic achievement in English or another language	Language arts					
	Mathematics					
	Science					
	Social studies					

Source: Adapted from Gottlieb, 2006, p. 180.

According to Ron Berger (2014), effective student-led conferences with family members consist of the following features:

- *There are clear agendas and structures.* Students are familiar with the material they are to share and the amount of time of the conference. For linguistically and culturally diverse students whose family members are more comfortable speaking in languages other than English, students should interact in the language or languages of the home.

Figure 8.6 Side 2 of a Summary Sheet: Sample Criteria for a Standards-Referenced Assessment Portfolio

Based on the evidence of learning in the assessment portfolio, mark or circle the cells that indicate whether the student is addressing, approaching, or attaining the integrated set of standards for the language(s) of instruction—in English (E), in another language (OL), or in both.

		1—Addresses Standards	2—Approaches Standards	3—Attains Standards
Language proficiency/ development standards and	E	• Work remains at same level of quality over time. • Emerging evidence of language learning and academic achievement • Skills/concepts/ideas and related language sporadically or loosely linked. • Some reasoning or learning strategies	• Work quality shows clear progress and growth over time. • Moving toward consistent evidence of language learning and academic achievement • Skills/concepts/ideas and related language communicated meaningfully • A variety of reasoning or learning strategies, along with some notion of metacognitive and metalinguistic awareness	• Work quality exemplifies that expressed in grade-level standards. • Strong evidence of language learning and academic achievement • Skills/concepts/ideas and related language integrated and applied to new situations • A repertoire of reasoning or learning strategies, along with metacognitive and metalinguistic awareness
	OL			
Academic content standards	E			
	OL			

Source: Adapted from Gottlieb, 2006, p. 181.

- *Students have multiple opportunities to reflect on and present their work in class.* Students are able to prepare and practice until they are confident in their presentations.
- *A teacher helps each student prepare for the conference.* At the elementary level, the classroom teacher, perhaps in collaboration with others, models and facilitates the process; at the secondary level, perhaps an advisor or counselor provides support.
- *Students show evidence for learning and meeting learning targets.* They explain why they have chosen a course of action and reflect on their personal progress toward meeting their goal.
- *Student portfolios anchor the conference* and the entries tell the story of student growth and learning.
- *Students set goals* for academic and personal growth, with assistance from their teachers and families.
- *Student accomplishments outside school are acknowledged*, including sports, arts, internships, service learning, or community service.
- *School leaders support this effort.* The school or district might create a handbook that includes procedures for student-led conferences so there is uniformity in implementation. The school might devote dedicated time for the conferences and post the schedule in the welcoming packet and on the school's Web site.

Student-led conferences might be folded into or serve as a precursor to portfolio nights where students come to school with family members and share their portfolios. Although assisted by teachers when necessary, students take the lead in preparing their portfolios and developing key questions in English and/or their home language (as applicable) to use when displaying their work samples. In this way, students take pride and ownership in their portfolio, and parents or other family members gain insights into what their children do at school.

Teacher/family member/student conferences are a powerful tool as they nurture relationships among these important stakeholders. In addition, a more complete understanding of the expectations of teaching and learning can be gained by examining student work samples, criteria of success, and goals for learning. As a result of this transparency, there is a building of trust and a commitment to excellence in education.

An interesting occurrence these days is that some districts are resurrecting the notion of having high school graduation portfolios that are built from a student's personalized learning plan and exemplify a student ready to face twenty-first-century challenges. Another mark of school success is a growing number of states and school districts with strong dual language programs that are moving towards having students demonstrate literacy in two languages.

Graduation Portfolios and the Seal of Biliteracy

High school graduation portfolios were inaugurated in the states of Kentucky and Vermont in the early 1990s as a means of offering a more comprehensive portrait of students' accomplishments than a score on a single high-stakes test. Today these graduation portfolios are reemerging as a mark of college and career readiness. In particular they reflect a systematic way of collecting and displaying students' academic, technical, and dispositional competencies. Entries include representative samples of student work from different subject areas, such as research essays and reports, multiliteracy presentations, and other in-depth projects that cannot be captured through traditional exit exams (Iasevoli, 2015; Bae & Darling-Hammond, 2014).

In increasing numbers of high schools across the country, seniors are defending their graduation portfolios in front of a panel of judges, which generally consists of a school administrator, counselor, teacher, and former student. In one high school devoted to the arts, students have a time slot of about 45 minutes to present three "artifacts" of their learning—one academic with a research base, one artistic, and one that is personal selection (Iasevoli, 2015). In other schools selections may include community service or service learning, examples of entrepreneurship, internship experience, personal statements (such as for a college essay), and self-reflection. Still other schools require a senior exit interview or for students to submit a flash drive with prescribed contents.

Submitting portfolios to online third parties is a recent attempt on the part of some school districts to take the subjectivity out of the evaluation process and to have a centralized data warehouse. One such effort has involved students earning digital badges for performance tasks. A student can, for example, upload an essay or research report to the site, and then his or her teacher can evaluate the writing according to a scoring rubric. A series of different colored dots represents the progress of the product through the system. When the product is deemed proficient, the student earns a badge. This online platform serves as a repository for students to share videos, audio files, photos, writing samples, resumés, applications, and, where applicable, cover letters, all of which showcase students' qualifications for colleges and potential employers.

Another trend at the high school level has been the recognition of students' proficiency in English and additional languages. The Seal of Biliteracy is affixed to the high school diploma of language learners who meet a specified set of criteria. Beginning as a California initiative, the notion of the seal has spread eastward across the country to New York. Given by a school, district, or county office of education, this award becomes part of a student's high school transcript.

The Seal of Biliteracy is intended to promote social and economic advancement within our interconnected, international marketplace. It is the hope that the seal will elevate the status of world languages, promote high levels of language learning, and applaud language learners. When the educational community comes to accept bilingualism as beneficial and advantageous in this competitive global society of ours, then the possibility of sustaining educational equity becomes closer to reality.

FINAL REACTION AND REFLECTION

Historically, grading students has been a rather subjective exercise. It has been most challenging for teachers to assign grades to ELLs, whose English language proficiency may preclude them from accessing grade-level content and demonstrating their true content knowledge when instruction is in English. In recent years standards have provided teachers guidance in identifying learning targets for their units and objectives for their lessons, deciding how to measure these targets and objectives, and translating the results into grades. While academic content standards offer the criteria for interpreting student performance for all students, language proficiency/development standards offer the stepping-stones for scaffolding language learning so ELLs can reach those criteria for academic success. Together, both sets of standards offer a means to interpret students' total growth and performance.

Assessment portfolios are one way in which teachers and students can gather information and provide evidence of teaching and learning. This purposeful collection of student work, including common rubrics and student self-assessment, provides documentation of students' language development alongside their academic progress from year to year. It also serves as a communication tool to be shared among students, family members, and teachers.

Language learners, teachers, and school leaders cross many bridges in their educational careers. For assessment, we must ensure that students have clear and well-marked pathways to success and a voice in their journey toward their destination. As educators, it is our responsibility to prepare today's students for tomorrow so they can reach their full potential and have the brightest future. We will have crossed the bridge to sustained educational equity when we (a) honor bilingualism and multiculturalism within an assets-based educational system, (b) agree that language varieties are integral to individuals' identities and their sociocultural interactions with others, and (c) accept the use of language for academic purposes as the grounding for assessment *as*, *for*, and *of* learning. With that in mind, here are some final questions to ponder:

- Since the inauguration of college and career readiness standards in 2010, have grading practices changed in your school or district, and, if so, how? How are standards represented and reported internally from unit to unit of instruction and externally to family members at the end of a quarter through grades? To what extent do the internal and external reporting of standards match each other?

- Are language proficiency/development standards included in report cards for all ELLs alongside their language proficiency level? Are the ELP/ELD standards given equal status with college and career readiness standards?

- Do you agree with Black and Wiliam's conclusion about formative assessment (inclusive of *as* and *for* learning) that grades are not as effective as feedback and, in some cases, may even be counterproductive? How would you convince middle school or high school students of this finding? How might you approach family members and school board members with this research?

- Has your school or district dabbled with assessment portfolios as a means of documenting what students can do linguistically and academically? If so, what are the contents of the portfolios and do they represent a full complement of student projects over the year? To what extent have students been involved in the process of selecting entries?

- To cross the bridge to sustained educational equity, there has to be solid consensus among educators and strong leadership supporting the effort. There must be a mission, vision, and commitment to excellence throughout a school and district that is foremost on the minds of educators. Ultimately there must be a belief in the potential of every student and an acceptance of multilingualism and multiculturalism as the bedrock of this potential. Based on these statements, to what extent do you believe that your school has crossed the bridge to sustain educational equity for its students and community?

RESOURCE 8.1

An Assessment Portfolio Checklist

This checklist may be helpful in planning the design and contents of a student assessment portfolio, with special attention paid to ELLs and other language learners.

Considerations

- ☐ The student's age
- ☐ The student's prior experiences with portfolios
- ☐ The language(s) of instruction for each content area
- ☐ Student self-reflection
- ☐ College and career readiness standards
- ☐ Language proficiency/development standards (for ELLs and other language learners)
- ☐ Levels of language proficiency in one or more languages and accompanying instructional supports (for ELLs and other language learners)
- ☐ The number of entries
- ☐ Digital or paper format

Potential Contents of Assessment Portfolios

- ☐ A student's inviting, personalized cover sheet
- ☐ A student summary sheet, including a self-reflection on the process and the final product
- ☐ Teacher and student mutual learning goals and action plan
- ☐ Standards addressed in student work samples
- ☐ Original samples of student work (products, projects, or performances) and accompanying rubrics or narrative feedback including

  - o Academic achievement—language arts
  - o Academic achievement—mathematics
  - o Academic achievement—science
  - o Academic achievement—social studies
  - o Cross-disciplinary samples, including the arts and engineering design
  - o Language proficiency—oral language development in one or more languages (for ELLs and other language learners)
  - o Language proficiency—literacy development in one or more languages (for ELLs and other language learners)

- ☐ Multimedia samples, including tapes, streaming videos, and photographs
- ☐ Peer and student self-assessment of common instructional products, projects, or performances

Source: Adapted from Gottlieb, 2006, p. 183.

Glossary

Academic achievement: student demonstration of the concepts, skills, and knowledge base associated with content-area curriculum.

Academic language: the language of school related to acquiring new and deeper understandings of content related to curriculum, communicating those understandings to others, and participating in the classroom environment. These understandings revolve around specific dimensions of language, including discourse, sentence, and words/expressions within sociocultural contexts.

Academic language development: the course of acquiring and using a variety of genres, language structures, and words/expressions required in processing, understanding, interpreting, and expressing curriculum-based content.

Accessibility: supports for assessment that are intended for all students to better access content and achieve academic success or to demonstrate their language proficiency, depending on the construct being measured.

Accommodations: modifications to a test or setting that do not affect the validity of the measure, intended to assist students with disabilities, including ELLs with disabilities with an individualized education program (IEP) or a 504 plan.

Accountable talk: teachers modeling forms of discussion and leading the interchange of ideas within classroom activities as a means of expanding students' thinking as they engage in academic conversations.

Activity: a series of related questions or single in-depth questions that are generally embedded in a lesson.

Alignment: the extent of the match or agreement between or among components in an educational system, such as among standards, assessments, and curriculum.

Alternate assessment of English language proficiency: standards-referenced language measures for ELLs with significant cognitive disabilities.

Analytic scales: a type of developmental rubric, usually in the form of a matrix, in which a construct, such as speaking or writing, or a project is defined by its dimensions or traits and levels of performance.

Assessment: the planning, collection, analysis, interpretation, and use of data from multiple sources over time that communicate student performance in relation to standards, learning goals, learning targets, or differentiated learning objectives.

Assessment *as* learning: enabling students to have agency by engaging in the assessment process to further their own learning; practices include student self-reflection, setting personal goals and criteria for success, and interacting with others, such as with peers and family members, to communicate their learning.

Assessment *for* learning: enabling teachers to plan and use evidence from assessment that is internal to their classrooms or mutually agreed upon by teachers across classrooms; to adjust instruction and to provide students with descriptive, criterion-referenced feedback on their learning.

Assessment *of* learning: enabling school leaders and administrators to use assessment data generally external to the classroom, such as that from high-stakes tests, to report on students' language proficiency and achievement in regards to specific learning expectations related to standards and to help inform decision making at a school or district level.

Assessment portfolio: a systematic collection of original work samples that serves as evidence of a student's accomplishments and achievements, along with criteria for judging the work, in one or more school subjects.

Backward design: frontloading standards, learning targets, and assessment in the instructional cycle to guide the crafting and implementation of activities and tasks for student learning.

Checklist: a dichotomous scale (one with two options) where traits, language functions, skills, strategies, or behaviors are marked as being either present or absent.

Cognates: words in one language that correspond in both meaning and form to words in another language (e.g., *solid* in English and *sólido* in Spanish).

Cognitive function: the mental processes used in processing thoughts and making sense of the world, often interpreted in terms of Bloom's revised taxonomy, from *remembering* at the lowest level to *creating* at the top.

College and career readiness standards: K-12 grade-level content expectations, minimally in English language arts and mathematics, depicting twenty-first-century knowledge and skills.

Collocations: a combination of words that generally co-occur (e.g., "strong tea" v. "powerful computer").

Common assessment: a multistep process by which measures have been crafted based on mutually agreed-upon decisions by educators for use in multiple classrooms, or a uniform set of procedures for collecting, interpreting, reporting, and using data across multiple classrooms.

Communities of practice: a process for sharing information and experiences with a group of individuals who learn from each other, such as a classroom of students.

Complex noun phrases: a series of connected adjectives and nouns that add to the linguistic density of written or oral text (e.g., "kidney transplant patient").

Confidence band: the amount of error surrounding a scale score that depicts the upper and lower limits of a range of data from a test.

Constructed response: types of assessment or test items where the students supply the answers or produce original work.

Content-based instruction: an approach in which discipline-specific content is integrated with language teaching; the concurrent teaching of academic subject matter along with language skills.

Content objectives: a component of a curricular framework or design that identifies observable student behavior or performance expected at the end of a lesson related to specific concepts or skills of a discipline.

Content standards, including college and career readiness standards: the skills and knowledge descriptive of student expectations, minimally in English language arts, mathematics, and literacy in history/social studies, science, and technical subjects, for each grade.

Content target: a component of a curricular framework or design that identifies the overall concepts, ideas, or knowledge of a topic expected of all students for a unit of learning.

Co-teaching: the collaboration of two or more educators who share the responsibility for instructing some or all of the students in a classroom.

Criteria for success: specific, measurable descriptors for learning, often tied to standards and related targets or objectives that are shared by teachers and students.

Criterion-referenced testing: a type of measure that is based on and reported by established criteria, such as standards, rather than by ranking the performance of students.

Cultural resources: the traditions, values, experiences, and artifacts that are part of students' lives that bridge home and community to school.

Curricular design: systematically organizing learning experiences that are relevant and meaningful for students; the process of developing an academic plan.

Curricular framework: an academic plan that defines the processes and products of a unit of instruction that, for example, includes academic language use associated with both grade-level content and language.

Descriptive feedback: a feature of the formative assessment cycle where students gain understanding of their performance in relation to the learning objectives, targets, or standards.

Differentiated instruction: an approach based on the philosophy "all students can learn" that provides groups of students with different avenues to acquire content based on challenging teaching materials.

Differentiated language objectives: defining language expectations for grade-level content so that teachers gear lessons according to ELLs' levels of language proficiency.

Digital literacy: making meaning by critically navigating, collecting, and evaluating information using a range of digital technologies, such as hand-held devices, the Internet, educational software, and cell phones.

Discourse: broadly, the many different ways in which oral and written language are connected and organized.

Discrete-point measures: tests that are skill based or measures of isolated skills.

Dual language learners: young children participating in early childhood education programs who speak a language other than English at home and are in the process of developing English; also applied to students, generally starting in kindergarten, who are systematically instructed content in two languages.

Dual language models (two-way): educational programs where proficient English speakers learn content and language side-by-side in two languages with their ELL peers.

e-portfolio: a digital collection of student work that can be used for instructional or assessment purposes.

Emergent bilinguals: language learners who, through school and acquiring English, become bilingual and have the ability to function in both their home language and in English.

English Language Learners (ELLs): linguistically and culturally diverse students who are in the process of developing English as an additional language as they access grade-level content.

English language proficiency levels: designations that are descriptive of where ELLs are positioned on the language development continuum.

Evaluation: using the evidence from assessment data to judge the worth or effectiveness of services or programs.

Expressive language: domains or modalities associated with the production of language—namely, speaking and writing.

Face validity: the extent to which a test is judged to measure the construct it purports to measure; its appearance at "face value."

Feedback: descriptive constructive information that students give teachers or that teachers give students about content or language learning and progress towards learning goals, targets, or objectives; a critical component of assessment *as* and *for* learning.

Formative practices: providing timely, descriptive, and relevant feedback related to student progress toward meeting learning targets or objectives; a process in which information is gathered during the instructional cycle for teachers to ascertain the effectiveness of their instruction.

Functional language: the purpose for communicating ideas, concepts, and information; in other words, what one does with language or how language is used (e.g., to describe, explain, or argue).

General academic vocabulary: words and expressions applicable to a wide range of contexts and content areas (e.g., strategies, instructions).

Genres: ways to organize and define various types of oral and spoken language (e.g., blog, oral book report).

Heritage language learners: students generally born and raised in the United States who have varying degrees of language proficiency in or a cultural connection to languages other than English.

Holistic scales: a type of developmental rubric in which there is an overall description of competencies for each performance level.

Home language: students' primary language spoken at home and generally one of their first languages acquired.

Informational texts: factual or nonfiction material whose purpose is to inform about the natural or social world.

Instructional activities: a component of curricular frameworks that describes the opportunities students have to interact with each other, with media or independently, to acquire or reinforce concepts, skills, or language.

Instructional assessment: varied measures of learning used in classrooms, such as performance tasks, that are embedded in teaching; assessment occurring during instruction.

Instructional supports: sensory (e.g., photographs), graphic (e.g., T-charts), linguistic (e.g., learning walls), and interactive resources (e.g., paired collaborative learning) embedded in instruction and assessment used to assist students at various levels of language proficiency in constructing meaning from language and content.

Interactive journals: a nonjudgmental communication tool shared between students and teachers that provides some insight into students' feelings, thoughts, and learning strategies.

Interim measures: the periodic administration throughout the school year of commercial measures that help educators determine the progress of students and, at times, to predict the performance of students on high-stakes tests.

Inter-rater reliability: the extent of consensus among judges (e.g., teachers) in interpreting student performance (e.g., oral or written language samples), usually calculated as a percentage of agreement.

Language allocation: the percentage of time used for each language of instruction or the subject areas assigned to each language.

Language domains or modalities: the division of language into the areas of listening, speaking, reading, or writing.

Language forms: the grammatical structures, syntax, and mechanics associated with sentence-level meaning.

Language functions: the purposes for which language is used to communicate (e.g., describe, compare/contrast, justify).

Language objectives: specified, observable language outcomes designed for individual lessons and often differentiated by ELLs' levels of language proficiency.

Language proficiency: demonstration of a person's competence in processing (through listening and reading) and producing (through speaking and writing) language at a point in time.

Language proficiency/development standards: language expectations for students marked by grade or grade-level cluster performance definitions and descriptors/performance indicators of language proficiency levels across the language development continuum.

Language targets: overall literacy and/or oral language outcomes designed for all students for a unit of learning.

Language use argument: a means of validating assessment by specifying proposed interpretations of the results and then evaluating the feasibility of the interpretation and uses of the data.

Large-scale measures: standardized norm-referenced or criterion-referenced tests used across multiple classrooms, generally at the school, district, or state levels.

Learning logs: an instructional assessment tool where students make entries on a regular basis that show student growth in language development or knowledge of content over time.

Levels of language proficiency: stages along the pathway of language development, generally expressed as descriptors of performance.

Lexicon: the vocabulary or words of a language.

Linguistic complexity: the amount or density of information in oral or written discourse as determined by the compactness of words and morphological and syntactic structures.

Linguistic resources: the availability of language-related capital that can be brought into the classroom to enhance instruction, such as the reference or use of the students' home language.

Linguistically and culturally responsive education: instruction and assessment that support students' learning by using resources and experiences from the students' homes and communities to relate to and build on what they know.

Linguistically diverse students: students who are exposed to languages in addition to English in their home backgrounds.

Long-term ELLs (LTELLs): linguistically and culturally diverse students in middle and high schools who have not met linguistic parity with their English-proficient peers although they have generally participated in language support programs for 7 or more years.

Metacognitive awareness: the understanding and expression of the thinking process involved in how one learns.

Metacultural awareness: the understanding and expression of one's sociocultural identity in shaping the lens through which one learns and sees the world.

Metalinguistic awareness: the understanding and expression of the nuances and uses of language, including the process of reflecting on the features and forms of language.

Model performance indicators: example representations of language development standards that are geared to each language proficiency level and consist of three elements: a language function, a content stem, and an instructional support.

Multiliteracies: a twenty-first-century approach to making meaning that relies on multimodal ways, in addition to print, to make sense of the world, such as through digital, visual, and gestural means.

Multimodal tools: the use of visual, digital, and print materials that give students opportunities to creatively show their learning.

Multiple meanings: words or expressions that have more than one interpretation in social situations or within or across content areas (e.g., *base* or *ring*).

Multiple measures: the reliance on two or more types of data sources at different points in time to make educational decisions.

Multi-tier system of supports (MTSS): an instructional framework similar to but broader in scope than response to intervention (RtI). MTSS addresses academic as well as social, emotional, and behavioral development of students from early childhood to graduation.

Newcomer ELLs: students who are recent arrivals to the United States (generally within the last 2 to 3 years) whose conceptual understanding and communicative skills are most likely in a language other than English.

Next Generation Science Standards: proposed student expectations on three dimensions: practices, cross-cutting concepts, and disciplinary core ideas based on the Framework for K-12 Science Education developed by the National Research Council.

Norm-referenced testing: comparison of standard scores representing the performance of individual or groups of students against the student sample that was originally tested

Peer assessment: descriptive feedback on student work given by fellow students, generally based on standards-referenced criteria.

Performance assessment: the planning, collection, and analysis of original student work, such as curriculum-related hands-on tasks, products, and projects, that is interpreted based on specified criteria, such as in a rubric.

Performance definitions: descriptions of the range of standards-referenced student performance; for language proficiency/development standards, criteria or descriptions include listening/reading (receptive language) and speaking/writing (productive language) across designated language proficiency levels.

Performance indicators: sample observable and assessable descriptions of what students can do to demonstrate progress toward or attainment of standards.

Personal learning network: a type of professional development experience where educators reach into cyberspace to create online communities in pursuit of self-directed academic learning and connections with others who share interest in the same topic.

Phonology: the sound system of a language.

Pragmatics: the social uses of language.

Productive language: domains or modalities associated with the expression of language—namely, speaking and writing.

Professional learning community (PLC): a group of educators, including teachers and school leaders, that meets, communicates, and collaborates on a regular basis to ensure that all students learn.

Professional learning team (PLT): a group of educators, such as grade-level teachers, that collaborates on a regular basis to work toward a mutually agreed upon goal.

Proficient English speakers: linguistically and culturally diverse students who are former ELLs or students who are fully functional in English.

Projects: a series of related performance tasks that allows students to explore a topic or theme in depth and can be used for common instructional products at the culmination of a unit of learning (e.g., an oral presentation—a task—and a written report—another task—serve as the basis for a debate, a project).

Rating scales: a type of rubric where traits, language functions, skills, strategies, or behaviors are defined by their frequency of occurrence (how often) or quality (how well they are achieved).

Raw scores: the total number of correct items on tests or questions answered correctly in assignments.

Receptive language: domains or modalities associated with the processing of language—namely, listening and reading.

Reclassification or redesignation: a set of criteria that is used to change the category or label of a student's status or participation in an educational program, often used in language education to distinguish ELLs from former ELLs.

Register: a variety of language used according to the setting or purpose of the communication (e.g., the language students use when speaking to their peers versus their principal).

Reliability: the internal cohesiveness of a measure, the uniformity of interpretation from rater to rater, or the consistency in use of the results for making decisions.

Response to intervention (RtI): a general education initiative that is an evidence-based, multitiered problem-solving model intended to provide high-quality instruction and intervention matched to student needs.

Rubrics: criterion-referenced tools that enable teachers and students to interpret student work using the same set of descriptors.

Scaffolding: the act of a knowledgeable person, such as a parent or a teacher, providing individual learners with exactly the support they need to move their learning forward.

Scaffolds: the use of instructional supports or strategies to allow students to work within their 'zones of proximal development' to facilitate learning.

Scale scores: the conversion of students' raw scores on a test to a common standard scale that allows for a numerical comparison of student performance.

Selected response: types of test items where the possible answers are listed, such as in multiple-choice or true/false questions.

Self-assessment: students' application of performance criteria or descriptors to monitor and interpret their own work as a means of reflecting on their language and content learning.

Sheltered instruction: a set of strategies associated with content-based methodologies whereby teachers deliver grade-level subject matter content in ways that are accessible and comprehensible to language learners.

Social media: a highly interactive means of communication in which people create, share, and exchange information and ideas in virtual communities and networks using mobile and Web-based technologies.

Sociocultural awareness: familiarity with the nuances, norms, traditions, histories, and perspectives of different cultural groups and their impact on learning.

Sociocultural context: the social and physical settings that provide the backdrop for individuals to understand the circumstances for language use and how to interact with others.

Specialized academic vocabulary: words or expressions representative of a content area or discipline (e.g., mixed fractions is a mathematical concept).

Standard error of measurement: an estimate of the amount of variance around a student's score on a test that forms the confidence band.

Standardized testing: tests (historically with a multiple-choice format) that require students to answer the same questions or questions in the same way and produce standard scores so that performance of individual or groups of students can be compared to one another or to a specified criterion.

Students With Limited or Interrupted Formal Education (SLIFE): older ELLs who are recent arrivals to a country and have not been afforded continuous opportunities for schooling.

Summative assessment: the "sum" of evidence for learning gathered at a point in time, such as at the culmination of a unit of learning, that is generally used for grading or tests that are administered annually on a large-scale basis used for accountability purposes.

Syntax: the rules that govern the ways words are arranged to form phrases, clauses, and sentences.

Tasks: two or more related instructional activities that generally involve multiple modalities or language domains (e.g., a summary of research requires reading different sources, taking notes, and synthesizing the information, often with the use of technology).

Task-specific rubrics: types of holistic or analytic scales that are designed for a single instructional assessment task or project.

Technical academic vocabulary: words or expressions tied to a specific topic within a content area (e.g., *patella* is the scientific name for a part of the anatomy).

Test: a systematic procedure for collecting a sample of student behavior or performance at one point in time.

Text types: different forms or genres, mainly of writing, with distinct purposes and features (e.g., a state of the union speech).

Transadaptation: translation of test items that makes adjustments for the unique linguistic and cultural characteristics of the students' home language.

Translanguaging or translinguistic transfer: a linguistic repertoire that includes more than one language used as a communication tool by bilingual speakers; the oral or written interaction of persons in two or more languages in naturally occurring situations.

Universal design: adapted from the field of architecture, principles for products and environments extended to educational testing that are used for all individuals to the greatest extent possible without the need for adaptation or specialized treatment.

Validity: the extent to which the assessment measures what it purports to measure and data are appropriate for the decisions to be made about students; the extent to which a test or measure matches its stated purpose.

Validity argument: providing evidence and justification for the proposed interpretations and uses of data from assessment.

Visual literacy: ability for students to express complex concepts and ideas without heavy reliance on print, such as through photographs, images, and film, among other media.

Vocabulary: the specificity of words, phrases, or expressions used in a given context.

Zone of proximal development (ZPD): A Vygotskyan concept that can be defined as the distance between the developmental level of learners as determined by their independent problem-solving abilities and their level of potential development through problem-solving under adult guidance or in collaboration with more advanced peers.

References

Abedi, J. (2004). The No Child Left Behind Act and English Language Learners: Assessment and accountability issues. *Educational Researcher, 33*(1), 4–14.

Abedi, J. (2010). Research and recommendations for formative assessment with English Language Learners. In H. L. Andrade & G. J. Cizek (Eds.), *Handbook of formative assessment* (pp.181–197). New York, NY: Routledge.

Abedi, J., & Linquanti, R. (2012, January). *Issues and opportunities in strengthening large-scale assessment systems for ELLs.* Paper presented at the Understanding Language Conference, Stanford University, CA.

American Educational Research Association. (2000, July). *AERA position statement concerning high-stakes testing in pre-K-12 education.* Washington, DC: Author. Retrieved from http://www.aera.net/AboutAERA/AERARulesPolicies/AERAPolicyStatements/PositionStatementonHighStakesTesting/tabid/11083/Default.aspx

August, D., & Shanahan, T. (Eds.). (2006). *Developing literacy in second-language learners: Report of the National Literacy Panel on language-minority children and youth.* Mahwah, NJ: Lawrence Erlbaum.

Bachman, L. F., & Palmer, A. S. (2010). *Language assessment in practice: Developing language tests and justifying their use in the real world.* Oxford, UK: Oxford University Press.

Bae, S., & Darling-Hammond, L. (2014). *Recognizing college and career readiness in the California school accountability system.* Stanford, CA: Stanford Center for Opportunity Policy in Education.

Bailey, A. L. (Ed.). (2007). *The language demands of school: Putting academic English to the test.* New Haven, CT: Yale University Press.

Bailey, A. L., & Butler, F. A. (2003). An evidentiary framework for operationalizing academic language for broad application to K-12 education: A design document. *CSE Report 611.* Los Angeles, CA: CRESST/University of California.

Bailey, A. L., & Carroll, P. E. (2015). Assessment of English Language Learners in the era of new academic content standards. *Review of Research in Education, 39,* 253–294.

Bailey, A. L., & Heritage, M. (2008). *Formative assessment for literacy grades K-6: Building reading and academic language skills across the curriculum.* Thousand Oaks, CA: Corwin.

Bailey, A. L., & Wolf, M. K. (2012). *The challenge of assessing language proficiency aligned to the Common Core State Standards and some possible solutions.* Retrieved from http://ell.stanford.edu/sites/default/files/pdf/academic-papers/08-Bailey%20Wolf%20Challenges%20of%20Assessment%20Language%20Proficiency%20FINAL_0.pdf

Basterra, M., Trumbull, E., & Solano-Flores, G. (Eds.). (2011). *Cultural validity in assessment: Addressing linguistic and cultural diversity.* New York, NY: Routledge.

Batalova, J., & McHugh, M. (2010). *Top languages spoken by English Language Learners nationally and by state.* Washington, DC: Migration Policy Institute. Retrieved from http://migrationpolicy.org/research/top-languages-spoken-english-language-learners-nationally-and-state

Bazron, B., Osher, D., & Fleischman, S. (2005). Creating culturally responsive schools. *Educational Leadership, 63*(1), 83–84.

Bergan, J. R., Bergan, J. R., & Burnham, C. G. (2009). *Benchmark assessment in standards-based education: The Galileo K-12 online educational management system.* Tucson, AZ: Assessment Technology, Incorporated.

Berger, R. (2014, March). When students lead their learning. *Educational Leadership, 71*(6). Retrieved from http://www.ascd.org/publications/educational-leadership/mar14/vol71/num06/When-Students-Lead-Their-Learning.aspx

Biber, D. (1988). *Variation across speech and writing.* Cambridge, UK: Cambridge University Press.

Black, P., & Wiliam, D. (1999). *Assessment for learning: Beyond the black box.* Cambridge, UK: University of Cambridge.

Brisk, M. E. (2006). *Bilingual education: From compensatory to quality schooling* (2nd ed.). Mahwah, NJ: Lawrence Erlbaum Associates.

Brisk, M. E. (2015). *Engaging students in academic literacies: Genre-based pedagogy for K-5 classrooms.* New York, NY: Routledge.

Brookhart, S. (2010). *Formative assessment strategies for every classroom* (2nd ed.). Alexandria, VA: ASCD.

Buck, G. (2001). *Assessing listening.* Cambridge, UK: Cambridge University Press.

Bunch, G. C., Kibler, A., & Pimentel, S. (2012, January). *Realizing opportunities for English learners in the Common Core English language arts and disciplinary literacy standards.* Paper presented at the Understanding Language Conference, Stanford University, CA.

Burr, E., Haas, E., & Ferriere, K. (2015). *Identifying and supporting English learner students with learning disabilities: Key issues in the literature and state practice* (REL 2015–086). Washington, DC: U.S. Department of Education, Institute of Education Sciences, National Center for Education Evaluation and Regional Assistance, Regional Educational Laboratory West. Retrieved from http://ies.ed.gov/ncee/edlabs

Cardenas, G., Jones, B., & Lozano, O. (2014). A window into my family and community. In M. Gottlieb & G. Ernst-Slavit (Series Eds.), *Academic language in diverse classrooms: Promoting content and language learning, English language arts, grades K-2* (pp. 45–77). Thousand Oaks, CA: Corwin.

Carr, J. F., & Harris, D. E. (2001). *Succeeding with standards: Linking curriculum, assessment, and action planning.* Alexandria, VA: ASCD.

Carrasquillo, A. L., & Rodriguez, V. (2002). *Language minority students in the mainstream classroom* (2nd ed.). Tonawanda, NY: Multilingual Matters.

Celic, C., & Seltzer, K. (2011). *Translanguaging: A CUNY-NYSIEB guide for educators.* New York, NY: CUNY-NYSIEB, City University of New York.

Chapman, C., & King, R. (2005). *Differentiated assessment strategies: One tool doesn't fit all.* Thousand Oaks, CA: Corwin.

Chatterji, M. (2003). *Designing and using tools for educational assessment.* Boston, MA: Allyn and Bacon.

Christian, D., & Genesee, F. (Eds.). (2001). *Bilingual education.* Alexandria, VA: TESOL.

Cloud, N., Genesee, F., Hamayan, E. (2009). *Literacy instruction for English Language Learners: A teacher's guide to research-based practices.* Portsmouth, NH: Heinemann.

Cohen, A. D. (1994). *Assessing language ability in the classroom.* Boston, MA: Heinle & Heinle.

Collard, S. B. (1998). *Our wet world: Aquatic ecosystems.* Watertown, MA: Charlesbridge.

Collier, V. P., & Thomas, W. P. (2009). *Educating English learners for a transformed world.* Albuquerque, NM: Dual Language Education of New Mexico—Fuente Press.

Connell, B. R., Jones, M., Mace, R., Mueller, J., Mullick, A., Ostroff, E., . . . Vanderheiden, G. (1997, April). *The principles of universal design. Version 2.1.* Raleigh, NC: NC State University, Center for Universal Design. Retrieved from https://www.ncsu.edu/ncsu/design/cud/about_ud/udprinciplestext.htm

Cook, H. G., & MacDonald, R. (2014). *Reference performance level descriptors: Outcome of a national working session on defining an "English proficient" performance standard.* Washington, DC: Council of Chief State School Officers.

Cope, B., & Kalantzis, M. (Eds.). (2000). *Multiliteracies: Literacy learning and the design of social futures.* New York, NY: Routledge.

Costa, A. L., & Kallick, B. (2013). *Learning and leading with habits of mind: 16 essential characteristics for success.* Alexandria, VA: ASCD.

Council of Chief State School Officers (CCSSO). (2012). *Distinguishing formative assessment from other educational assessment labels.* Washington, DC: Author.

Crafton, L. K., Brennan, M., & Silvers, P. (2007). Critical inquiry and multiliteracies in a first-grade classroom. *Language Arts, 84*(6), 510–518.

Crandall, J. A. (Ed.). (1987). *ESL through content-area instruction: Mathematics, science, social studies.* Englewood Cliffs, NJ: Prentice Hall Regents.

Cummins, J. (1981). The role of primary language development in promoting educational success for language minority students. In California State Department of Education (Ed.), *Schooling and language minority students: A theoretical framework* (pp. 3–49). Los Angeles, CA: California State University, Evaluation, Dissemination and Assessment Center.

Cummins, J. (2000). *Language, power, and pedagogy.* Clevedon, UK: Multilingual Matters.

Darian, S. (2003). *Understanding the language of science.* Austin: University of Texas Press.

Davies, A. (2011). *Making classroom assessment work* (3rd ed.). Bloomington, IN: Solution Tree.

Derewianka, B. (1991). *Exploring how texts work.* Newtown, Australia: Primary English Teaching Association.

Dillon, R. (2015, July). *Tech tip: Five elements of the connected classroom.* Retrieved from http://smartblogs.com/education/2015/07/07/tech-tip-5-elements-of-the-connected-classroom/

Dove, M. G., & Honigsfeld, A. (2013). *Common Core for the not-so-common learner: English language arts strategies, grades K-5.* Thousand Oaks, CA: Corwin.

Dove, M. G., Honigsfeld, A., & Cohan, A. (2014). *Beyond core expectations: A schoolwide framework for serving the not-so-common learner.* Thousand Oaks, CA: Corwin.

Durgunoglu, A. U. (2002). Cross-linguistic transfer in literacy development and implications for language learners. *Annals of Dyslexia, 52,* 189–204.

Earl, L. M. (2013). *Assessment as learning: Using classroom assessment to maximize student learning* (2nd ed.). Thousand Oaks, CA: Corwin.

Echevarria, J., Vogt, M. E., & Short, D. J. (2012). *Making content comprehensible for English learners: The SIOP model* (4th ed.). Boston, MA: Pearson.

Elliott, S. N., Kettler, R. J., Beddow, P. A., & Kurz, A. (2010). Research and strategies for adapting formative assessments for students with special needs. In H. L. Andrade & G. J. Cizek (Eds.), *Handbook of formative assessment* (pp. 159–180). New York, NY: Routledge.

Ernst-Slavit, G., Gottlieb, M., &. Slavit, D. (2013). Who needs fractions? In M. Gottlieb & G. Ernst-Slavit (Series Eds.), *Academic language in diverse classrooms: Promoting content and language learning: Mathematics, grades 3-5* (pp. 81–121). Thousand Oaks, CA: Corwin.

Ernst-Slavit, G., & Mason, M. (2012). Making your first ELL home visit: A guide for classroom teachers. ¡Colorín Colorado! Retrieved from http://www.colorincolorado.org/article/59138/

Escamilla, K., & Hopewell, S. (2013). *Biliteracy from the start: Literacy-squared in action.* Philadelphia, PA: Caslon.

Eshet, Y. (2004). Digital literacy: A conceptual framework for survival skills in the digital era. *Journal of Educational Multimedia and Hypermedia, 13*(1), 93–106. Norfolk, VA: Association for the Advancement of Computing in Education (AACE).

Estrada, P. (2004). Patterns of language arts instructional activity and excellence in first- and fourth-grade culturally and linguistically diverse classrooms. In H. C. Waxman, R. G. Tharp, & R. S. Hilberg (Eds.), *Observational research in U.S. classrooms* (pp. 122–143). Cambridge, UK: Cambridge University Press.

Fairbairn, S., & Jones-Vo, S. (2010). *Differentiating instruction and assessment for English Language Learners: A guide for K-12 teachers.* Philadelphia, PA: Caslon.

Farr, P. B., & Trumbell, E. (1997). *Alternate assessments for diverse classrooms.* Norwood, MA: Christopher-Gordon.

Farr, R., & Tone, B. (1994). *Portfolio and performance assessment: Helping students evaluate their progress as readers and writers.* Fort Worth, TX: Harcourt Brace.

Farrell, T. S. C. (2009). *Teaching reading to English Language Learners.* Thousand Oaks, CA: Corwin.

Feldman, J. (2015, July 16). How our grades support inequity and what we can do about it. *SmartBlog on Education.* Retrieved from http://smartblogs.com/education/2015/07/16/how-our-grading-supports-inequity-and-what-we-can-do-about-it/

Finocchiaro, M., & Brumfit, C. (1983). *The functional-notional approach.* Oxford, UK: Oxford University Press.

Fisher, D., & Frey, N. (2008). *Better learning through structured teaching: A framework for the gradual release of responsibility.* Alexandria, VA: ASCD.

Fisher, D., & Frey, N. (2014). *Checking for understanding: Formative assessment techniques for your classroom* (2nd ed.). Alexandria, VA: ASCD.

Fisher, D., Frey, N., & Rothenberg, C. (2008). *Content-area conversations: How to plan discussion-based lessons for diverse language learners.* Alexandria, VA: ASCD.

Flannery, M. E. (2015, March). Parents and educators to lawmakers: Testing is not learning! *neaToday.* Retrieved from http://neatoday.org/2015/03/12/parents-educators-lawmakers-testing-not-learning/

Francis, D. J., Rivera, M., Lesaux, N., Kieffer, M., & Rivera, H. (2006). *Research-based recommendations for instruction and academic interventions.* Portsmouth, NH: Center on Instruction. Retrieved from http://www.centeroninstruction.org/files/ELL1-Interventions.pdf

Frantz, R. S., Starr, L. E., & Bailey, A. L. (2015). Syntactic complexity as an aspect of text complexity. *Education Researcher 44*(7), 387–393.

Frey, N., & Fisher, D. (2011). *The formative action assessment plan: Practical steps to more successful teaching and learning.* Alexandria, VA; ASCD.

García, O., Kleifgen, J. A., & Falchi, L. (2008). From English Language Learners to emergent bilinguals. *Equity Matters: Research Review, 1,* 1–59.

García, O., & Wei, L. (2013). *Translanguaging: Language, bilingualism and education.* London, UK: Palgrave Macmillan.

García, S. B., & Ortiz, A. A. (2006). Preventing disproportionate representation: Culturally and linguistically responsive prereferral interventions. *Teaching Exceptional Children, 38*(4), 64–68.

Gauvain, M. (2005). Sociocultural contexts of learning. In A. E. Maynard & M. I. Martini (Eds.), *Learning in cultural context: Family, peers, and school* (pp. 11–40). New York, NY: Springer.

Gay, G. (2002). *Culturally responsive teaching.* New York, NY: Teachers College Press.

Gibbons, P. (2009). *English Learners, academic literacy, and thinking: Learning in the challenge zone.* Portsmouth, NH: Heinemann.

Goertz, M.E., Oláh, L. N., & Riggan, M. (2010). *From testing to teaching: The use of interim assessments in classroom instruction.* CPRE Research Report # RR-65. Consortium for Policy Research in Education: Author.

Goldenberg, C. (2013, Summer). Unlocking the research on English Learners: What we know— and don't yet know—about effective instruction. *American Educator, 37*(2), 4–11.

Gómez, E. L. (1998). *Perspectives on policy and practice: Creating large-scale portfolios that include English Language Learners.* Providence, RI: Education Alliance at Brown University.

González, N., Moll, L., & Amanti, C. (2005). *Funds of knowledge: Theorizing practices in households, communities and classrooms.* Mahwah, NJ: Lawrence Erlbaum Associates.

Gottlieb, M. (1995). Nurturing student learning through portfolios. *TESOL Journal, 5*(1), 12–14.

Gottlieb, M. (1999). *The language proficiency handbook: A practitioner's guide to instructional assessment.* Springfield, IL: Illinois State Board of Education.

Gottlieb, M. (2003). *Large-scale assessment of English Language Learners: Addressing accountability in K-12 settings.* TESOL Professional Papers #6. Alexandria, VA: Teachers of English to Speakers of Other Languages.

Gottlieb, M. (2006). *Assessing English Language Learners: Bridges from language proficiency to academic achievement.* Thousand Oaks, CA: Corwin.

Gottlieb, M. (2012a). *Common language assessment for English Learners.* Bloomington, IN: Solution Tree.

Gottlieb, M. (2012b). Common instructional assessment for English Learners: A whole school effort. In M. Calderón (Ed.), *Breaking through: Effective instruction & assessment for reaching English Learners* (pp. 167–182). Bloomington, IN: Solution Tree.

Gottlieb, M. (2013). *Essential actions: A handbook for implementing WIDA's framework for English language development standards.* Madison, WI: Board of Regents of the University of Wisconsin System, on behalf of the WIDA Consortium (www.wida.us).

Gottlieb, M. (2015). What is the value of formative classroom assessment in the era of Common Core State Standards? In G. Valdés, K. Menken, & M. Castro (Eds.), *Common Core, bilingual and English Language Learners: A resource for educators* (pp. 258–259). Philadelphia, PA: Caslon.

Gottlieb, M., & Ernst-Slavit, G. (Series Eds.). (2013). *Academic language in diverse classrooms: Promoting content and language learning: Mathematics, grades K-2, 3-5, and 6-8.* Thousand Oaks, CA: Corwin.

Gottlieb, M., & Ernst-Slavit, G. (2014a). *Academic language in diverse classrooms: Promoting content and language learning: Definitions and contexts.* Thousand Oaks, CA: Corwin.

Gottlieb, M., & Ernst-Slavit, G. (Series Eds.). (2014b). *Academic language in diverse classrooms: Promoting content and language learning: English language arts, grades K-2, 3-5, and 6-8.* Thousand Oaks, CA: Corwin.

Gottlieb, M., & Hamayan, E. (2007). Assessing language proficiency of English Language Learners in special education contexts. In G. B. Esquivel, E. C. Lopez, & S. Nahari (Eds.), *Handbook of multicultural school psychology.* New York: Lawrence Erlbaum.

Gottlieb, M., Katz, A., & Ernst-Slavit, G. (2009). *Paper to practice: Implementing TESOL's preK-12 English language proficiency standards.* Alexandria, VA: Teachers of English to Speakers of Other Languages.

Gottlieb, M., & Nguyen, D. (2007). *Assessment and accountability in language education programs: A guide for administrators and teachers.* Philadelphia, PA: Caslon.

Graves, M., August, D., & Mancilla-Martinez, J. (2012). *Teaching vocabulary to English Language Learners.* New York, NY: Teachers College Press.

Greenstein, L. (2010). *What teachers really need to know about formative assessment.* Alexandria, VA: ASCD.

Guskey, T. R., & Bailey, J. M. (2001). *Developing grading and reporting systems for student learning.* Thousand Oaks, CA: Corwin.

Guskey, T. R., & Bailey, J. M. (2010). *Developing standards-based report cards.* Thousand Oaks, CA: Corwin.

Halliday, M. A. K. (1976). *System and function in language.* London, UK: Oxford University Press.

Hamayan, E., Marler, B., Sanchez-Lopez, C., & Damico, J. (2013). *Special education considerations for English Language Learners: Delivering a continuum of services* (2nd ed.). Philadelphia, PA: Caslon.

Hammond, Z. (2015). *Culturally responsive teaching and the brain: Promoting authentic engagement and rigor among culturally and linguistically diverse students.* Thousand Oaks, CA: Corwin.

Harlen, W. (2007). *Assessment of learning.* London, UK: Sage.

Hartnell-Young, E., & Morriss, M. (2007). *Digital portfolios: Powerful tools for promoting professional growth and reflection* (2nd ed.). Thousand Oaks, CA: Corwin.

Hattie, J. (2008). *Visible learning: A synthesis of over 800 meta-analyses relating to achievement.* New York, NY: Routledge.

Hattie, J., & Timperley, H. (2007). The power of feedback. *Review of Education Research, 77,* 81–112.

Hein, G. E., & Price, S. (1994). *Active assessment for active science: A guide for elementary school teachers.* Portsmouth, NH: Heinemann.

Heller, M. (1999). *Linguistic minorities and modernity: A sociolinguistic ethnography.* New York, NY: Longman.

Heritage, M. (2010). *Formative assessment: Making it happen in the classroom.* Thousand Oaks, CA: Corwin.

Honigsfeld, A., & Giouroukakis, V. (2011, Summer). High-stakes assessment and English Language Learners. *The Delta Kappa Gamma Bulletin,* 6–10.

Horwitz, A. R, Uro, G., Price-Baugh, R., Simon, C., Uzzell, R., Lewis, S., & Casserly, M. (2009, October). *Succeeding with English Language Learners: Lessons learned from urban school districts.* Washington, DC: Council of Great City Schools.

Hymes, D. H. (1972). On communicative competence. In J. B. Pride & J. Holmes (Eds.), *Sociolinguistics.* Harmondsworth, UK: Penguin.

Iasevoli, B. (2015, August 7). Should high school students have to "defend" their diploma like a Ph.D.? California's new way of ranking school performance could open the door to portfolio assessments. *Hechinger Report.* Retrieved from http://hechingerreport.org/should-high-school-students-have-to-defend-their-diploma-like-a-ph-d/

International Reading Association. (2013–2014). *Using high-stakes assessment for grade retention and graduation decisions.* Retrieved from http://www.reading.org/Libraries/position-statements-and-resolutions/ps1081_high_stakes.pdf

Jacobs, G. E. (2013, May). Designing assessments: A multiliteracies approach. *Journal of Adolescent & Adult Literacy, 56*(8), 623–626.

Kagan, S. (1989). The structural approach to cooperative learning. *Educational Leadership, 47,* 12–15.

Kahl, S. (2010). *Making data & classroom assessments work for you.* Washington, DC: American Federation of Teachers.

Kersaint, G., Thompson, D. R., & Petkova, M. (2009). *Teaching mathematics to English Language Learners.* New York, NY: Routledge.

Klingner, J. K., Hoover, J. J., & Baca, L. M. (2008). *Why do English Language Learners struggle with reading? Distinguishing language acquisition from learning disabilities.* Thousand Oaks, CA: Corwin.

Kohn, A. (2011). The case against grades. *Educational Leadership, 69*(3), 28–33.

Kopriva, R. J., & Sexton, U. (2011). Using appropriate assessment processes: How to get accurate information about the academic content knowledge and skills of English Language Learners. In M. del Rosario Basterra, E. Trumbull, & G. Solano-Flores (Eds.), *Cultural validity in assessment.* New York, NY: Routledge.

Krashen, S. D. (1992). *The input hypothesis: Issues and implications.* New York, NY: Longman.

Krogstad, J. M., & Fry, R. (2014, August 18). Department of Education projects public schools will be "majority-minority" this fall. *Pew Research Center.* Retrieved from http://www.pewresearch.org/fact-tank/2014/08/18/u-s-public-schools-expected-to-be-majority-minority-starting-this-fall/?hd#utm_campaign=2014-08-20%20pnn&utm_medium=email&utm_source=eloqua

Kuhn, T. S. (1962). *The structure of scientific revolutions.* Chicago, IL: University of Chicago Press.

Lam, E. Y., Low, M., & Tauiliili-Mahuka, R. (2014). Legends and life. In M. Gottlieb & G. Ernst-Slavit (Series Eds.), *Academic language in diverse classrooms: English language arts, grades 6–8* (pp. 79–116). Thousand Oaks, CA: Corwin.

Lave, J., & Wenger, E. (1991). *Situated learning: Legitimate peripheral participation (Learning in doing: Social, cognitive and computational perspectives).* Cambridge, UK: Cambridge University Press.

Lee, O., & Quinn, H. (2012, January). *Next Generation Science Standards and English Language Learners.* Paper presented at the Understanding Language Conference, Stanford University, CA.

Lemke, J. (1990). *Talking science: Language, learning, and values.* Norwood, NJ: Ablex.

Linquanti, R., & Bailey, A. L. (2014). *Reprising the Home Language Survey: Summary of a national working session on policies, practices, and tools for identifying potential English Learners.* Washington, DC: Council of Chief State School Officers.

Linquanti, R., & Cook, H. G. (2013). *Toward a "common definition of English Learner": Guidance for states and state assessment consortia in defining and addressing policy and technical issues and options.* Washington, DC: Council of Chief State School Officers.

Louis, K. S., Leithwood, K., Wahlstrom, K., & Anderson, S. (2010). *Learning from leadership: Investigating the links to improved students learning.* Minneapolis, MN: Center for Applied Research and Educational Improvement.

Lucas, M. R., & Corpuz, B. (2007). *Facilitating learning: A metacognitive process.* Manila, Philippines: Lorimar.

MacDonald, R., Boals, T., Castro, M., Cook, H. G., Lundberg, T., & White, P. A. (2015). *Formative language assessment for English learners.* Portsmouth, NH: Heinemann.

Madsen, H. S. (1983). *Techniques in testing.* New York, NY: Oxford University Press.

Mahn, H. (2013). Vygotsky and second language acquisition. In C. A. Chapelle (Ed.), *The encyclopedia of applied linguistics* (pp. 6150–6157). Oxford, UK: Blackwell.

Mariotti, A. S., & Homan, S. P. (1994). *Linking reading assessment to instruction: An application worktext for elementary classroom teachers.* New York, NY: St. Martin's.

Martin, J. R. (1992, March). Genre and literacy-modeling context in educational linguistics. *Annual Review of Applied Linguistics, 13,* 141–172.

Martiniello, M. (2008). Language and the performance of English-Language Learners in math word problems. *Harvard Educational Review, 78*(2), 333–368.

Marzano, R. J. (2010). *Formative assessment & standards-based grading: Classroom strategies that work.* Bloomington, IN: Marzano Research Laboratory.

Mathis, W. J. (2015, October). *Research-based options for education policymaking: School accountability, multiple measures and inspectorates in a post-NCLB world.* Boulder, CO: National Education Policy Center.

McBride, A., Richard, J., & Payan, R. M. (2008). The language of acquisition and educational achievement of English-Language Learners. *ETS Policy Notes 6*(2), 1–3.

McCloskey, M. L., & New Levine, L. (2014). In M. Gottlieb & G. Ernst-Slavit (Series Eds.), *Academic language in diverse classrooms: Promoting content and language learning: English language arts, grades 3-5* (pp. 131–178). Thousand Oaks, CA: Corwin.

Menken, K. (2008). *English learners left behind: Standardized testing as language policy.* Tonawanda, NY: Multilingual Matters.

Menken, K. (2015). What have been the benefits and drawbacks of testing and accountability for English Language Learners/emergent bilinguals under No Child Left Behind and what are their implications under the Common Core State Standards? In G. Valdés, K. Menken, & M. Castro (Eds.), *Common Core, bilingual and English Language Learners: A resource for educators* (pp. 246–247). Philadelphia, PA: Caslon.

Menken, K., & Kleyn, T. (2015). What do teachers need to understand about the challenges that the CCSS and NGSS present for long-term ELLs/emergent bilinguals? In G. Valdés, K. Menken, & M. Castro (Eds.), *Common Core, bilingual and English Language Learners: A resource for educators* (pp. 220–222). Philadelphia, PA: Caslon.

Menken, K., Kleyn, T. & Chae, N. (2012, August). Spotlight on "long-term English Language Learners": Characteristics and prior schooling experiences of an invisible population. *International Multilingual Research Journal, 6*(2), 121–142.

Miller, E. C., & MacDonald, R. (2015). Rethinking language goals in science with three-dimensional learning. ¡Colorín Colorado! Retrieved from http://www.colorincolorado.org/article/rethinking-language-goals-science-three-dimensional-learning

Minaya-Rowe, L. (2014). A gothic story: The Cask of Amontillado. In M. Gottlieb & G. Ernst-Slavit (Series Eds.), *Academic language in diverse classrooms: Promoting content and language learning: English language arts, grades 6-8* (pp.137–182). Thousand Oaks, CA: Corwin.

Miramontes, O. B., Nadeau, A., & Commins, N. L. (2011). *Restructuring schools for linguistic diversity: Linking decision making to effective programs* (2nd ed.). New York, NY: Teachers College.

Mohan, B. (1986). *Language and content.* Reading, MA: Addison-Wesley.

Mora-Flores, E. (2014). Bombarding students with informational texts: Writing across the curriculum. In M. Gottlieb & G. Ernst-Slavit (Series Eds.), *Academic language in diverse classrooms: Promoting content and language learning. English language arts, grades K-2* (pp. 79–116). Thousand Oaks, CA: Corwin.

Mordaunt, O. G., & Olson, D. W. (2010). Listen, listen, listen and listen: Building a comprehension corpus and making it comprehensible. *Educational Studies, 36*(3), 249–258.

Moschkovich, J. (2012, January). *Mathematics, the Common Core, and language recommendations for mathematics instruction for ELs aligned with the Common Core.* Paper presented at the Understanding Language Conference, Stanford University, CA.

Moss, C. M., & Brookhart, S. M. (2009). *Advancing formative assessment in every classroom: A guide for instructional leaders.* Alexandria, VA: ASCD.

Mota-Altman, N. (2006). Academic language: Everyone's "second" language. *National Writing Project.* Retrieved from http://www.californiawritingproject.org/uploads/1/3/6/0/13607033/academic_lang.pdf

Muñoz, M. A., & Guskey, T. R. (2015, April). Standards-based grading and reporting will improve education. *Phi Delta Kappan, 96*(7), 64–68.

Murphy, S., & Underwood, T. (2000). *Portfolio practices: Lessons from schools, districts, and states.* Norwood, MA: Christopher-Gordon.

Nagaoka, J., Farrington, C. A., Ehrlick, S. B., Heath, R. D. (2015). *Foundations of young adult success: A developmental framework.* Chicago, IL: University of Chicago.

National Center for Education Statistics. (2014). *Racial/ethnic enrollment in public schools.* Retrieved from http://nces.ed.gov/programs/coe/indicator_cge.asp

National Council of Teachers of English. (2015, February). *NCTE position statement: Resolution on mandatory grade retention and high-stakes testing.* Retrieved from http://www.ncte.org/positions/statements/grade-retention

National Council of Teachers of Mathematics. (2012). *Large-scale mathematics assessments and high-stakes decisions.* Retrieved from http://www.nctm.org/Standards-and-Positions/Position-Statements/Large-Scale-Mathematics-Assessments-and-High-Stakes-Decisions/

National Research Council. (2012). *Education for life and work: Developing transferable knowledge and skills in the 21st century.* Pellegrino, J., & Hilton, M. (Eds.), Center for Education, Board on Testing and Assessment, Division of Behavioral and Social Sciences and Education. Washington, DC: National Academies Press.

Neumann, F., & Associates. (1996). *Authentic achievement: Restructuring schools for intellectual quality.* San Francisco, CA: Jossey-Bass.

Noguera, P. A. (2014, October 24). *Creating school conditions that support academic achievement for immigrant and ELL students.* Keynote address, WIDA National Conference, Atlanta, GA.

O'Connell, M. J., & Vandas, K. (2015). *Partnering with students: Building ownership of learning.* Thousand Oaks, CA: Corwin.

Office of Head Start. (2008). *Dual language learning: What does it take? Head Start dual language report.* Arlington, VA: National Head Start Training and Technical Assistance Resource Center, Pal-Tech, Inc.

Olson, L. (2005, November 30). Benchmark assessments offer regular checkups on student achievement. *Education Week.* Retrieved from http://www.edweek.org/ew/articles/2005/11/30/13benchmark.h25.html

O'Malley, J. M., & Pierce, L. V. (1996). *Authentic assessment for English Language Learners: Practical approaches for teachers.* New York, NY: Addison-Wesley.

Pearson, P. D., & Gallagher, M. C. (1983). The instruction of reading comprehension. *Contemporary Educational Psychology, 8,* 317–344.

Peregoy, S., & Boyle, O. (1993). *Reading, writing, and learning in ESL: A resource book for teachers.* White Plains, NY: Longman.

Pintrich, P. R., & Zusho, A. (2002). The development of academic self-regulation: The role of cognitive and motivational factors. In A. Wigfield & J. S. Eccles (Eds.), *Development of achievement motivation* (pp. 249–284). San Diego, CA: Academic Press.

Popham, W. J. (2008). *Transformative assessment.* Alexandria, VA: Association for Supervision and Curriculum Development.

Quinn, H., Lee, O., & Valdés, G. (2012). *Language demands and opportunities in relation to Next Generation Science Standards for English Language Learners: What teachers need to know.* Palo Alto, CA: Stanford University, Understanding Language.

Reeves, D. B. (2008). Leading to change/effective grading practices. *Educational Leadership, 65*(5), 85–87.

Regional Equity Assistance Centers. (2013). *How the Common Core must ensure equity by fully preparing every student for postsecondary success: Recommendations from the Regional Equity Assistance Centers on implementation of the Common Core State Standards.* San Francisco, CA: WestEd.

Rhodes, L., & Shanklin, N. L. (1993). *Windows into literacy; Assessing learners K-8.* Portsmouth, NH: Heinemann.

Richard-Amato, P. A., & Snow, M. A. (Eds.). (2005). *Academic success for English Language Learners: Strategies for K-12 mainstream teachers.* White Plains, NY: Pearson Education.

Riches, C., & Genesee, F. (2006). Literacy: Crosslinguistic and crossmodal issues. In F. Genesee, K. Lindholm-Leary, W. M. Saunders, & D. Christian (Eds.), *Educating English Language Learners: A synthesis of research evidence* (pp. 64–87). New York, NY: Cambridge University Press.

Sadler, D. R. (1989). Formative assessment and the design of instructional systems. *Instructional Science, 14,* 119–144.

Sadler, D. R. (1998, March). Formative assessment: Revisiting the territory. *Assessment in Education, 5*(1), 77–85.

Saifer, S., Edwards, K., Ellis, D., Ko, L., & Stuczynski, A. (2011). *Culturally responsive standards-based teaching: Classroom to community and back* (2nd ed.). Thousand Oaks, CA: Corwin.

Saunders, W., Goldenberg, C., & Marcelletti, D. (2013, Summer). English language development: Guidelines for instruction. *American Educator,* 13–39.

Scanlan, M., & López, F. A. (2015). *Leadership for culturally and linguistically responsive schools.* New York, NY: Routledge.

Schmidt, W. H., & Burroughs, N. A. (2013, Spring). How greater educational equality could grow from the Common Core mathematics standards, *American Educator, 32*(1), 2–9.

Scriven, M. (1967). The methodology of evaluation. In R. W. Tyler, R, M. Gagne, & M. Scriven (Eds.), *Perspectives of curriculum evaluation* (pp. 39–83). Chicago, IL: Rand McNally.

Scriven, M. (1991). Beyond formative and summative evaluation. In M. W. McLaughlin & E.C. Phillips (Eds.), *Evaluation and education: A quarter century.* Chicago, IL: University of Chicago Press.

Selber, S. A. (2004). *Multiliteracies for a digital age.* New York, NY: Routledge.

Shohamy, E. (2011). Assessing multilingual competencies: Adopting construct valid assessment policies. *The Modern Language Journal, 95*(3), 418–429.

Short, D. J., & Fitzsimmons, S. (2007). *Double the work: Challenges and solutions to acquiring language and academic literacy for adolescent English Language Learners: A report to the Carnegie Corporation of New York.* Washington, DC: Alliance for Excellent Education.

Silvers, P., & Shorey, M. (2012). *Many texts, many voices: Teaching literacy and social justice to young learners in the digital age.* Portland, ME: Stenhouse.

Silvers, P., Shorey, M., Eliopoulis, P., & Akiyoshi, H. (2014). Making a difference in the world: Civil rights, biographies, and the southeast region. In M. Gottlieb & G. Ernst-Slavit, (Series Eds.), *Academic language in diverse classrooms: Promoting content and language learning. English language arts, grades 3-5* (pp. 87–129). Thousand Oaks, CA: Corwin.

Smith, M. (1986). A model for teaching native oriented science. In J. J. Gallagher & G. Dawson (Eds.), *Science education and cultural environments in the Americas*. Washington, DC: National Science Teachers Association.

Soltero-González, L., Escamilla, K., & Hopewell, S. (2012). Changing teachers' perspectives about the writing abilities of emerging bilingual students: Towards a holistic bilingual perspective on writing assessment. *International Journal of Bilingual Education and Bilingualism, 15*(1), 71–94.

Soto, I. (2014). *Moving from spoken to written language with ELLs*. Thousand Oaks, CA: Corwin.

Spolsky, B. (1989). *Conditions for second language learning*. Oxford, UK: Oxford University Press.

Staehr Fenner, D. (2014). *Advocating for English learners*. Thousand Oaks, CA: Corwin.

Stiggins, R. (2006, November/December). Assessment for learning: A key to motivation and achievement. *Phi Delta Kappa International, 2*(2), 1–19.

Stiggins, R. J. (2005). *Student-involved assessment FOR learning* (4th ed.). Upper Saddle River, NJ: Pearson.

Swales, J. M. (1990). *Genre analysis: English in academic and research settings*. New York, NY: Cambridge University Press.

Teachers of English to Speakers of Other Languages (2003, March). *Position paper on high-stakes testing for K-12 English Language Learners in the United States*. Retrieved from http:// www.tesol.org/docs/pdf/375.pdf?sfvrsn=2

Teachers of English to Speakers of Other Languages (TESOL) International Association. (2013, March). *Overview of the Common Core State Standards initiatives for ELLs*. Alexandria, VA: Author.

Thomas, W. P., & Collier, V. P. (2002). *A national study of school effectiveness for language minority students' long-term academic achievement*. Santa Cruz, CA: Center for Research on Education, Diversity & Excellence, University of California-Santa Cruz.

Trumbull, E., & Farr, B. (Eds.). (2000). *Grading and reporting student progress in an age of standards*. Norwood, MA: Christopher-Gordon.

Underhill, N. (1987). *Testing spoken language: A handbook of oral testing techniques*. Cambridge, UK: Cambridge University Press.

U.S. Department of Education Office for Civil Rights (2000, December). *The use of tests as part of high-stakes decision-making for students: A resource guide for educators and policy makers*. Washington, DC: Author.

U.S. Department of Justice and U.S. Department of Education. (2015, January). *Dear colleague letter: English learner students and limited English proficient parents*. Retrieved from http:// www2.ed.gov/about/offices/list/ocr/letters/colleague-el-201501.pdf

van Lier, L., & Walqui, A. (2012). *Language and the Common Core State Standards*. Retrieved from http://ell.stanford.edu/sites/default/files/pdf/academic-papers/04-Van%20 Lier%20Walqui%20Language%20and%20CCSS%20FINAL.pdf

Vandergrift, L. (2012). Listening: Theory and practice in modern foreign language competence. *Centre for Language, Linguistics and Area Studies*. Retrieved from https://www.llas .ac.uk//resources/gpg/67

Villegas, A. M., & Lucas, T. (2007). The culturally responsive teacher. *Educational Leadership, 64*(6), 28–33.

Vygotsky, L. S. (1978). *Mind in society: The development of higher psychological processes*. Cambridge, MA: Harvard University Press.

Walqui, A., & van Lier, L. (2010). *Scaffolding the academic success of adolescent English Language Learners*. San Francisco, CA: WestEd.

Walsh, D., & Staehr Fenner, D. (2014). Diving into the depths of research. In M. Gottlieb & G. Ernst-Slavit (Series Eds.), *Academic language in diverse classrooms: Promoting content and language learning: English language arts, grades 6-8* (pp. 101–135). Thousand Oaks, CA: Corwin.

Weir, C. J. (2005). *Language testing and validation: An evidence-based approach*. London, UK: Palgrave Macmillan.

WIDA Consortium (2015, June 29). *ACCESS for ELLs 2.0® accessibility and accommodation guidelines*. Retrieved from https://www.wida.us/assessment/WIDA_AccessAccGuidelines_5-28-15.pdf

Wiggins, G. (2012, September). Seven keys to effective feedback. *Educational Leadership, 70*(1), 10–16.

Wiggins, G. P., & McTighe, J. (1998). *Understanding by design*. Alexandria, VA: Association for Supervision and Curriculum Development.

Wiliam, D. (2011). *Embedded formative assessment*. Bloomington, IN: Solution Tree.

Wiliam, D., & Leahy, S. (2015). *Embedding formative assessment: Practical techniques for K-12 classrooms*. West Palm Beach, FL: Learning Sciences International.

Wilson, D. M. (2011). Dual language programs on the rise. *Harvard Educational Letter, 27*(2), 1–2.

Wolf, M. K., Guzman-Orth, D., & Hauck, M. C. (2014). *Next-generation summative English language proficiency assessments for English learners: Priorities for policy and research*. Princeton, NJ: Educational Testing Service.

Young, T. A., & Hadaway, N. L. (2014). Taking a closer look at our changing environment. In M. Gottlieb & G. Ernst-Slavit (Series Eds.), *Academic language in diverse classrooms: Promoting content and language learning: English language arts, grades 3-5*, (pp. 45–86). Thousand Oaks, CA: Corwin.

Zacarian, D. (2011). *Transforming schools for English learners: A comprehensive framework for school leaders*. Thousand Oaks, CA: Corwin.

Zwiers, J. (2008). *Building academic language: Essential practices for content classrooms, grades 5-12*. San Francisco, CA: Jossey-Bass.

Zwiers, J., & Crawford, M. (2011). *Academic conversations: Classroom talk that fosters critical thinking and content understandings*. Portland, ME: Stenhouse.

Zwiers, J., O'Hara, S., & Pritchard, R. (2014). *Common Core Standards in diverse classrooms: Essential practices for developing academic language and disciplinary literacy*. Portland, ME: Stenhouse.

Sources for Standards and Standards-Related Documents

Alaska standards for culturally responsive schools. (2013). *Alaska Native Knowledge Network*. Retrieved from http://ankn.uaf.edu/Publications/Standards.html

Arizona Department of Education. (2015). *English language proficiency standards.* Retrieved from http://www.azed.gov/english-language-learners/elps/

California Department of Education. (2012). *California English language development standards.* Retrieved from http://www.cde.ca.gov/sp/el/er/eldstandards.asp

Common Core en español. (2012). *Common Core State Standards in Language Arts and Literacy in History/Social Studies, Science, and Technical Subjects: Spanish language version.* Retrieved from https://commoncore-espanol.sdcoe.net/CCSS-en-Espa%C3%B1ol/SLA-Literacy

Common Core en español. (2012). *Common Core State Standards in Mathematics: Spanish language version.* Retrieved from https://commoncore-espanol.sdcoe.net/CCSS-en-Espa%C3%B1ol/Mathematics

Common Core State Standards Initiative. (2010). *English language arts standards.* Retrieved from http://www.corestandards.org/ELA-Literacy

Common Core State Standards Initiative. (2010). *Mathematics standards.* Retrieved from http://www.corestandards.org/Math

Council of Chief State School Officers. (2012). *Framework for English language proficiency development corresponding to the Common Core State Standards and the Next Generation Science Standards.* Washington, DC: Author.

Council of Chief State School Officers. (2014). *English language proficiency (ELP) standards with correspondences to K-12 English Language Arts (ELA), Mathematics, and Science practices and 6–12 Literacy standards.* Retrieved from http://www.elpa21.org/sites/default/files/Final%204_30%20ELPA21%20Standards_1.pdf

Dynamic Learning Maps. *Essential elements.* Retrieved from http://dynamiclearningmaps.org

Engage NY. (2013). *Home language arts progressions by grade.* Retrieved from https://www.engageny.org/resource/new-york-state-bilingual-common-core-initiative

Engage NY. (2013). *New language arts progressions.* Retrieved from https://www.engageny.org/resource/new-york-state-bilingual-common-core-initiative

International Society of Technology in Education. *ISTE Standards.* Retrieved from www.iste.org.

National Center and State Collaborative. *Core content connectors.* Retrieved from http://www.ncscpartners.org

National Coalition for Core Arts Standards. (2014). *National core arts standards*. Retrieved from http://nationalartsstandards.org

National Council for the Social Studies. (2013). *College, career, and civic life: C3 Framework for Social Studies State Standards: Guidance for enhancing the rigor of K-12 civics, economics, geography, and history*. Silver Spring, MD: Author.

National Research Council. (2012). *A framework for K-12 science education: Practices, crosscutting concepts, and core ideas*. Washington, DC: National Academies Press.

The Next Generation Science Standards. (2013). Retrieved from http://www.nextgenscience .org/next-generation-science-standards

Normas para la enseñanza de las artes del lenguaje en español para programas de inmersión doble. (2011). Washington, DC: The Mid-Atlantic Equity Center at the George Washington University. Retrieved from http://www.trenton.k12.nj.us/Downloads/NormasDL_ MAECSu20111.pdf

Partnership for Assessment of Readiness for College and Careers. (2014). *PARCC accessibility features and accommodations manual: Guidance for districts and decision-making teams to ensure that PARCC mid-year, performance-based, and end-of-year assessments produce valid results for all students* (3rd ed.). Retrieved from http://www.parcconline.org/images/Assessments/ Acccessibility/PARCC_Accessibility_Features__Accommodations_Manual_v.6_01_ body_appendices.pdf

Smarter Balanced Assessment Consortium. (2014). *Usability, accessibility, and accommodations implementation guide*. Retrieved from http://www.smarterbalanced.org/wordpress/ wp-content/uploads/2014/03/Usability-Accessibility-and-Accommodations- Implementation-Guide.pdf

Spanish language arts and reading: Texas essential knowledge and skills, kindergarten-grade 6. (2009). Austin, TX: University of Texas System/Texas Education Agency.

Texas English language proficiency standards (ELPS). (2009). Retrieved from http://www.elltx .org/docs/English_Language_Proficiency_Standards.pdf

WIDA Consortium. (2004). *English language proficiency standards, Kindergarten through grade 12*. Madison, WI: Board of Regents of the University of Wisconsin System.

WIDA Consortium. (2005). *Spanish language arts standards*. Madison, WI: Board of Regents of the University of Wisconsin System.

WIDA Consortium. (2007). *English language proficiency standards, Prekindergarten through grade 12*. Madison, WI: Board of Regents of the University of Wisconsin System.

WIDA Consortium. (2012). *Amplification of the English language development standards, Kindergarten– grade 12*. Madison, WI: Board of Regents of the University of Wisconsin System.

WIDA Consortium. (2013). *Los estándares del desarrollo del lenguaje español de WIDA, desde Kínder hasta el Grado 12°, Edición 2013*. Madison, WI: Board of Regents of the University of Wisconsin System.

WIDA Consortium. (2014). *The early English language development standards, 2.5-5.5 years*. Madison, WI: Board of Regents of the University of Wisconsin System.

WIDA Consortium. (2015). *ACCESS for ELLs 2.0*®. Retrieved from https://www.wida.us/ assessment/access20-prep.aspx

WIDA Consortium. (2015). *Guía de consulta: Los estándares del desarrollo del lenguaje temprano del español de WIDA de los 2.5 hasta los 5.5 años, Edición 2015*. Madison, WI: Board of Regents of the University of Wisconsin System.

WIDA Consortium. (2016). Can Do descriptors, Key uses edition. Madison, WI: Board of Regents of the University of Wisconsin System.

Index

A SAGE Publishing Company

Helping educators make the greatest impact

CORWIN HAS ONE MISSION: to enhance education through intentional professional learning.

We build long-term relationships with our authors, educators, clients, and associations who partner with us to develop and continuously improve the best evidence-based practices that establish and support lifelong learning.